Strong Religion, Zealous Media

Strong Religion, Zealous Media

Christian Fundamentalism and Communication in India

Pradip Ninan Thomas

Los Angeles • London • New Delhi • Singapore
www.sagepublications.com

First published in 2008 by

 SAGE Publications India Pvt Ltd
B-1/I-1, Mohan Cooperative Industrial Area
Mathura Road, New Delhi 110 044, India

SAGE Publications Inc
2455 Teller Road
Thousand Oaks, California 91320, USA

SAGE Publications Ltd
1 Oliver's Yard, 55 City Road
London EC1Y 1SP, United Kingdom

SAGE Publications Asia-Pacific Pte Ltd
33 Pekin Street
#02-01 Far East Square
Singapore 048763

Published by Vivek Mehra for SAGE Publications India Pvt Ltd, typeset in 10.5/12.5 pt Garamond by Excellent Laser Typesetters, Delhi and printed at Chaman Enterprises, New Delhi.

Library of Congress Cataloging-in-Publication Data Available

ISBN: 978-81-7829-834-4 (HB)

The SAGE Team: Rekha Natarajan, Samprati Pani, Anju Saxena and Trinankur Banerjee

CONTENTS

LIST OF ABBREVIATIONS

ACO	Access Cable Operator
AIADMK	All India Anna Dravida Munnetra Kazhagam
AICs	African Independent Churches
AIMS	Accelerating International Mission Strategies
AIR	All India Radio
AOG	Assemblies of God
BJP	Bharatiya Janata Party
CACS	Christian Arts and Communication Service
CAMERA	Committee for Accuracy in Middle East Reporting in America
CBC	Canadian Broadcasting Corporation
CBN	Christian Broadcasting Network
CMC	Christian Media Centre
CMD	Centre for Mission Direction
CMS	Christian Missionary Society
CSI	Church of South India
DMK	Dravida Munnetra Kazhagam
DTH	Direct-to-Home
EWTN	Eternal Word Television Network
FEBA	Far Eastern Broadcasting Association
FEBC	Far Eastern Broadcasting Corporation
FKWW	Fox Kids Worldwide
GFA	Gospel for Asia
HBI	Hindustan Bible Institute
IFE	International Family Entertainment
ISP	Internet Service Provider
IT	Information Technology

LMS	London Missionary Society
MP	Member of Parliament
MSO	Multi-Service Operator
NCCI	National Council of Churches of India
NCCUSA	National Council of Churches USA
NDA	National Democratic Alliance
NGO	Non-Governmental Organisation
PHDCCI	PHD Chamber of Commerce and Industry
RSS	Rashtriya Swayamsevak Sangh
SISWA	South India Soul Winner's Association
SLBC	Sri Lanka Broadcasting Corporation
TBN	Trinity Broadcasting Network
VHP	Vishwa Hindu Parishad
WACC	World Association for Christian Communication
WCC	World Council of Churches

ACKNOWLEDGEMENTS

This study was shaped by the work environment at my former work place, the World Association for Christian Communication (London) and, in particular, the freedom I was given to explore critical media issues including Christian fundamentalism. I would also like to acknowledge my present employers, University of Queensland, and the start-up grant that I received to pursue this study. I would like to thank Prof. Cindy Gallois, Philip Lee, Dr Zala Volcic, Randy Naylor, Dennis Smith, Adan Medrano, Prof. Stewart Hoover and the late Michael Traber, among numerous others, for their practical and intellectual support. The study would have been close to impossible to complete if it were not for the support that I got from family and friends in India including my mother Anna, sister-in-law Beena, brother Prem, nieces Sneha and Shruthi, wife Preetha, and children Nitin and Prianka. I would like to acknowledge the many people that I interviewed in Chennai and Bengaluru, and hopefully did not take advantage of, including Jesudas Athyal, K.C. Abraham, Prabhu, Nehru and Ashwin Dhyriam, Swarna Felix, Roger Hedlund, Gracy Thomas, Shobha Samuel and John Solomon, among numerous others. And SAGE for all the encouragement for this project, in particular Sugata Ghosh, Rekha Natarajan and Samprati Pani. Last but not least, my absent father, T.K. Thomas, who played a formative role in my life, and who encouraged me to not take religion as the 'Big Picture' too seriously. This one is for you mate.

INTRODUCTION

Fundamentalism and the Media

O Believers! What is the matter with you? When you are said: 'March in the way of Allah', you tend to the earth. Are you pleased with the life of the world leaving the Hereafter...if You do not go forth. He will give you a painful chastisement, and will bring in return different people other than you, and you will not injure him aught.... (Al-Quraan, 9: 38–39, quoted from Taliban Online).

Even the Taliban use the Internet.

From time immemorial, the media has been a fertile and well-used (manipulated) tool for religious fundamentalists. This is to be expected since one of the primary aims of the religious fundamentalist is to persuade people to accept the authenticity of an eternal message, valid for all times and for all people. Fundamentalists have employed scribes and Pharisees, preachers and mullahs as well as used dance and drama, song and verse, edict and artifice to communicate eternal and unchanging truths. However, the modern-day fundamentalist operates in a very different milieu to that which prevailed even half a century ago. The marketing of Paradise is big business today. God sells. There is a battle on for the souls of the global community as much as for its purse in a context teeming with a variety of communication options—video and audio, terrestrial, cable and satellite broadcasting, and the Internet, along with print and older forms of communication. Islamic fundamentalists, in particular those who have taken on the 'Great Satan', are savvy users of mobile phones and computing, as was evident in the aftermath of 9/11. Christian fundamentalists, in particular, rank among the world's foremost users of the media, because in their way of thinking, every medium of communication is a gift from God and a potential ally in the dissemination of God's unvarying, eternal truth. Instrumentalism, professionalism and pragmatism are typical attitudes underlying media use by religious fundamentalists.

It is one of the central paradoxes of our time that precisely when we have been told that we are moving forward to a qualitatively new era—characterised by sisterhood, brotherhood, global unity and togetherness, aided by the technologies of networking—our familiar world is perceptibly and imperceptibly breaking up into an unfamiliar, unforgiving landscape. This landscape is home to a variety of fundamentalists. The term fundamentalism, meaning an entirely self-sufficient and self-referential doctrine or worldview, is often used to describe the worldview of an individual or a group and their interpretation of things immanent and eschatological. In common usage, it is specifically applied to the doctrinaire beliefs and action of religious zealots everywhere, regardless of their religious affiliation. In the words of Giddens (1999), 'Fundamentalism is beleaguered tradition. It is tradition defended in the traditional way—by reference to ritual truth—in a globalising world that asks for reasons.' Overt and covert wars aimed at establishing the primacy of one religious worldview over another is commonplace today and unites the world in a fratricidal embrace. Such crusades link the most unlikely of countries—USA, Sudan, Egypt, Israel, Italy, India, Pakistan, Indonesia and numerous others.

The Word of God says in John 4 that we should lift up our eyes and see the fields of the world because they are ready to be harvested. One of the great fields to which our Lord is referring is the Hindu world. Sadly, Western Christians have almost forgotten about these people whom God loves, and so 14% of the world's population is silently passing away not to the realisation of another birth in the endless cycle of reincarnation, but to eternal hell (Centre for Mission Direction [CMD]).

Religious fundamentalists normally have a political agenda and the media are used to further this agenda. The meticulous, systematic uses of the media by Hindu nationalist forces in India, the Vishwa Hindu Parishad (VHP) and the Bharatiya Janata Party (BJP), as much as by Pat Robertson and others of his ilk in the USA, backed by the technologies of marketing, have played a key role in their ascendance in the public domain. The family and community as much as the nation are targets for the fundamentalist. The fundamentalist message is simple, straightforward and literal, and promises an important value-added extra—it guarantees all believers the promise of salvation. Fundamentalists neither have time for irony nor do they subscribe to diversity. In fact, in their way of thinking, Satan lurks in every outsider opposed to their cause.

> The Hindu culture is the life-breath of Hindusthan. It is therefore clear that if Hindusthan is to be protected, we should first nourish the Hindu culture. It is therefore the duty of every Hindu to do his best to consolidate the Hindu society....(Keshav Baliram Hedgewar, founder of the Rashtriya Swayamsevak Sangh [RSS]).

The use of the media by religious fundamentalists has varied from context to context. Hindu fundamentalists in India have used video to great effect and more recently satellite television. Their mass leaders such as Sadhvi Rithambara are what they are today because of their cassette ministries—a tradition perfected by the late Ayatollah Khomeini, whose popularity was boosted by his sermons delivered via audio cassettes. In USA, Christian fundamentalists such as Pat Robertson control vast media empires and, in addition, have substantive interests in wealth-creation activities such as banking and education. His Christian Broadcasting Network (CBN) is one of the largest cable providers in USA. Synergies and links with secular media moguls such as that effected through the sale of the channel International Family Entertainment (IFE) to Rupert Murdoch illustrate the inroads made by fundamentalist media in the mainstream.[1] Tele-evangelism, however, is a lot more than an adaptation of television for religious ends. It has also, perhaps in a fundamental sense, changed the way religion is experienced by a vast number of people.

The Chapters in the Book

This book is an exploration of new Christianity in Chennai, India, and in particular the communication strategies adopted by Christian fundamentalist groups that belong primarily to the Pentecostalist and neo-Pentecostalist traditions within the Protestant tradition. It does not address issues related to the 'charismatic' movement in India linked to the Roman Catholic Church in India, except in passing. It, however, does acknowledge the fact that there are close doctrinal and 'performative' links between the charismatics and the neo-Pentecostalists. The book is divided into four sections. Section I, consisting of Chapters 1–4, fore-grounds the context of the study, with separate chapters on religious fundamentalism, the media and religious fundamentalism, Christianity in India, and Pentecostalism and neo-Pentecostalism. It provides a broad introduction to some of the key issues related to religious fundamental-ism and to Christian fundamentalism in particular; deals with the theory and practice of fundamentalist media against the background of issues related to media, religion and culture, with the contested history and contemporary status of the Protestant Christian mission in India; and presents an extensive understanding of the global–local nature of Pentecostalism and neo-Pentecostalism.

Section II, consisting of Chapter 5, provides the theoretical scaffolding for the study and uses concepts popularised by the French sociologist Pierre Bourdieu—habitus, field, distinction, symbolic capital and symbolic violence—to illumine the contested nature of Christianity and mediated Christianity in India. Bourdieu offers a theoretical framework that enables an understanding of the relationship between agency and structure, cultural and material power, and the global and the local.

Section III, consisting of Chapters 6–8, focuses on core aspects of this study—the specificities of Christian broadcasting in India, in particular the status of Christian cable and satellite broadcasting, both foreign and local channels; the use and abuse of cyberspace by Christian mission agencies, in particular an analysis of the virtual wars being fought by Christian and, to a lesser extent, Hindu groups; followed by an analysis of a Christian crusade held in Bengaluru in January 2005 by the global evangelist Benny Hinn. I argue that Benny Hinn as well as other evangelists and tele-evangelists are involved in the cultivation of 'distinction'; use religion and practices such as 'faith healing' as a means to facilitate a fundamental 'misrecognition' of their real, material interests; and are key enablers and reinforcers of a fundamentalist Christian identity and a global Christian fundamentalist *umma*.

Section IV consists of the concluding chapter, which explores the theory and practice of communication for inter-subjective futures in India and suggests another approach to religious broadcasting from a collaborative, inter-faith perspective.

The era of Pentecostalism that began in the 1920s in India has experi-enced extraordinary growth between the years 1980–2005. Pentecostalism is fast becoming the face of Christianity in India. These new Christian churches are in themselves indicative of the changing landscape of Chris-tianity in India. This tradition, with its strong commitment to the media, and in particular broadcasting, has begun to communicate a selective understanding of Christian identity that is particular, triumphalistic and conservative. While some expressions of Pentecostalism in Latin America, for example, espouse a version of what one may call the Social Gospel, many of the churches associated with neo-Pentecostalism, including the ones present in India, deliberately eschew this tradition and instead embrace both the market and a triumphalist version of Christianity. While one can argue that the Pentecostal churches in India have contributed to the strengthening of Christian identity among Dalit communities, it remains to be seen whether conversion has led to the making of quiescent Dalit Christianity or to the enabling of a truly liberating tradition. The beliefs and agendas of some Pentecostalist and neo-Pentecostalist traditions can be termed 'fundamentalist' precisely because it is based on an implicit politics of eventual Christian global domination. That agenda includes conversion, an aggressive stance towards non-Christians and the use of the media to extend their sphere of influence.

Why Chennai?

I chose Chennai for my study not only because of a familiarity with the city of my birth, but also because the various denominations representative of Protestant Christianity have had a significant historical presence in the state of Tamil Nadu. The Church of South India, the first expression of the ecumenical movement, was established in Madras in 1948. The Pentecostals have been around for decades (Burgess, 2001), so has Christian broadcasting, and this city today is considered the fastest growing hub of Christianity in South Asia.

1. According to the 2001 Census, 5.2 per cent (3.8 million) of the 62 million people in Tamil Nadu are Christians. This figure, along with figures for the whole of India that suggests a decline in Christian numbers between 1991 and 2001 (2.4–2.3 per cent), is contested.
2. Southern Tamil Nadu was the first mission field in India to be actively wooed by Protestant missionaries starting with the Tranquebar Mission, that was established by the Royal Danish Missionaries represented by two Germans, Bartolomaus Ziegenbalg and Heinrich Plutschau, in July 1706 (Hudson, 2000).
3. In terms of Christian revival, the first recorded outpourings of the Spirit, manifestation of tongues and other gifts was reported in 1860 at a mission in Tirunelveli in Tamil Nadu (Hedlund, 2001).

4. Tamil Nadu has had a strong presence of Pentecostal churches and conservative forms of Christianity that led to the religions scholar Lionel Caplan (1987) to write what is perhaps the first writings on Christian fundamentalism in India—'Fundamentalism as a Counter-Culture: Protestants in Urban South India'. Susan Bayly's (1994) study 'Christians and Competing Fundamentalisms in South Indian Society', based in southern Tamil Nadu and Kerala, furthers understandings of the growth and development of fundamentalisms in South Asia.

5. Despite an increase in inter-religious tensions elsewhere in India, Tamil Nadu continues to be relatively free of such tensions. While north India and central India have witnessed a rise in anti-Christian feelings during the last two decades, the south has remained relatively free of attacks on Christians. The repeal of the anti-conversion laws by the government of Tamil Nadu that was promulgated in 2002 and withdrawn in 2005 is an indication of the religious dynamics that continue to favour minority communities, unlike in north and west India, where the conflict between Christians and Hindus has become a lot sharper.

To focus on Christian fundamentalists in Chennai would seem an idiosyncratic choice given the world's many urgent entanglements with Islamic fundamentalism. Christian fundamentalists in Chennai are not Jihadists and do not have plans to blow up Saudi Arabia or convert the Taliban. Be that as it may, I argue that Christian fundamentalists, like their Islamic counterparts, belong to a global *umma* and harbour real and perhaps imagined, even delusional, longings directed towards making all of God's people Christian. This nostalgic yearning can be dismissed as a mere fancy, although if one were to assess the efforts and capital that had been invested in plans for Lumen 2000 by the Catholics and in the Joshua Project by evangelical groups, a different, altogether less wholesome, picture of Christian mission becomes immediately apparent. These Christian groups may not use real physical violence, though they are well-versed in using the media and non-media means to propagate 'symbolic violence' that is often backed up by economic enticements to persuade or coerce individuals and communities to become Christian. While there is need for circumspection in assessments of the grand projects of global conversion given the existence of real gaps between the often striking intentions and actual reality, there is also a need to recognise the existence of these many 'grand projects' and the many armies of evangelicals, beavering away in every corner of the world, determined to save every sinner, homosexual, whore, Muslim, Hindu and other 'fallen' human being from the clutches of Satan. This is a billion dollar project that is generously supported by right-wing politics, the right-wing church in USA, Christian broadcasting and global Christian mission. It has a global audience and foot soldiers who are from Tamil Nadu, Andhra Pradesh and Kerala in India, as well as South Korea, numerous European countries, North America and the Pacific, including Australia.

In the context of India, I believe that the mainstream churches, in spite of their accommodations with the charismatics, evangelicals and fundamentalists, have an obligation to study the rise of Christian fundamentalism, at least for the sake of members like myself, who would like to believe in a vision of Indian Christianity that is inclusive, that accepts the richness of other faiths and that is socially responsible. Indian Christian identities are multifarious. There is no singular Indian Christian identity and it is important that this diversity is maintained and strengthened, not weakened by the viral spread of exclusive, triumphalistic, divisive understandings of Christianity. Having said this, it is equally important to study these new traditions of Christianity, to understand their vision and beliefs, their organisational and ideological patterns, and the specificity of their traditions. Moreover, on a global scale, as in India, these new traditions of Christianity are steadily becoming the 'face' of Christianity. Mainstream churches in India are, for the most part, in denial mode and are not willing to acknowledge that these new churches have become their equals. Why is it that large numbers of Indian Christian youth are deserting the mainstream church and worshipping in these new churches? What strengths do these new churches possess? And would it be fair to say that these churches represent a Christianity that is deeply and intensely global and local? While I continue to remain critical and sceptical of the specific politics of these new Christian traditions, I do acknowledge that the spiritual yearnings of millions of Christians around the world are being fulfilled by these new Christian churches. It is, in other words, important to distinguish and respect the spiritualities and traditions of faith represented by these new churches. I also strongly believe that before Christians point their fingers at other fundamentalisms and fundamentalists, they have a responsibility to 'clean their own stables', and nodal and apex church bodies need to rein in Christian fundamentalists who are doing their utmost best to wreck inter-faith relationships in India.

Note

1. International Family Entertainment (IFE) was part of the media stable owned by the conservative Pentecostal tele-evangelist Pat Robertson. It was sold to Rupert Murdoch in 1997 who merged IFE with Fox Kids Worldwide (FKWW).

References

Bayly, S. 1994. 'Christians and Competing Fundamentalisms in South Indian Society', in M.E. Marty and R.S. Appleby (eds), *Accounting for Fundamentalisms: The Dynamic Character of Movement*. Chicago & London: The University of Chicago Press.

Burgess, S.M. 2001. 'Pentecostalism in India: An Overview', *Asian Journal of Pentecostal Studies*, 4(1): 85–98.

Caplan, L. 1987. 'Fundamentalism as a Counter-Culture: Protestants in Urban South India', in L. Caplan (ed.), *Studies in Religious Fundamentalism*, pp. 156–76. Basingstoke/London: Macmillan Press.

Centre for Mission Direction (CMD). Available at http://www.cmd.org.nz/hindu07.html, accessed on 10 December 2001.

Giddens, A. 1999. 'Tradition'. BBC Reith Lectures 3. Available at http://news.bbc.co.uk/hi/english/static/events/reith_99/week3/week3.htm, accessed on 15 May 2007.

Hedgewar, Keshav Baliram. Available at http://www.rss.org/www/mission.htm, accessed on 10 December 2001.

Hedlund, R.E. 2001. 'Previews of Christian Indigenity in India', *Journal of Asian Mission*, 3(2): 213–30.

Hudson, D.D. 2000. *Protestant Origins in India: Tamil Evangelical Christians, 1706–1835*. Grand Rapids, Michigan/Cambridge, UK: William B. Eerdmans Publishing Company; Richmond, UK: Curzon Press.

Taliban Online. Available at http://www.taliban.com/main.htm, accessed on 10 December 2001.

SECTION **1**

LOCATING THE STUDY

I

CHRISTIAN FUNDAMENTALISM AND OTHER FUNDAMENTALISMS

An Era of Fundamentalisms?

It is one of the central paradoxes of our time that the world's tryst with modernity and, more recently, the belief in global futures based on market integration and democracy has not led to the much-heralded global unity and togetherness, but to many inflected varieties of globalisation, even anti-globalisation, that is best reflected in the fissures, strains, and polarisations caused by resurgent nationalisms, religious fundamentalisms and inter-civilisational conflict. This landscape has become a fertile staging post for covert and overt religion-inspired struggles aimed at asserting control over material and symbolic resources, territories, people and their identities, allegiances and futures. Stand-alone expressions of religious fundamentalism along with expressions that are closely integrated with nationalism typify conflict in many parts of our world today, from Sudan to Indonesia. Overt and covert struggles aimed at establishing the primacy of one religious worldview over another are commonplace today and unite the world in a fratricidal embrace. Such crusades link the most unlikely of countries—the USA, Sudan, Egypt, Israel, Italy, India, Pakistan, Indonesia and UK—and have led to unlikely alliances between fundamentalist groups, for instance, the Jewish and Hindu religious right against their common enemy, Islam.

During the preceding two decades, the study and exploration of mainly religious and also other types of fundamentalisms have become a growth

3

industry in academic, policy and political circles. Politicians, particularly in the West, have conflated the war on terror as a war against religious fundamentalism, thereby contributing to 'security' panics as is the case in USA today, where there are daily alerts. Conferences, symposia, think tanks, books and treatises, and national, regional and international projects have debated, discussed and dissected religious fundamentalism. A variety of organisations at governmental and inter-governmental levels have explored the ways and means to curb the spread of religious fundamentalism, in particular Islamic fundamentalism. To a large extent, interest in this subject has been a response to the rise of a variety of chauvinistic religious, nationalist and secessionist movements in different parts of the world that have, in a real sense, thrown down the gauntlet and taken on the powers that be. The overthrow of the Shah in the late 1970s by Ayatollah Khomeini, struggles over religious identification in Bosnia, Chechnya and India, the rise of militant Islam from the simmering ashes of the struggles in Palestine, the continuing struggles in Iraq, the war against the Taliban in the post 9/11 period, the proxy wars waged by the Israeli government on behalf of USA against the militant Islamic groups Hamas and Hezbollah, the political role of the Christian right wing in USA—each is characterised in some measure by a hardening of religious identities and dispositions, and the drawing of boundaries between 'us' and 'them'. The war against terror is often couched in the language of the apocalypse—battles between the forces of good and evil (Western, Christian civilization vs the Muslim hordes) is a familiar trope in media discourses throughout the world. The slippage between identifying terrorists within the Islamic world and, by extension, affirming the culpability of all Muslims for the present world situation of war and unrest does suggest that a renewed, much starker version of Orientalism has been manufactured for public consumption by the proponents of a muscular Occidentalism. At the very same time, there is a need to recognise that the lack of, or at best the limited number of, interpretive options within the Islamic tradition makes it an easy target for a variety of liberal interrogations.

The media of course plays the key role in the manufacture of and circulation of stereotypes, and functions as a conduit for the transmission of tropes from official sources—'Islamofascism' and the 'axis of evil', to name just two signifiers that have global currency today. However, and despite the real wars being fought against Islamic fundamentalism in Asia, Africa and elsewhere, at any given time, there are numerous, far less violent expressions of religious fundamentalism that do not feature in the media and that are recognised as a public threat. The crusadic dimension of religious fundamentalism today is a reality that cannot be downplayed. Just as Bin Laden and his compatriots are committed to saving the world for the cause of Islam, Christian mission, albeit in a less confrontationist, although equally aggressive manner, is extensively involved in resisting the spread of Islam and other faiths, and is committed to the project of converting people to the Christian faith. Hindu revivalists, who occupy spaces outside of this global struggle between two cognate religions within the Judaic tradition, are nevertheless committed to keeping India Hindu—a further indication that in the 21st century, wars and negotiations with a variety of religious fundamentalisms are a given.

Making Sense of Religious Fundamentalism

The roots of religious fundamentalism are by no means singular or clear-cut. While the term 'fundamentalism' itself was coined about a century ago to describe a series of booklets called *The Fundamentals,* produced by Baptists in USA in the 1920s in response and opposition to the perceived influence of liberal theology and the sway of modern scientific views, the term today is used to describe a far more complex, multi-faceted, multi-dimensional reality that is often linked to, and influenced by, the discourses of nationalism, patriotism, terrorism, democracy, the market economy and even global futures. It is, therefore, not surprising that the edited volume by M.E. Marty and S.R. Appleby (1995: 405–15) *Fundamentalisms Comprehended*, itself part of the five volume Fundamentalism Project, identifies a list of family resemblances or characteristics of fundamentalism rather than opt for a list of 'absolute' characteristics. This list includes five ideological and four organisational characteristics:

1. Reaction to the marginalisation of religion in the context of secularisation.
2. Selectivity in their response to modernity and in highlighting their own traditions.
3. Moral dualism—dividing the world into black and white, right and wrong.
4. Absolutism and inerrancy—in their interpretation of scripture and belief in core fundamentals.

5

5. Millennialism and messianism or belief in the end of times and victory for the faithful and just.
6. Elect membership—the belief that the faithful, who are ordained by God, will prevail over the unfaithful masses.
7. The drawing of sharp boundaries between those who are born again, those who are saved and those who have been damned.
8. Authoritarian organisation and belief in charismatic leaders such as Bin Laden.
9. Behavioural requirements that adherents follow a strict code of discipline including the expectation that the individual member's identity is subsumed into the larger collective identity.

The term religious fundamentalism is often used to describe individuals and communities who subscribe to an entirely self-sufficient and self-referential doctrine or worldview and in things immanent and eschatological. In common usage, it is specifically applied to the doctrinaire beliefs and action of religious zealots everywhere, regardless of their religious affiliation. It is clear that the meaning of fundamentalism, in its broadest sense, refers to the cognitive, emotive attachment to absolutes and to the ideological, material and productive practices that extend such absolutisms. However, according to the meaning ascribed to it in this study, *religious fundamentalists are those who implicitly and explicitly employ low intensity and high intensity politics to advance their specific, normative project of singular religious identifications at global and local levels.* In other words, the religious fundamentalist is one who actively espouses politics to advance the cause of a single religion, at the expense of other religions and traditions of belief. Christian religious fundamentalism in USA, for example, is mutually constituted by politics as is the case with that of the Taliban in Afghanistan. In this sense, the meanings given to the term in this book differs from the 'normal' ways in which it is used to describe 'doctrinaire believers'—from the Amish, to the Jehovah's Witnesses, to the Shias. It is notoriously difficult to define fundamentalism in this way or to fix its meaning, for there simply are many gradations of openness and closeness in religious beliefs. While it is tempting to label all Bible-thumping Pentecostalists fundamentalist simply because their approach to worship is different from that practised by 'mainstream' Christians, such seductions must be avoided because the right to worship is a human right and should not be prescribed or, for that matter, proscribed. The ascetic and extreme Agoras too have a place in religion and society.

6

The Roots of Religious Fundamentalism

Colonialism

The roots of religious fundamentalism are inextricably linked to the project of modernity that started with the Enlightenment in 17th century Europe. This project resulted in the displacement of religious worldviews of creation—the meaning of life and individual destiny overseen by the arbitrary, cavalier, even whimsical fiat of omnipotent Gods and Goddesses—by scientific explanations advanced by the individual, the increasingly secular, rational, scientific man. It led to struggles to restrict the influence of religion to the private sphere and to the emergence of the state as the public representative of rational man. The advocacy of 'secularism' in the 17th century in Europe that was, in an essential sense, directed towards the expropriation of church property must be seen in the context of the vast powers exercised by the church for many centuries, and the real correspondences between monarchs and their exercise of temporal power, on one hand, and the church and its exercise of power over life after death, on the other (the latter famously explored in T.S. Eliot's *Murder in the Cathedral*). This gradual displacement of religion and the clear demarcation of boundaries between the church and state, the private and the public, unfolded in different ways in different climes, most dramatically in France after the French Revolution. The pace of this change was influenced by the growth of the market economy and liberal politics, processes that themselves were mediated by colonialism between the 16th and 19th centuries and by neo-colonialism in the post-World War II period.

The relationship between colonialism and Christian mission has been the focus of studies (see, for example, Dharmaraj, 1993; Vishwanathan, 1989). The military conquest of countless heathens and their religious conquest through forced conversion—a binary relationship that involves real and symbolic violence—continues to be practised in our contemporary world. The grand project of Christianising the world—for example, the US-based, although global, Joshua Project—is complemented by the Christian broadcasting station SAT-7's objective to convert Muslims in the Middle East, a sub-text that surfaced repeatedly during the US invasion of Iraq (see Mokhiber and Weissman, 2003). The perceived slighting of cultures and religions in the past, along with the habitual, routine degradations heaped on certain religions in the present, continues to rankle and remains a potent reason for contemporary forms of religious

---

7

fundamentalism. The founders of Hindu nationalism, Keshav Baliram Hedgewar (1889–1940) and Madhav Sadashiv Golwalker (1940–73), bristled against the dismissal of Hinduism as a religion based on superstition and magic (Andersen and Damle, 1987), a slight that Arun Shourie (1994, 2000), the most prominent critic of Christian mission in India, has continued to question and challenge. Post-colonial writers, for example, Gandhi (1998) and Viswanathan (1989), have cited Lord Macaulay's (1835) infamous Minute on Education as an example of the classic put-down of Hinduism by the colonisers:

> It is, I believe, no exaggeration to say that all the historical information which has been collected in the Sanscrit language is less valuable than what may be found in the paltry abridgements used at preparatory schools in England.... It is said that the Sanscrit and Arabic are the languages in which the sacred books of a hundred millions of people are written, and that they are, on that account, entitled to a peculiar encouragement.... Assuredly it is the duty of the British government in India to be not only tolerant, but neutral on all religious questions. But to encourage the study of a literature admitted to be of small intrinsic value, only because that literature inculcates the most serious errors on the most important subjects, is a course hardly reconcilable with reasons, with morality, or even with that very neutrality which ought as we all agree, to be sacredly preserved.... We are to teach it because it is fruitful of monstrous superstitions. We are to teach false history, false astronomy, false medicine, because we find them in company with a false religion (quoted in Kuriakose 1999).

The sub-texts within the extraordinary expression of civilisational superiority remain present in the many mission statements of Christian organisations currently working in India.

While the East India Company did, at least initially, and in direct contrast to the Portuguese colonisers (who, apart from routinely massacring Hindus, Muslims and Syrian Christians, instituted the Inquisition in Goa), try to remain committed to its primary goal of economic exploitation and to the expropriation of surplus value, this intent to dissuade missionaries from spreading the Gospel in India was contested by Christian missionaries and colonial administrators in England resulting in a policy volte-face in the mid-17th century. This inevitably led to India becoming a fertile environment for competing missions. Jesupatham (2005: xiv), in a book on the Tranquebar Mission and the Danish missionary

Bartholomaus Ziegenbalg, has observed that the objective of this mission to the native

> was not exploratory in nature, but an accomplishment in deriving attempts, converting *heathens* who were subjects of the Danes. The Evangelical Conversion has conspicuous facets, namely: (i) *Converting Heathens*, (ii) *Instructing the New Converts in the Doctrines*, (iii) *Baptizing the Converts*, and (iv) *Helping them sustain in the Faith through Catechetical Tools*.

While there were numerous Christian missionaries in India and elsewhere who contributed to the development of local language, education, Indian nationalism and to the social betterment of marginalised communities, the suspicion that such examples of service, however progressive, were ultimately meant for the fulfilment of a larger cause, the conversion of the *heathen* to the true religion of Christianity, has remained to this day. Mahatma Gandhi (1927: 26) in an article in the *Young Indian* once famously remarked:

> I have ventured at several meetings to tell English and American missionaries that if they could have refrained from 'telling' India about Christ and had merely lived the life enjoined upon them by the Sermon on the Mount, India instead of suspecting them would have appreciated their living in the midst of her children and directly profited by their presence.

While there are numerous contemporary expressions of Christian mission that have intentionally tried to humanise Christianity, it has become more than apparent in our post-colonial contexts that the memory of 'mission' remains a vital, affirmative aspect in many institutional contexts of contemporary Christian mission today. Christianity, like Islam, is a universalising religion. Global Christianity, in spite of the presence of non-Western forms of Christianity, is essentially Western in outlook, character and expression. Its symbols of identification are unapologetically Western and its inability to take root as an authentic expression of faith in India and in other contexts around the world has contributed to the perception of Christianity as an exclusive, monolithic juggernaut, the basis for a religious pandemic spreading a singular vision of global Christianity. In the words of the late Indian social theorist Sebastien Kappen (quoted in Samartha, 1994: 36): 'We have become mental immigrants in our own country.' The ecumenical theologian Stanley Samartha (1994) goes on to observe that:

> This is truer of Christians in India than people of other religions. Our theology and religious life, our liturgy and music, and our ecclesiastical structures, even our attitudes towards neighbours of other faiths, are dominated by powerful forces from the West. The vast majority of books in the library of theological colleges come from the West. This is true of books on liberation theology as well.

While issues related to Indian Christian identity have been debated in journals (such as *Religion & Society*), books and treatises, and have been the subject for numerous symposia, this has not led to any significant mainstream Christian efforts at indigenising Indian Christianity or to the fashioning of a distinctive Indian Christian identity, with perhaps the obvious exception of the Syrian Orthodox.

Secularism

One of the key battles being fought today is between secularism and religion. The idea of secularism, as Ashis Nandy (1990) and others (Chatterjee, 1995; Rai, 1990) have argued, is based on a false dichotomy, an 'imperialism of categories' that was a heritage of Orientalism and colonial rule. The absolutism of the secular state, and in particular its attempts to demarcate and contain religion and culture, has, interestingly enough, not only riled traditionalists in the developing world, but also in the developed world. To a certain extent, this critique of secularism is warranted, given that India's tryst with secularism, for instance, has not resulted in the making of a rational society or to the establishment of traditions of religious tolerance. Modern India has witnessed a massive rise in inter-religious tension that has led to thousands of deaths, most recently in 2003 in Godhra, Gujarat. In Nandy's words: 'It is not modern India which has tolerated Judaism in India for nearly two thousand years, Christianity from before the time that it went to Europe, and Zoroastrianism for more than twelve hundred years; it is traditional India which has shown such tolerance'(1990: 84). While Nandy can be accused of over stating his case, there is a need to recognise the fact that India's tryst with secularism has not been without serious strain.

However, the propensity to blame secularism for all the problems of the modern state's relationship with religion needs to be treated with circumspection precisely because religious nationalists have used anti-secularism as a pretext for reining in the project of multi-culturalism and communitarianism, and for replacing it with a vision of majoritarian futures. Both Hindutva in India and the Christian right wing in USA, to cite two examples, have used the threat of secularism as a pretext to extend their own political agendas. The Christian right in USA has used the pretext of secularism to roll back the gains of democracy, science and human progress. They have been at the forefront of campaigning for a number of issues—anti-abortion, creationism, support for Zionism—and have been among the most vocal supporters of the wars in Iraq and the Middle East. Television programmes such as Pat Robertson's widely-syndicated *The 700 Club* that is featured daily on Robertson's Christian Broadcasting Network (CBN) and other channels are a barometer for gauging the extent and depth of issues favoured by the Christian right in USA—be it calls to what is euphemistically referred to as the 'taking out' of Saddam Hussein, Hugo Chavez, and others, who stand in the way of the geo-political interests of USA or public lobbying for the extension of support for countries in the developing world that are in favour of the US government's foreign policy (see *BBC News*, 2005; Coomerasamy, 2006).

Mr Robertson, 75, said on Monday's edition of the 700 Club: 'We have the ability to take him out, and I think the time has come that we exercise that ability.' 'We don't need another $ 200 bn war to get rid of one, you know, strong-arm dictator.' 'It's a whole lot easier to have some of the covert operatives do the job and then get it over with' (*BBC News*, 2005).

While the project of modernisation attempted to further marginalise religion and culture to the levels of epiphenomena—perhaps best illustrated by Daniel Lerner's (1958) now infamous book *The Passing of Traditional Societies*—this project's end result was multiple modernities, characterised by different and varied balances between religion and the state in different contexts around the world. For all the modern nation-state's attempt to keep the influence of religion at bay—for example, through Sukarno's Pancasila or Nehru's secular Constitution—the influence of religion was palpable in these contexts in an everyday sense. Modernity did lead to the creation of modern 'social imaginaries' (Taylor, 2002) that were shaped by the economy, the public sphere, the ideas and practices of democratic self rule, and, despite the best efforts by secularists, religion. The inability of the Indian State to advance the project of substantive secularism, while failing to curb the upsurge of inter-religious conflict, remains a tangible example of the very real difficulties faced by many plural societies in the world today that have not been able to manage the tension between secularism and religion. The post-Independence Congress government's involvement in the religious affairs of the majority community, its non-involvement in the affairs of minority communities and its selective exploitation of minorities as an electoral vote bank has remained a source of tension, particularly during the last three decades (D'Cruz, 1988; Hasan, 1990). This is a concern that has been highlighted by Hindu nationalists. However, minority communities argue that for all this non-interventionism, the Indian State, its institutions and its accented identity have putatively and implicitly communicated a national culture that is co-terminus with a Brahminical Hindu identity. In this sense, one can argue that it is not secularism per se that is the problem but the selective operationalisation of secularist policies by governments throughout the world. Alok Rai (1990: 41) has observed that secularism must advance a social imaginary conducive to the making of democratic practice and to the fulfilment of people's aspirations. Secularism

> must, in practice, fabricate that democratic legitimacy without which it is condemned to remaining alienated, a set of unassimilated attitudes. However such a process of 'fabrication' inevitably involves a process of redefining 'democracy' itself, so that it is no longer congruent with the reproduction of existing social categories of prejudice and association, but seeks to accord ever greater numbers of people control over the conditions of their existence.

Core Values and Fundamentalist Identity

A key characteristic shared by all religious fundamentalists is their commitment to a collective and individual identity based on the affirmation of 'certainty' in 'essential, core values' sourced from religious texts perceived to be valid for all time, in contrast to the loose and shifting values undergirding individual identities in the 21st century. The affirmation of 'certainty' in core values has been debated by, on the one hand, the heirs of the Enlightenment who believe that it is uncertainty that is the basis for creativity and innovation and who defend their right to use reason rather than received knowledge to advance human futures, and, on the other hand, by those who believe in limits to human possibility and to the efficacy of transcendentally-inspired normative values for life and order. The latter believe that Western forms of rationality do not have answers to the larger meanings of life that are divinely ordained and inspired. The global media routinely dismiss 'Jihadists' as dysfunctional, mis-educated, mis-informed and misfits, although there probably are multiple, real and imagined reasons for people to choose such a drastic remedy. Living life as a refugee for more than half a century in Palestine while Israelis next door enjoy an enviable quality of life does not encourage rational solutions in the matter of peace and reconciliation. Similarly, the fall-out of the Salman Rushdie affair over the publication of *Satanic Verses* arguably needs to be also seen from the perspectives of marginalised Muslims living in Bradford and other ghettoes in Europe and elsewhere, whose only source of certainty is the Koran.

While reason and rationality have certainly been the basis for human freedom and creativity, in a world characterised by disparities in the distribution of material resources and knowledge, there is a need to understand why the other half behaves in the way that it does and a need for honest explorations of the realities of difference. The fact remains that fundamentalist beliefs remain implicit in all societies. North American Christian fundamentalists use reason and a technocratic rationality when it suits them, while at the same time promoting the global dissemination of 'universal' American values. Coreno (2002: 356–57) has argued that North American Protestant fundamentalism is a class culture.

> Fundamentalism is an extreme religious response to modernity, but its sanctification of piety, asceticism, personal responsibility, and salvation and its general distaste for liberalism are all part of a common strand of a broader conservative value structure that has always defined a wide swathe of the American upper classes.

While the same can be said of upper classes in other societies, for example, elite Brahmins in India and the Wahabis in Saudi Arabia, I would argue that the upper class on its own right is not a sufficient marker of religious fundamentalist identification today, given the real, active presence of other markers including caste, race, gender, ethnicity and, of course, the active involvement of lower classes in the discourses and making of fundamentalism today.

13

It can be argued that the West's cherished values—human freedom, market freedom, value freedom—often become fundamentalist absolutes. These values are difficult to contest precisely because they are globally extensive and are part of the values of the global hegemon. Religious fundamentalists contest this hegemony of values from within and without. While North American Protestant fundamentalists contest value freedoms that undergird the liberal societies of North America and Europe, they actively support the global extension of market values. Islamic fundamentalists contest the US government's support for an aggressive Zionism in Israel and for their perceived marginalisation of Islam as a worthy religion and cultural reality in large swathes of the world today. Their project is dedicated to making an 'imagined community' a real community. This is achieved through a variety of mechanisms of identification, rituals, rites and the granting of rewards that facilitate the project of attaining salvation or God-head. This process of identification varies from religion to religion. Adult baptism, for example, is a prerequisite for 'born again' Christians who value this distinction and use this marker to distinguish themselves from other Christians. The battle against secularism in Christian circles has been defined by attempts to reclaim the moral high ground that has been lost to secular forces. This process of pursuing and defining the moral high ground is often selective. It always involves the sacralisation of narratives consisting of stories, symbols, practices and identifications that in their totality offer a complete meaning system for their followers, in contrast to the shifting values of secular Godless societies.

Religion and Politics

The term Christian fundamentalism as used in this book describes the doctrines and attitudes of Christian groups and sects who are united in their belief that Christian triumphalism is mandated in the Gospels and that, as such, Christians are duty-bound to translate this vision into political reality through the ballot box, by influencing the political agenda of their governments and by engaging and supporting Christian conversions. The alliances between successive US Presidents—Reagan, Ford, Bush Sr and Bush Jr—and the religious right in a country that constitutionally mandates the separation between the church and the state is illustrative of this tendency. Such obvious identifications—iconically represented by Franklin Graham's triumphal entry into the newly 'liberated' Baghdad atop a US armoured carrier, Pat Robertson's daily exclusivisms of those who do not belong to the Christian faith on *The 700 Club*, and Alec and Wendy's support for Christian Zionism on GOD TV—are reminders of the neo-imperialist nature of this project. This identification between religion and politics is by no means the exclusive preserve of fundamentalists from the Bible-belt in USA, for the call to arms and for jihad by imams in different parts of the world against Judeo-Christian civilisation is another side of what essentially is the same struggle. The tragedy of 9/11 was, without a doubt, the clearest expression of the strength of globalised Islamic fundamentalism pitted against its obverse, that is, Judeo-Christian fundamentalism and all that it is perceived to stand for—moral decay, social and political arrogance typified by the continued posturing over Palestine, the invasion of Iraq and its chaotic aftermath, and the mediations of prejudice, such as the 12 cartoons of Mohammed that were published in the Danish newspaper *Jyllands-Posten* in September 2005. Joshua Hoops (2006: 3) in a paper on the cartoons in the Danish newspaper describes the fundamentalist position taken by the Danish authorities that merely inflamed an already difficult situation:

> Two Danish *imams*, Ahmad Akkari and Ahmed Abu Laban, toiled to obtain conciliation from the newspaper and the Danish government, but to no avail. A petition of 17,000 signatures submitted to Danish Prime Minister Anders Fogh Rasmussen elicited no response. The Prime Minister refused to meet with eleven ambassadors from Muslim countries regarding the cartoons, citing freedom of the press.

Theocratic rule in Khomeni's Iran and in Afghanistan under the Taliban are of course paradigmatic cases of religious fundamentalism, although the specific extensions of what one may call consensual fundamentalism—under the cloak of the freedom of expression, the right to propagate and profess religion, and as a strategic option in the context of populist electoral politics—is, in my opinion, a far more widespread and under-theorised process than theocratic, fundamentalist politics. The launch by the US government of its Arabic language satellite television news station for Muslim Iraq on 2 May 2003 in collaboration with the US-based Christian organisation Grace Digital Media is a contemporary example of the way in which religion, politics and the media are aligned in low-intensity struggles aimed at making Christianity more global that it is at the moment. Such examples—along with other forms and varieties of Christian mission located throughout the world, from the work of the Summer School of Linguistics that is involved in translating the Bible into all the world's languages, to the Joshua Project, whose main aim is to take the Gospel to the unreached peoples of the world in order to convert them—feed into and support the project of global Christian fundamentalism.

There have also been less well-known alliances between state leaders and conservative Christian groups. Paul Mbiya (Cameroon), Frederick Chiluba (Zambia), Laisenia Qurase (Fiji), Bill Skate (Papua New Guinea) and Efraín Ríos Montt (Guatemala), among others, have actively wooed the religious right. The Guatemalan President, Efrain Mott, was an elder of a mission of the California-based Gospel Outreach network during his presidency. In 2003, he campaigned for re-election using his 'born again Christianity' badge as a vote winner in impoverished rural districts where American evangelical churches have mushroomed and cater to the Mayan population (*The Guardian*, 2003). Montt's Christian credentials were supported extensively by the US tele-evangelist Pat Robertson to legitimise the struggle against the Communists and anti-Christians in Guatemala (see Marty and Appleby, 1993). In a study of Christianity and television in Guatemala and Brazil, Smith and Campos (2005: 55) describe the active role played by Pentecostals in both countries in supporting conservative politicians. In 2004, the Guatemalan Pentecostalist Jorge Lopez 'organised an inter-denominational prayer service for newly elected President Oscar Berger, a Roman Catholic and his cabinet on the lines of the Te Deum Evangelico by Chilean Pentecostals held in support of the Pinochet regime in Chile' (ibid.). In a study of the relationship between Chiluba and Christian groups in Zambia, Phiri (2003: 405–06) refers to the cleansing ceremony at the state house held on 31 October 1991, followed by the anointing ceremony for Chiluba initiated by the charismatic and Pentecostal churches, and leading to the declaration by the newly elected President on 29 December 1991 affirming Zambia's identity as a Christian nation. General Pinochet, who ruled Chile with an iron fist in the 1970s and 1980s, was avidly supported by the Chilean Evangelical Church. A muscular Christian fundamentalism deeply entangled in politics has emerged as a major force in many parts of the world, in USA in particular and also in Australia, Latin America, Africa, Asia and the Pacific. In USA, as a recent study by Alan Gold (2006) reveals, American Christian nationalists have become, in effect, an unelected shadow government, pulling the strings on a range of policy issues and enjoying financial support from the government to bring the 'disposed' to Jesus Christ, while using this opportunity to marginalise unbelievers and undesirables. Gold's book is one among the many published during the first half of 2006 that has explored the links between Dominion Theology and politics, economics and geo-politics in USA. Other publications include Lerner (2006), Philipps (2006) and Hendricks (2006).

Christian Fundamentalism

Nancy Ammerman (1991: 4–8) has described North American Protestant fundamentalism as based on

1. Evangelism: 'aimed at convincing the unconvinced that eternity in heaven is better than the eternal damnation in hell that surely awaits the unsaved'.
2. Inerrancy: 'a faith in Jesus Christ grounded in unwavering faith in an inerrant Bible'. They (the Christian fundamentalists) 'are confident that everything in Scripture is true' and that 'true Christians must believe the whole Bible';
3. Premillennialism: 'They...expect to find in Scripture clues to the future destiny of this world, what will happen in the End Times... the idea of the Rapture', of what will happen 'when the Son of Man comes...lends both urgency to the evangelistic task and comfort to persecuted believers'. Along with the need to be prophetic 'Believers are not content to know that Jesus is coming for them; they want to know when and what will happen next'.
4. Separatism: 'Fundamentalists insist on uniformity of belief within the ranks and separation from others whose beliefs and lives are suspect.'

To reiterate, Christian fundamentalists abide by a handful of Bible-inspired core tenets—evangelism and the salvation of souls, belief in the inerrancy of Scripture, belief in premillennialism (Bible-based knowledge of the end times) including a belief in prophecy, the 'Rapture' ('Then shall two be in the field; the one shall be taken, and the other left' [Mathew, 24: 37–41]; 'caught up together with them in the clouds, to meet the Lord in the air' [1 Thessalonians 4: 15–18]) and separatism. I would argue, that in addition to harbouring such predispositions, militant Christian fundamentalists are actively involved in either using politics in order to legitimise their national and global projects related to social change or are involved in covert acts of mission that, in the final analysis, are oriented towards the fulfilment of the goal of Christianising the world. I argue that militant Christian fundamentalists include those who are actively and publicly involved in the project of global evangelism through fair means or foul, along with those who are involved in low intensity mission work. In this light, the Australia-based preacher Danny Nalliah, who belongs to a group called Catch the Fire and who is routinely in the headlines for his anti-Muslim remarks, and the low-key operations of the Summer School of Linguistics involved in indigenous language translations of the Bible are implicated in the business and activities of Christian fundamentalism. I also argue that global forms of conservative Christian broadcasting offer these groups the necessary 'oxygen of publicity'.

Some Reasons for the Rise of Christian Fundamentalism

1. Christians who for one reason or another have been dissatisfied with the services and pastoral care offered by mainstream churches have been drawn to the many mediated Gospels of Prosperity, to weekly encounters with an accessible, personal God and to events that provide space for individual validations of God in one's life. Healing, testimonials, prayer and free forms of worship are the props that broadcasting has used to create symbolic dramas and spectacles around universal themes—the struggles between good and evil, the meaning of life, the spiritual basis for health and prosperity, and the basis for sin and salvation.

    There is little doubt that these new forms of mediated worship have resulted in forms of community, strengthened personal self-esteem and given people hope in the context of the many disruptions caused by rapidly modernising societies throughout the world. The fastest growing churches in many parts of the world are those outside of the mainstream. Given the strength of these churches, their global remit, market-based acknowledgement of their services and the relative decline of the traditional power of the mainstream churches, the latter are not in a position to challenge this new form. In fact, mainstream churches have, in some contexts, opted to join the bandwagon and offer more of the same.

2. While mainstream Christianity's understanding of God's active, salvific presence in our world has undergone major changes as a result of the church's encounter with other faiths, economic and political structures, ideologies and issues of concern, such as gender justice, violence, sexuality, war, the environment and marginality,

---

the further that one is away from the centres of denominational power, the more likely it is that understandings of faith are layered and informed by authoritative, received interpretations of tradition and culture. 'Progressive' understandings of Christianity adopted by a church synod often take a long time to filter down to the level of the local parish. More often than not, the journey of a position or idea from centre to periphery is fraught and involves dilution, adaptation, reinterpretation and even rejection.

The continuing furore in the Anglican Church over the ordination of gay priests illustrates the point that there are different wings within Christian denominations who routinely contest issues and theological interpretations. The India-based Mar Thoma Church, a member of the World Council of Churches, has a strong evangelical wing and tolerates separate churches for Dalits within its fold. The Roman Catholic Church actively endorses its right-wing arm Opus Dei and many charismatic movements within its midst, for instance, Father Rossi in Brazil, Mother Angelica in USA and the Potta Movement in India.

3. The ecumenical movement in general and the progressive strands of mainstream Christianity have been in a crisis for more than two decades. A crisis of resources, vision, structures, interpretation, education and even credibility. While the mainstream church is willing to dialogue with the conservative churches on certain controversial issues such as 'abortion' and 'women's rights', they are not similarly motivated to take on the theology, the politics and the structures of the well-resourced ultra-conservative churches, for example, those aligned to the religious right in USA. To Christian fundamentalists, the ecumenical movement is a sign of all that is wrong with Christianity. The Social Gospel, tolerance of other faiths and lifestyles, rabid inclusiveness and the contextualisation of faith are all seen as antithetical to the original Christian mandate, often cited as reasons for the decline of Christian civilisation.

While the more zany and explicitly brash intentions of Christian zealots are often criticised by the mainstream churches, for instance, Rev. Franklin Graham's triumphal entry into Iraq along with US troops, the critique has not been sustained. The mainstream church neither has the political will nor the resources to challenge the ultra-conservatives.

4. Fundamentalist positions are tolerated because in an increasingly divided world across religious lines, a world in which religious

identities are at stake, there are implicit moves to stand by one's faith, warts and all. For example, the National Council of Churches of India (NCCI) consistently defended all Christians in India during inter-religious tensions, but failed to point fingers at members belonging to ultra-conservative Christian groups who had a hand in stirring up inter-religious tension. The NCCI would argue that this is not the time to engage in a Christian fundamentalism project in India but, such a position begs the question, when is a good time?

Christian Fundamentalism and Market Fundamentalism

Fundamentalism can also be explored from an altogether different angle—for instance, the perceived influence of market fundamentalism supported by the neo-liberal economy, the globalisation of trade, intellectual property rights, the knowledge economy and the global banking system. While religious and economic fundamentalisms may not, at first glance, have anything in common, it can be argued that there are enduring relationships between these two forms of fundamentalism. The global market economy is founded on the free market, global flows of cultures, lifestyles, finances, ever closer integrations between the global and the local, liberal politics and global extensions of democracy. This is the 'free world' that is endorsed by President Bush and Prime Minister Blair. This global, universalising project has been contested by those who either have been disenfranchised by this process or marginalised or whose identities and aspirations are inspired by an altogether different, transcendentally inspired code of ethics and way of life. The rhetoric and reality of a singular, universal, mono-civilisation, valid for all nations and for all time, remains a vision that is antithetical to the hopes and dreams of communities around the world. It is in this sense that one can claim that religious fundamentalism is pitted against fundamentalist modernity, although this cannot be taken in an absolute sense given that religious fundamentalists, in varying degrees, often do make selective peace with modernity, while concurrently excoriating its perceived defence of, and contributions to, the making of a Godless world (Farley, 2005). The very fact that contemporary forms of terrorism piggy-back and make full use of new technologies—mobile phones, computing, websites and planes—indicates that religious fundamentalists are not averse to using the tools of the West to destroy its power or at least make a dent in its aura of power.

North American Protestant fundamentalists are of course great supporters of the free market that they believe in a divinely-inspired system that will lead to the greatest good in society. Iannaconne (1993: 346–47), in a chapter on the economics of Christian fundamentalists, refers to an affirmation in a paper entitled the 'Christian Worldview of Economics' by an evangelical organisation called the Coalition on Revival that states the following:

> We affirm that the free market economy is the closest approximation that man has yet devised in this fallen world to the economy set forth in the Bible, and that, of all the economies known to man, it is the most conducive to producing a free, just and prosperous society for all people.... We deny that central planning and other coercive interferences with personal choice can increase the productivity of society; that the civil government has the authority to set the value of property; and that the Bible teaches any just price other than that resulting from the interaction of supply and demand in a marketplace of free people.

While the market orientations of religious fundamentalists vary, Christian fundamentalists in general are great believers in the market precisely because economic globalisation has played an important role in the export of this tradition from the West to the rest of the world. Having said that, and given the reality of complexity in any social formation, there are bound to be those within the Christian fundamentalist fold who eschew the embrace of the market because it is perceived to be tainted by the hands of 'fallen' human beings. For every Christian fundamentalist backed up by corporate mission bodies and agencies, there are those who do lead relatively simple lives and are committed to converting the world to Christ. Some of the most vociferous opponents of the free market in India also include members of the Rashtriya Swayamsevak Sangh (RSS), a right-wing Hindu organisation that provides the ideological framework for the Sangh Parivar (the family of right-wing Hindu organisations built around the RSS).

In the case of neo-Pentecostals, the spiritual dimension is underlaid by ultra-conservative worldviews related to politics and economics—obedience to market fundamentalism, to the established order of politics. In the words of Dennis Smith and Rolando Pérez (2003):

> The Neo-pentecostals offer individualised consumer religion ... consumers enter the marketplace and take from the shelf those symbolic goods they need to get them through the week: an ounce of self-esteem,

21

a packet of hope, a portion of pardon, essence of encounter with the divine. All this is mixed according to one's personal recipe and used as needed.

Exploring Christian Fundamentalism in India

The existence of Christian separatism in India has been highlighted in Edna Fernandes' (2006) study *Holy Warriors: A Journey into the Heart of Indian Fundamentalism*, which includes separate chapters on the rise of Christian fundamentalism in Goa and Nagaland in northeast India. I believe that India, indeed, is home to many incipient, dispersed traditions of exclusive Christianity that correspond with Christian fundamentalism as discourse, thought and deed. However, any correspondence with an explicit politics, with the exception of the situation in northeast India, is less noticeable, although intriguingly present.

While the rise and fall of Hindu fundamentalism in India during the last two decades has inspired a number of publications (Basu et al., 1993; Das, 1990; Hansen and Jaffrelot, 1998; Juergensmeyer, 1993; Ludden, 1996; Nandy et al., 1997) that have specifically dealt with issues related to Hindu nationalism and its implications for the democratic project in India, there is very little information available on other expressions of religious fundamentalism in India. Arvind Rajagopal (2001) has written a well-researched book on the relationship between televised serials in India, on one hand, and the rise of the Bharatiya Janata Party (BJP) and the electoral fortunes of the Hindu right wing, on the other. Yet, very little work has been carried out on other types of religious fundamentalisms in India, in particular minority fundamentalisms involving Christians who are actively involved in muscular forms of mission and evangelism work throughout the country. There are a handful of writings on fundamentalism among Christians including the studies by Caplan (1987) and Bayly (1994). Caplan was perhaps the first to describe the reality of multi-church attendance within the Church of South India—of Protestant Pentecostals paying tithes, becoming 'born again' and turning into itinerant evangelists. Bayly (1994: 727), in her study of the growth of Christian fundamentalism on the southern coast of Tamil Nadu and in its hinterlands, claims that 'fundamentalist movements' in South Asia 'can only be understood as a product of conflicts emanating from within its own complex societies', a claim that I have contested in this book, given the real time connections between neo-Pentecostal groups in Chennai and the

West, and the reality of global exports of Christian fundamentalism. While the rise of Hindu nationalism in India has certainly led to a response from radical Muslim and Christian groups, and there are examples of indigenous Christianity, I would agree that Bayly's (1994: 728) prediction that 'greater standardisation and mutual interconnections may be in prospect' has, a decade later, become a reality. Augustine (1987) has contested Caplan's labelling of Pentecostals fundamentalist, given that they were not involved in an explicit politics during the 1980s. However, in the context of globalising India, the relationship between economics, politics and society has become a lot more pronounced. There has been a blurring of whatever distinctions there once were between Pentecostals, neo-Pentecostals and the charismatics and instead there are closer, shared identifications that are supportive of a triumphalist Christianity. Augustine (1987: 132) has observed that church growth has been most significant outside of the mainline churches:

> For example, the Assemblies of God exhibited a growth of 264 per cent and the Pentecostal mission 327 per cent. The Maranatha Full Gospel Church in Tamil Nadu showed a growth of 94 per cent. In addition to churches numbering more than in any other city in South Asia, Madras has a large number of Christian institutions sponsored by the churches. Among them are 11 Bible correspondence schools, 10 book shops, 4 broadcasting studios, more than 75 children's homes and orphanages...20 communication centres.

These statistics need to be revised given the tremendous church growth that has taken place in Chennai and in Tamil Nadu in general.

Christianity and Politics in India

Unlike the pre-colonial and colonial eras when the church in India did enjoy close ties to colonial politics, in post-colonial India, the church, for the most part, was not actively aligned with politics except in states that had a majority or sizeable Christian population such as in Nagaland, Mizoram, Meghalaya and Kerala. The church, for the most part, kept its distance from the nationalist struggles, although there were a handful of Christian leaders, notably the Gandhians C.F. Andrews and S.K. George, who advocated for a church and Christian expression supportive of a politically independent India. For Christians, the Congress party, with its avowedly secularist leanings, was the political party of choice and, in return for Christian votes, the party followed a hands-off policy with respect to Christians and, for that matter, with all minority religions. The Communist government's intention in Kerala to collectivise land in 1959, following that party's accession to power on the basis of a free ballot, was opposed by the church, Christian landlords and Nehru's Congress party. In contrast to this hands-off policy related to minorities, the secular state was involved in managing the affairs of the Hindu majority, a contradiction that Hindu nationalists have turned to their political advantage and which they have used to create an image of an anti-majority Congress party. During the post-Independence period, the mainstream churches built a reputation in areas such as education, health and development. Among the only active Indian Christian leaders involved in a humanist politics during the post-Independence era were M.M. Thomas, who served as the Governor of Nagaland in the mid-1990s, and Juhanon Mar Thoma, the Metropolitan of the Mar Thoma Church. They were both actively involved in resisting the Emergency rule that was promulgated by Indira Gandhi during 1975–77.

In the context of Tamil Nadu, Dravidian politics with its broadly secular, anti-Brahmin, pro-minority stance appealed to local Tamil Christians, while Christians from other parts of India living in Tamil Nadu continued to support the Congress Party. In the historic mission fields in the extreme south, where there still are sizeable Christian communities, the church has remained keenly involved in party politics. However, the advent of new Christianity in this region has taken the relationship between the politics and the church to new levels.

1. While the presence of the church in Chennai and in Tamil Nadu in general is strong and bishops belonging to the Church of South India have been courted by politicians, it is clear that in the era of economic globalisation and India's tryst with liberalisation, the groups actively involved in politics are factions within the Pentecostal church who are aligned to the two key Dravidian parties—the Dravida Munnetra Kazhagam (DMK) and the All India Anna Dravida Munnetra Kazhagam (AIADMK). Bishop Ezra Sargunam, who heads the Indian Pentecostal Church, and who is a former member of the minorities commission, is a supporter of the incumbent DMK party. When the AIADMK is in power, it is the turn of Bishop M. Prakash, who heads the Synod of Independent Churches, to take over as the Christian representative on the minorities commission. These two

church representatives from the Pentecostal/independent traditions have been recognised by politicians for the vote banks that they represent. While both leaders stand for 'family values' and express their social conservativeness on Christian television, they are not in a position to advance their agenda on secular Chennai. In fact given the minority status of Christians in India, any pan-Indian project is bound to remain a case of wishful thinking. They have, however, used their connections and politics to smoothen the way for the continuation of uninterrupted mission work in the south; actively, publicly supported the right to convert; played an instrumental role in organising Pentecostal-led Christian rallies and conventions; and, more importantly, taken a lead role in manufacturing and communicating globally the changing nature of Christian identity in India. Bishop Ezra Sargunam's support for Dalit Christians would seem to suggest that some expressions of Pentecostalism in India are socially grounded. This example does suggest that there indeed may be a case to consider certain variants of socially grounded Pentecostalism as expressions of subalternity.

2. While the relationship between Christian leaders and an explicit politics is absent at the national level, at the state level, in the majority Christian, so-called 'tribal' states in northeast India and some of the states in southern India, this relationship is both visible and sometimes explicit. While there is, to date, scant evidence to suggest that these two leaders are actively involved in advocating separatism, their commitment to muscular forms of mission and evangelism and, in particular, to conversion has taken them on a collision course with Hindu nationalists and secularists. It has also resulted in their becoming the de facto spokespersons for Indian Christians and in their being featured on Capital Hill in USA, at the US Commission on International Religious Freedom and the US State Department's annual report on international religious freedom. They have played a key role in the consolidation of the independent and Pentecostal churches, and have used their political power to get the government of Tamil Nadu to repeal the bill against 'forced conversions' that was promulgated by the previous AIADMK government and to leverage space and support for Christian conventions and rallies that are a platform for conversion. Furthermore, some of these leaders feature regularly on Christian cable and satellite channels, where they reinforce their brand of conservative Christianity. The former president of the minorities commission in the state of Tamil Nadu,

M. Prakash, who is the founder of the South India Soul Winner's Association, is also the president of the Synod of the Independent Churches of India (1700 churches) and the national coordinator of the US-based Trinity Broadcasting Network (TBN), the world's largest Christian broadcasting network. The present head of the state minorities commission, Ezra Sargunam, leads the Evangelical Church of India and is a vocal supporter of conversion. The present chief minister of Andhra Pradesh, Samuel Rajasekhar Reddy, is a Seventh Day Adventist who has allegedly provided tacit support for Christian missions, including Christian broadcasting. Incidentally, Hyderabad, the capital of Andhra Pradesh, is the location of the CBN's Indian operations. The mainstream churches, the Catholic Church in particular, is in a state of denial on the issue of the inroads made by these new churches. While the charismatic movement has provided the space for a renewal within the mainstream church, Pentecostalism as a movement is deeper, wider, better resourced and networked, and has been able to reinvent itself in the myriad contexts of globalising India.

3. The Pentecostal churches have played an extremely important role in popularising a specific transnational Christianity based on the cultivation of 'distinctions' that include the organisation of the church, preaching styles, modes of worship, and pastoral outreach that includes cell churches, houses of prayer and care cells. These distinctions, which have been reinforced through Christian broadcasting, have become a powerful draw for youth belonging to the mainstream churches who, in turn, have pushed their own churches to adapt and accommodate such forms of worship. In other words, there has been a sharing of distinctions between charismatics from the mainstream church, evangelicals and Pentecostals. While the sharing of these distinctions has led to a renewal in churches that had become bogged down in tradition, it has also led to congregational demands that Christian pastors belonging to the mainstream churches follow styles of worship perfected by Pentecostal preachers.

4. The relationship of these new churches with mainstream politics is public. At the Every Tongue Every Tribe convention organised by the Indian Pentecostal Church that I attended in January 2006 in Chennai—the first national convention specifically devoted to celebrating the missionising of tribal India—the chief guests included India's present finance minister, P. Chidambaram, along with a host of politicians from the Congress government and the then

opposition DMK government. That this convention was specifically convened to celebrate the conversion of 'tribals' was not an issue of concern for these politicians. The relationship between politicians and religion in India is an explicit relationship. Politicians are present at all major religious rallies, from Benny Hinn conventions to Hindu meetings, and can be seen actively seeking spiritual guidance and blessings from religious leaders. The grey area of correspondences between religion and politics, public expression and private morality involving politicians from the Hindu right and fundamentalist Christian groups, is indicative of the reality of real politik that certainly involves real money transfers, but also respect for Christian miracle healers. While interviewing employees at the Chennai-based Jesus Calls, run by the Dhinakarans, and one of the largest evangelical organisations in India, I was told of liaisons and 'understandings' between prominent members of the BJP and this organisation. While such relationships may seem far-fetched, the logistics of a Benny Hinn rally requires that a range of connectivities need to be forged, for instance, as was the case in Mumbai, with the Shiv Sena, a rightwing Hindu group that controls a number of local municipalities.

5. These new churches have certainly played an important role in paving the way for mission and missionaries in India, and in the strengthening of transnational networks of Pentecostal and neo-Pentecostal missions.

Religious Fundamentalism Problematised

Scholars have debated and continue to debate the slippery nature of the term 'fundamentalism' (Marty and Appleby, 1993) and the tendency of critics to apply the term indiscriminately to describe a number of tendencies in any given religion and, in the specific case of Christianity, to label those in the charismatic and Pentecostal movements fundamentalists. The rise of Hindutva in India has led to the study of Hindu religious nationalism and to a questioning of the universal validity of terms like fundamentalism to describe the efflorescence of politically inspired forms of revivalism in non-Judeo-Christian religions such as Hinduism and Buddhism. All religions adhere to fundamentals. This is probably more true of the Judeo-Christian religions (Judaism, Christianity and Islam) than Eastern religions such as Buddhism and Hinduism that allow for a certain leeway, ambiguities, options in one's journey towards understanding one's faith and attaining Godhead. In Hinduism, you have a choice of your *ishta daivam* (preferred God/Goddess) and different paths to the knowledge of God—the path of knowledge, the path of action, and so on. The rise of right-wing Hinduism is often described as an instance of 'revivalism' and not as an instance of 'fundamentalism'.

As Nehring (1994:18) has observed:

> If we define fundamentalism as movement that calls for a return to the original fundamentalisms of a certain doctrine, ideology or religion, then the term seems not appropriate to the Indian context, especially not appropriate to Hindusim because such a monistic fundament is not to be found in [this]...religion.

This position is supported by Peter Beyer (1998) and articulated in Romila Thapar's (1990: 10) characterisation of Hinduism as 'a mosaic of distinct cults, deities and sects', without a common centre or core, but that is now being shaped and unified by the proponents of 'syndicated Hinduism'. One can argue that the rise of 'syndicated Hinduism' is a response to the perceived value of a centrally-organised religion against a type of dispersed religion. The need for a centrally-organised religious system is arguably a vital requirement for the project of majoritarian identity making. Others have pointed out that even within a specific religious tradition, for instance, Protestant Christianity, the habitual inclination to label different groups fundamentalist leads to a blurring of real differences between these groups. There are, for instance, clear doctrinal differences between Christian fundamentalists and the 'charismatics', given that the latter's 'Gifts of the Spirits' (glossolia, that is, speaking in tongues) in the context of the Azuza Street Revival in USA was described as the last 'vomit of the Devil' by Christian fundamentalists in USA (attributed to Campbell Morgan, quoted in Vinson, 1971).

While for academic purposes it is important that we have accurate descriptions of the integrity, uniqueness and distinctive character of conservative Christian denominations, it is clear that in spite of real doctrinal and ideological differences, there has been a closing of ranks between Pentecostal and neo-Pentecostal groups, and between these churches and churches within the mainstream churches which, for reasons of expediency and self-preservation, turn a blind eye to the many forms of crusadic Christian mission that are pervasive in India. To some extent, such expressions of Christian unity are a consequence of Hindu nationalism and the Christian-baiting that accompanied it. I have also argued in this book that global forms of conservative Christian broadcasting, for example, the CBN and GOD TV, have offered opportunities for a closing of ranks, for a suppression of difference in the pursuit of the larger goal of universal, Christian unity.

Christian unity remains an implicit discourse in dominant Christian broadcasting although its epistemological basis is very different from other discourses of Christian unity such as that shared by the ecumenical movement or promoted by the Vatican. Having said that, and in spite of the progressive, liberal core that is at the heart of the ecumenical movement, it can be argued that this movement's grand, universalising project of the 'oikoumene' for all God's people, based on the Johanine verse (17: 21) 'so that all may believe', is fraught precisely because its claims on behalf of all people can be interpreted as an instance of custodianship not shared by adherents of other faiths. As against the model of an imputed, universalising religion, the religions scholar Peter Beyer (2003: 361) argues that:

> Religions in today's world, to the extent that they are constructed as differentiated social forms, accomplish this result through a globally extended and multi-centred process which, rather than favouring a centre-periphery process such as, in the case of Christianity at least may have prevailed in the past, proceeds by way of the multiple particularisation of a general and somewhat imprecise universal model.

While there is no reason to doubt that the glocalisation of religion is an extra dimension that needs to be considered, I argue that for all the indigenity that is reflected in local churches around the world, their relationship with their mother church in USA or Germany or with mission agencies continues to be based on centre–periphery relationships. The financing of local Christian missions, irrespective of whether these are supported by the ecumenical movements and its agencies or by evangelical groups, remains, in spite of innovations in 'partnership', a centre–periphery relationship.

One can argue that the creation of an *umma* by Islamic fundamentalists is the mirror-image of what Christian fundamentalists have been trying to achieve for many decades. There is an implicit belief—be it by the Family First Party in Australia, the Christian right in USA or the Evangelical Church of India—that missionising the world is a God-given task. While there are any number of denominations divided along doctrinal, ritual and other lines, the core message of proclamation and conversion remains a constant that unites even seemingly disparate Christian groups.

This struggle to create an identity based on core Christian values is echoed in different contexts around the world. However, it is when mainstream churches in India begin to be influenced by fundamentalist dogma and remain silent when militant Christian fundamentalists attempt to break down idols in the precincts of Hindu temples or turn a blind eye to those involved in dubious forms of conversion, that the full extent of the influence of conservative Christianity becomes evident.

Fundamentalists have an explicitly political agenda. They can be described as grateful ultra-conservatives who fervently believe that they must share the message of God's redeeming presence in their lives with others thus contributing to fulfilling the great commission and playing their part in saving the unsaved. They fight against perceived lapses in Christian civilisation, they fight for a Christian world order, they fight with resources that they use as weapons, for example, broadcasting, they fight against others and they fight under a God-given mandate.

References

Ammerman, N.T. 1991. 'North American Protestant Fundamentalism', in M.E. Marty and R.S. Appleby (eds), *Fundamentalism Observed*, pp. 1–65. Chicago & London: The University of Chicago Press.

Andersen, W.K. and Damle, S.D. 1987. *The Brotherhood of Saffron: The Rashtriya Swayamsevak Sangh and Hindu Revivalism*. Boulder & London: Westview Press.

Augustine, J.S. (ed.). 1987. *Religious Fundamentalism: An Asian Perspective*. Bangalore: SATHRI, CCA, WARC.

Basu, T., P. Datta, S. Sarkar, T. Sarkar and S. Sen. 1993. *Khaki Shorts Saffron Flags*, Tracts for the Times/1. New Delhi: Orient Longman Ltd.

Bayly, S. 1994. 'Christians and Competing Fundamentalisms in South Indian Society', in M.E. Marty. and R.S. Appleby (eds), *Accounting for Fundamentalisms: The Dynamic Character of Movement*, pp. 726–69. Chicago & London: The University of Chicago Press.

BBC News. 2005.'Chavez Assassination Row Erupts', *BBC News*, 23 August. Available at http://news.bbc.co.uk/2/hi/americas/4178608.stm, accessed on 23 August 2005.

Beyer, P. 2003. 'De-Centring Religious Singularity: The Globalisation of Christianity as a Case in Point', *Numen*, 50(1): 357–86.

———. 1998. 'The Modern Emergence of Religions and a Global Social System for Religion', *International Sociology*, 13(2): 151–72.

Caplan, L. 1987. 'Fundamentalism as a Counter-Culture: Protestants in Urban South India', in L. Caplan (ed.), *Studies in Religious Fundamentalism*, pp. 156–76. Basingstoke/London: Macmillan Press.

Chatterjee, P. 1995. 'Religious Minorities and the Secular State: Reflections on an Indian Impasse', *Public Culture*, 8 (Fall): 11–39.

Coomerasamy, J. 2006. 'US Evangelicals Warn Republicans', *BBC News*, 17 March. Available at http://news.bbc.co.uk/2/hi/americas/4815912.stm, accessed on 17 March 2006.

Coreno, T. (2002), 'Fundamentalism as a Class Culture', *Sociology of Religion*, 63(3): 335–60.

D'Cruz, E. 1988. *Indian Secularism: A Fragile Myth*. New Delhi: Indian Social Institute.

Das, V. (ed.). 1990. *Communities, Riots and Survivors in South Asia*. Delhi: Oxford University Press.

Dharmaraj, J.S. 1993. *Colonialism and Christian Mission: Postcolonial Reflections*. New Delhi: ISPCK.

Farley, E. 2005. 'Fundamentalism: A Theory', *Cross Currents*, Fall, 55(3): 378–403.

Fernandes, Edna. 2006. *Holy Warriors: A Journey into the Heart of Indian Fundamentalism*. New Delhi: Penguin/Viking.

Gandhi, L. 1998. *Post-Colonial Theory: A Critical Introduction*. NY: Columbia University Press.

Gandhi, M. 1927. 'Why I am a Hindu', *Young Indian*, 27 October. Also available at http://www.gandhiserve.org/cwmg/VOL040.PDF, accessed on 12 March 2008.

Gold, A. 2006. *Kingdom Coming: The Rise of Christian Nationalism*. NY: W.W. Norton & Company.

Hansen, T.B. and C. Jaffrelot (eds). 1998. *The BJP and the Compulsions of Politics in India*. Delhi: Oxford University Press.

Hasan, Z. 1990. 'Changing Orientation of the State and the Emergence of Majoritarianism in the 1990s', *Social Scientist*, 18(8–9): 27–37.

Hendricks, S. 2006. *Wise Use, Dominion Theology and the Making of American Environmental Policy*. NY: Melville House Publishing.

Hoops, J.F. 2006. 'Muslim Protest: An Emic Analysis of the Ideograph in the Danish Cartoons of the Prophet Muhammed', paper presented at the conference on Fundamentalism and the Media, Boulder, Colorado, 9–12 October 2006.

Iannaconne, L.R. 1993. 'Heirs to the Protestant Ethic? The Economics of American Fundamentalists', in M.E. Marty and R.S. Appleby (eds), *Fundamentalisms and the State: Remaking Polities, Economies, and Militance*, pp. 342–66. Chicago & London: The University of Chicago Press.

Jesupatham, D.S. 2005. *Evangelical Conversion as the Design: The Tranquebar Mission in its Inception*. Bangalore: Sacrifices.

Juergensmeyer, M. 1993. *Religious Nationalism Confronts the Secular State*. Delhi: Oxford University Press.

Kuriakose, M.K. 1999. *History of Christianity in India: Source Materials*, pp. 122–25. New Delhi: ISPCK.

Lerner, D. 1958. *The Passing of Traditional Societies*. NY: Free Press.

Lerner, M. 2006. *The Left Hand of God: Taking Back our Country from the Religious Right*. San Francisco: Harper.

Ludden, D. (ed.). 1996. *Making India Hindu: Religion, Community, and the Politics of Democracy in India*. Delhi: Oxford University Press.

Marty, M.E. and R.S. Appleby (eds). 1993. *Fundamentalisms and the State: Remaking Polities, Economies, and Militance*. Chicago & London: The University of Chicago Press.

———. 1995. *Fundamentalisms Comprehended*. Chicago: University of Chicago Press.

Mokhiber, R. and R. Weissman. 2003. 'US Hires Christian Extremists to Produce Arabic News'. Available at http://www.alternet.org/story.html? Story ID = 15801, accessed on 2 April 2005.

Nandy, A. 1990. 'The Politics of Secularism and the Recovery of Religious Tolerance', in V. Das (ed.), *Mirrors of Violence: Communities, Riots and Survivors in South Asia*. Delhi: Oxford University Press.

Nandy, A., S. Trivedy, S. Mayaram and A. Yagnik. 1997. *The Ramjanmabhumi Movement and Fear of the Self: Creating a Nationality*. Delhi: Oxford University Press.

Nehring, A. 1994. 'Fundamentalism: A Radical Response to Post-Modern Secularism', in A. Nehring (ed.), *Fundamentalism and Secularism: The Indian Predicament*, pp. 16–27. Chennai: Gurukul Lutheran Theological College and Research Institute.

Philipps, K. 2006. *The Peril and Politics of Radical Religion, Oil and Borrowed Money in the 21st Century*. NY: Viking Books.

Phiri, I.A. 2003. 'President Frederick J.T. Chiluba of Zambia: The Christian Nation and Democracy', *Journal of Religion in Africa*, 33(4): 401–28.

Rai, A. 1990. 'Democracy and Secularism', *Seminar*, 374 (October): 37–41.

Rajagopal, A. 2001. *Politics after Television: Hindu Nationalism and the Re-Shaping of the Public in India*. Delhi: Cambridge University Press.

Samartha, S.J. 1994. 'The Causes and Consequences of Religious Fundamentalism', in A. Nehring (ed.), *Fundamentalism and Secularism: The Indian Predicament*, pp. 29–44. Chennai: Gurukul Lutheran Theological College and Research Institute.

Shourie, A. 2000. *Harvesting Our Souls: Missionaries, their Design, their Claims*. New Delhi: ASA Publications.

———. 1994. *Missionaries in India: Continuities, Changes, Dilemmas*. New Delhi: Rupa & Co.

Smith, D. and R. Pérez. 2003. 'The Churches, the Media and Cultural Power in Latin America', unpublished paper.

Smith, D.A. and L.S. Campos. 2005. 'Christianity and Television in Guatemala and Brazil: The Pentecostal Experience', *Studies in World Christianity*, 11(1): 49–64.

Synan, Vinson. 1971. *The Holiness-Pentecostal Movement*. Grand Rapids, MI: William B. Eerdman's Publishing Co.

Taylor, C. 2002. 'Modern Social Imaginaries', *Public Culture*, 14(1): 91–124.

Thapar, R. 1990. 'Communalism and the Historical Legacy: Some Facets', *Social Scientist*, 18(6–7): 4–20.

The Guardian. 2003. 8 September.

Vishwanathan, G. 1989. *Masks of Conquest: Literary Studies and British Rule in India*. NY: Columbia University Press.

2

CHRISTIAN FUNDAMENTALISM AND THE MEDIA

Christian fundamentalism is a complex phenomenon that is often shaped by a variety of factors including the perceived crisis of 'authentic' Christianity in the light of accentuated forms of secularisation; the dilution of the 'true' Christian faith by mainstream Christian groups; the desire to privilege 'true' belief, doctrines and identities; and an explicit and implicit politics linked to the project of mainstreaming Christianity through conversion, electoral politics and a variety of mission activities. Broadcasting is a potent transnational and national communication, mobilisation and educational tool for Christian fundamentalists the world over, and it is this relationship between Christian fundamentalism and broadcasting that will be explored in this chapter.

There are a number of observations that can be made on the contemporary rise of religious fundamentalism and the relationship between Christian fundamentalism and the media, inclusive of the following:

1. The failure of classical and modern social theorists inclusive of Auguste Comte, Karl Marx, Max Weber, Émile Durkheim and Anthony Giddens to theorise religion as more than just an epiphenomenon, 'false consciousness' or a metaphysics that was destined to wither away under the onslaught of modernisation and globalisation. Anthony Giddens (1999) has observed that, 'Fundamentalism is beleaguered tradition. It is tradition defended in the traditional way—by reference to ritual truth—in a globalising world that asks for reasons'. While fundamentalism may be a beleaguered

tradition from the point of view of sociologists, and fundamentalists belonging to every religious tradition certainly uphold the virtues of 'tradition', the fact remains that this tendency has established itself at the very core of many of the world's established religions—Christianity, Judaism, Islam and Hinduism.

2. The neglect by the media to report religion in spite of its extraordinary influence in the modern state, be it in USA or for that matter in the former Soviet Union, where the Russian Orthodox Church, under state patronage, played an important role in society. It is clear that secular media had, until very recently, little or no space to devote to news or analyses related to 'other worldly' concerns and to matters of faith. The media, true to its criteria for newsworthiness, took religion seriously when 'religion as overt conflict' became a key issue in global geo-politics. It took the end of the Cold War and the rise of theocratic Iran and conflicts in the Middle East, Indonesia, Bosnia and Chechnya, for the media to consider religion as a newsworthy item to report. To be fair, 'conflict in religion' had been considered newsworthy—scandals in the church, intra-denominational conflicts over gay clergy and the ordination of women, sex and celibacy, among other issues, featured in countries around the world that had traditions of a free press.

3. The globalisation of religious identities that has accelerated in the context of the globalisation and liberalisation of the economy, mobility, the growth of transnational cultures, and the role played by the market in enabling the transformations of religious goods into a global commodity available to be bought and sold in the religious marketplace. The market for Gospel music is among the largest in the music business. Globalisation has certainly impacted on religion and religious identities. It has provided opportunities for global evangelism and enabled movements such as Pentecostalism to become truly global. At the very same time, it has exposed the limitations of ossified religious traditions and expressions that are out of touch with modern expectations. This, in turn, has led to some mainstream churches adapting to the demands of change and to accommodating 'charismatic' traditions, 'exuberant forms of worship' and 'the gifts of the spirit' within their worship traditions.

4. The thoroughly 'modern' character of many of these fundamentalisms, aided by the technologies of computing and the Internet, despite their obvious adherence to essentialist, traditional values. The use of the media by the Hindu and Christian right and the many

accommodations with the economy, politics and culture does suggest that, in the context of contemporary wars of position between religions, the media have been invested with the power to marginalise 'the other'.

5. The ways in which culture and values have been assiduously reinforced through the media, and the manner in which the media have become an important nodal point in the production and circulation of fundamentalist ideologies. The media play a vital role in the overall mission of religious fundamentalists.

It is a recognised fact that the media play an important role in the formation of identity—personal, religious and national. While most religions have used one type of media or the other to propagate their truth to believers and non-believers, the Judaic faiths and mainstream Christianity, in particular, have had a reputation for being rather cautious in their use and support of the media. The origins of this attitude to the media are shrouded in history, the outcome of pietistic Christian interpretations of the sacred and the profane, inspired to some extent by the Biblical distrust of 'graven images'. The media, in particular cinema, was seen as the Devil's medium that was specifically created to tempt the faithful and lead them into the 'paths of unrighteousness'. This attitude towards cinema and broadcasting remains among the more traditional, conservative, older generation of Christians in India. I remember that my grandmother, who lived close to Thiruvalla, in the heart of Syrian Christian Kerala, and who liked watching films, was not allowed to go to the theatre because, her husband would not allow it, and the church and society were against cinema-going and cinema-goers—a rather ironic state of affairs in a country that produced the largest number of films per year and in which cinema, from its early beginnings, was routinely used as a medium to convey Hindu mythological stories. As Thomas and Mitchell (2005) have observed, the advent of cable and satellite television and opportunities for family viewing seem to have facilitated a greater acceptance by church and society in Kerala of broadcasting, although cinema-going is shunned by the more evangelically-minded Christians in Kerala and elsewhere.

Unlike the Marthomite Syrian Christians in Kerala, Christian fundamentalists have readily embraced the media. They believe that every successive technological innovation in communication is God-made and therefore should be used by fellow Christians to fulfil the promise of the Great Commission. An instrumentalist approach to the use of the media is a characteristic feature of Christian fundamentalists. Religious fundamentalists have from time immemorial assiduously used the media to proclaim the truth, mobilise the masses, protect the faithful and lay down the gauntlet to non-believers. Christian fundamentalists, in particular, are renowned for their pragmatic uses of the media. Broadcasting has traditionally been their forte and they have given transcendental meanings to the encounter between the media and individuals. The media environment, in their hands, has been transformed into a sacred space and place, where the divine is experienced through the discourses of healing, testimonials, speaking in tongues and being 'slain by the spirit'. A characteristic feature of Christian fundamentalist organisations today is their use of broadcasting and web-based information strategies as a part of their increasing multi-media campaigns (Thomas, 1999). Their communication campaigns support on-the-ground activities that include church planting, conversion and development.

The Media and Religion

Stewart Hoover and Knut Lundby (1997: 7), in an edited volume *Rethinking Media, Religion and Culture*, describe three broad rubrics under which the relationship between media, religion and culture has been explored—rallies, rituals and resistances. While the term 'rallies' refers to the intentional uses of media by formal religious institutions, 'ritual' offers the space to explore the 'quasi-religious role' played by the media in everyday life—in other words, the relationship between media consumption, media meanings and substantive meaning-making, and the way such meanings are engendered and negotiated. In this sense, the media offers us possibilities to ascribe sacramental meaning to everyday issues. Resistance relates to audience negotiations of meaning. Hoover and Lundby (1997: Chapter 2) provide an extensive overview of the available writings on the media, religion and culture. After a critical assessment of the key texts, in conclusion, they argue 'for a broader conception of religion that provides space for questions of meaning, identity and ontology to emerge in cultural studies'. It is interesting to note that Thomas and Mitchell (2005: 41), in an article on television and Christianity among the Mar Thoma community in Kerala, observe that 'Religion...is hardly thought to relate to the news or to entertainment programs. This finding is intriguingly different from those who have found television viewers appropriate religious meanings from many secular programs'. Commenting on the families that were studied, they also point to the fact that 'The families in this study do not consider secular television to have a religious dimension or mythic function. They reported gaining religions meanings from explicitly religious programs alone, and that too of one's own religion.' These findings would seem to suggest that in contexts where traditional religion is more than just an epiphenomenon and is part of one's primary identity, there is a need to privilege the mediation of established religion.

There have been numerous studies in USA that have explored specific uses of the media by the religious right—tele-evangelism, the use of the media to communicate the Gospel of Prosperity, media-based marketing of God, the relationship between ultra-conservative broadcasting, on one hand, and right-wing politics and their communication and media-based mobilisation strategies, on the other (see, for example, Hoover, 2006; Horsfield, 1984). Stewart Hoover—who has published numerous books on religion and the media, from tele-evangelism to religion in the news—has, as he has pointed out in his book *Religion in the Media Age* (2006), moved towards considerations of the 'significance of the media for religion in the context of media consumption and reception'. The question is not '*what* is the significance of the media age for religion?' but instead '*where* is that significance to be found?'. While studies of religious meaning-making and its consumption are certainly important, I argue that in the south, there is also a need for studies that explore the political economy of religious broadcasting. The role of Christian broadcasting in the global export of Christian fundamentalism not only needs to be explored in terms of its global–local correspondences, but also in terms of its specificities. Production occurs prior to consumption which is why the global circuit of Christian fundamentalist media needs to be mapped and assessed. One of the better critical texts on Christian fundamentalism and the media in USA from a political-economy perspective is *Media, Culture and the Religious Right* (1998) edited by Linda Kintz and Julia Lesage. I have yet to come across publications on the relationship between Christian fundamentalism and the media from other parts of the world, although there are a number of articles from Brazil, Guatemala and Ghana on tele-evangelism and the relationship between conservative religion, politics and the media (see Smith and Campos, 2005; De Witte, 2003).[1]

While there certainly is a case for cultural studies based on explorations that deal with the reception and consumption of a variety of 'religious' texts in contemporary life, one can argue that, at the very same time, this needs to be complemented by studies in the political economy of religion, media and culture from different parts of the world, precisely because formal religion and, in particular, a type of conservative Christianity are engaged in a global project supportive of a specific geo-politics—a project that has been globalised and given significance through the media, especially broadcasting (see Brouwer et al., 1996). This global project has certainly contributed to a shift in the meanings and practice of Christianity, from the mainstream to Pentecostalism, and to a strengthening of a transnational Christian unity, which has led to the shaping and making of a global Christian *umma*. While this *umma* certainly includes an indigenous, largely independent strand (De Witte, 2003; Hedlund, 2001, 2004; Hunt, 2002; Phiri, 2003; Smith and Campos, 2005), the correspondences with their compatriots in USA cannot be ignored. De Witte (2003: 186) in an article on the television programme (of the International Central Gospel Church headed by Mensa Otabil) *Living Word* in Ghana observes that: 'Much inspiration for making *Living Word* comes from American tele-evangelists like Benny Hinn, Billy Graham, Morris Cerullo, and Kenneth Hagin, who reach Ghana through Trinity Broadcasting Network (TBN), available on Cable TV.' To ignore the relationship between religion, media, politics, economics and power in contemporary society is, in my way of thinking, problematic precisely because it has become a global phenomenon. In the words of Linda Kintz (1998: 3): 'If we have learned anything from post-modern theory and cultural studies, it is the importance of symbolic meanings and culture in solidifying the power of political and financial interests, especially in the mass-mediated culture of an information society.' I have, in this book, strongly emphasised the need for a political-economy inspired approach, because in the context of studying religion, media and culture, the structures provide the scaffolding for meaning making.

While the relationship between Hindu religious nationalism, on one hand, and the media and its impact on communal strife, on the other, has been extensively documented (see Babb and Wadley, 1995; Manuel, 1993; Rajagopal, 2001), there is precious little material available on the relationship between Christian fundamentalism and the media in India or, for that matter, from other parts of the developing world. This is altogether surprising given that the export of Christian broadcasting from USA in particular to the rest of the world is a growing multi-million dollar industry, backed by some of the most conservative US Christians including Pat Robertson, the President of the Christian Broadcasting Network (CBN), and Ed Crouch, the President of the TBN. US-style Christian broadcasting has influenced the establishment of copy-cat indigenous Christian channels in places like Brazil, Ghana, Nigeria, Fiji and India. The project of globalising Pentecostal Christianity that is based on the establishment of mega churches, through conventions and rallies organised in sports stadiums, church planting, the spread of Dominion Theology and Christian popular culture, packaged and distributed through a mammoth marketing exercise, is a global phenomenon that is based on close correspondences between the global and the local. The ideological sub-texts within this Christian culture, in turn, influence the direction of local church policy on a host of social issues—from support for abstinence as a response to the AIDS pandemic, to the exclusion of gays and lesbians and their de-legitimisation as home-makers, care-givers and partners, to support for the war in Iraq and justifications for the occupation of Palestine. Apart from the occasionally critical article on Benny Hinn in the Indian press or on websites in the immediate aftermath of a convention, there is very little exploratory or in-depth material on the structures and political economy of Christian fundamentalism, politics and the media in India.

Media and Christian Fundamentalism

To recognize, source, create, package and present world-class anointed, prophetic, supernatural content in a spirit of excellence across the globe into every nation, reconciling man, woman and child with God by the power of the Holy Spirit(GOD TV, 'Vision Statement').

Christian fundamentalists use a variety of media to fulfil their mission. However, broadcasting, both radio and television, remains their favourite media. There are a number of defining characteristics of the media and Christian fundamentalism. These can be categorised in terms of structure, process, audience, policy, strategy and ideology.

1. While they have a massive presence in print, their core media is undoubtedly broadcasting and, of late, the Internet. Christian broadcasting is a multi-million dollar industry and while there are significant variations within this industry—from radio and television owned and operated by the mainstream churches, to broadcasting that is specifically oriented towards fulfilling the Great Commission, that is, taking the Word of God to the four corners of the Earth—it is also characterised by close correspondences with an explicit politics and political agendas. A well-known example of such correspondences is found in the US evangelist Pat Robertson's magazine programme

The 700 Club on CBN. This programme has regularly featured US politicians who have openly sought the electoral favour of the Christian right and who have, in turn, supported conservative social agendas flagged by these groups—for example, on issues such as gun control, gay marriage, stem cell research, the war on terror, Iraq, and the conflict between Israel and Palestine. Guests on this programme have included US Majority Whip Tom DeLay, Oliver North, Al Liberman, Al Gore, Jimmy Carter, Ronald Reagan, Mel Gibson and Charlton Heston. George Bush Jr is featured on a weekly radio programme. Using a format that includes interviews, special reports, commentary and news, this syndicated programme is carried across the world on ABC Family Channel, the TBN, Family Net and numerous other television stations in USA and elsewhere. The news coverage on *The 700 Club* deals with the following:

> International news coverage on the persecution of Christians around the world including Sudan, Pakistan, Cambodia, Bangladesh, Egypt, China, Burma and Indonesia; Israeli election; and the nuclear proliferation in Iraq, Iran, and North Korea were covered. Extensive political coverage of the 2000 election and post-election legal battle. Breaking news coverage of the September 2001 terrorist attacks against America. As well as up-to-date facts and forecasts on the stock market and the economy (CBN).

The CBN web page 'Inside Israel' (http://www.cbn.com/cbnnews/world/Israel/index.aspx) provides fascinating insights into Christian Zionism and the extent to which the Christian right have invested in Israel as a bulwark against the Islamic tide. This page has links to key Israeli news sources inclusive of *Ha'aretz* and the *Jerusalem Post* and to three sites—those of Palestinian Media Watch, Committee for Accuracy in Middle East Reporting in America (CAMERA) and the Middle East Media Research Institute—devoted to media reporting of the conflict in this region, establishing 'accuracy' and the re-presentation of stories in favour of the policies and military solutions advocated by the Israeli government. These sites are devoted to a contestation of meanings on the conflict and use liberal sub-texts to convey illiberal ideas. A story on the CAMERA website dated 7 November 2006, headlined 'Guardian Conceals Facts about Gaza Casualties' begins with this opening paragraph:

'In a newspaper prone to extreme anti-Israel coverage, readers now find shoddy reporting on casualty numbers that, not surprisingly, tilt against Israel'.

2. Since one of the key raisons d'être of Christian fundamentalism is the Great Commission, the media have traditionally been used to further the goals of outreach including church planting, preaching, conversion and global evangelism. Print, broadcasting and new information technologies have been used extensively. Today, when we speak of fundamentalist Christian broadcasting, it refers in the main to the networks owned and operated by conservative neo-Pentecostal churches and tele-evangelists aligned to such churches, most of whom are based in USA. Their networks are both global and local.

3. While the most aggressive expressions of Christian fundamentalism are represented by globally-networked Christian television stations such as the CBN, the TBN and GOD TV, there are also local/indigenous expressions of Christian fundamentalist media that are bounded by language, region and nation. Writing on mediated Christianity in Ghana, De Witte (2003: 177) has observed that the 'Church's extensive use of mass media has generated a religious, charismatic Pentecostally oriented public sphere...which is characterised by the intertwining of religion with both national and global politics and the field of commerce and entertainment.' Local Christian television supported by local entrepreneurs also plays a role in reinforcing a conservative politics and in the interpretation of Scripture at the local, regional or national levels. While Asamoah-Gyadu (2005) does point to the influence of US-based tele-evangelists such as Oral Roberts and Benny Hinn on local expressions of tele-evangelism in Ghana, he is of the opinion that despite such correspondences, 'the media ministries of Ghana's CMs reflect modern African ingenuity in the appropriation of neo-Pentecostal techniques, style and strategy in organisation and expression' (ibid.: 21). While it is certainly important that we treat indigenous expressions of mediated Christianity in context, I believe that it is also critical for such studies to explore the extent to which correspondences between the global and the local have contributed to the normalisation of a global Christian politics supported by the Christian right in USA and elsewhere.

4. Therefore, while there is need for more extensive global studies on the political economy of televangelism, and for a mapping of the

many levelled networks and synergistic partnerships that sustain conservative Christian broadcasting, there is also a need to interrogate the traditions of meaning making within mediated discourses of Christian fundamentalism. Moreover, there is a need to study the deliberate manner in which content is being used to marginalise those belonging to other faiths and explore the ways in which Christian symbols are manipulated for marketing ends. Pierre Bourdieu's contribution to understanding the play of power in society and the relationship between material and cultural power can, in this context, be drawn upon to throw light on the specific ways in which the global–local field of muscular Christianity is maintained through a cultural politics of 'misrecognition' (see Chapter 6, for an elaboration of the use of Bourdieun concepts for an analysis of mediated Christianity in India). Perhaps, as importantly, it is necessary for research to prise upon the gaps between religion as faith and religion as an institution, in order for it remain accountable to the communities that sustain it. Historian and leading advocate of Christian socialism Richard Tawney, in his classic study *Religion and the Rise of Capitalism* (1926: 55), reminds us of the enduring role that the church played in legitimising the framework for capitalist accumulation:

> Practically, the Church was an immense vested interest, implicated to the hilt in the economic fabric, especially on the side of agriculture and land tenure. Itself the greatest of land owners, it could no more quarrel with the feudal structure than the Ecclesiastical Commission, the largest of mineral owners today, can lead a crusade against royalties. The persecution of the spiritual Franciscans, who dared, in defiance of the Bull of John XXII to maintain St. Francis' rule as to evangelical poverty, suggests that doctrines impugning the sanctity of wealth resembled too closely the teaching of Christ to be acceptable to the princes of the Christian churches.

While the established churches, for the most part, continue to support the status quo, one can argue that the neo-Pentecostal churches and their flashy and muscular versions of Christianity have also become potent centres for the accumulation of religious and economic capital that are currently being used to support the extension of conservative values.

5. The mainstreaming of fundamentalist Christianity, which is an on-going process, has been achieved through global marketing strategies. Christian broadcasting is a multi-billion dollar business and it is, therefore, not at all surprising that its strategies at profit and audience maximisation mirror the objectives of mainstream broadcasting. Pat Robertson, for example, has used new technologies and his own entrepreneurial business skills to transform CBN into a multi-media conglomerate that sells everything from pharmaceutical products to products that enhance healthy living. Frankl (1998: 166), in a perceptive essay on Pat Robertson's transformation of his media business into a business empire, reveals the vertically integrated nature of the business, which is based on the acquisition of lucrative companies and the ownership of the complete production chain from production to delivery systems.

> Pat Robertson exemplifies this strategy, both producing *The 700 Club* and owning the cable network to carry it. From the cable network, the Family Channel and a variety of other enterprises developed—CBN television productions; CBN University (now Regent University, comprising graduate schools in business, communication, law and public policy); CBN Publishing offering a 'Superbook Audio Cassette and Colouring Book' for children ages four to eleven; 'Sing, Spell, read and Write', an instructional system for children in primary grades; and Video Tracts 'designed to be used by the individual or as a key element in a church's or organisation's overall evangelistic outreach' (ibid.).

CBN Travel and Operation Blessing became separate endeavours, as did American Benefits Plus.

6. Some of these networks, given their global operations, are no longer owned by strictly Christian interests. Today, Pat Robertson's CBN empire is, for instance, connected through inter-locking directorships to a variety of secular institutions that are broadly supportive of his ultra-conservative views. In 1997, CBN sold International Family Entertainment (IFE) to Rupert Murdoch and Murdoch merged his Fox Kids Worldwide with IFE. Pat Robertson remains co-chairman of the board. Similarly, the Brazilian neo-Pentecostalist Edir Macedo who runs the mega-church Universal Church of the Reign of God is a major player in commercial broadcasting in the region. He purchased a commercial television network Rede Record,

consisting of 30 stations, in 1989 for US$ 45 million. He also controls 400 temples, numerous radio stations, newspapers and a bank (see Smith and Campos, 2005). Sam Boerboom (2006), in a paper presented at the International Conference on Fundamentalism and the Media, shows how Christian fundamentalist media products, in particular the *Left Behind* film series, are part of a mobile commodity circuit that links production, distribution, exhibition and the home.

> In late 2005, Sony Pictures Home Entertainment became the first major film studio to back the release of a significantly evangelical film when it partnered with the Christian production team Cloud Ten and released *Left Behind: World at War* to over 3,200 churches.... Perhaps even more significant than a devoutly evangelical film receiving major studio backing is that the film was shown exclusively in churches. Each of the participating churches paid Cloud Ten a licensing fee ranging from $99 to $199, depending on how many people they expected to watch the film. In exchange for the fee participating churches received a copy of the film on DVD and were allowed to play the film as many times as they wanted. Four days after it released *LB: WW* to churches, Sony shipped 600,000 copies of the film to Wal Mart (ibid.).

Synergistic, multi-media strategies are a hallmark of contemporary Christian fundamentalist projects such as AD2003.

7. Since mainstreaming Christianity is a key objective, many Christian networks also broadcast wholesome, family entertainment— *Hill Street Blues*, *The Mary Tyler Show*, and the like. In fact, family values are a widespread trope that Christian broadcasters the world over strongly espouse. The Chennai-based production house Good News TV is in fact set to launch a family values-based cable television channel that offers wholesome entertainment for the family. Rather than an 'in your face Christianity', the objective is to convey Christian values through a range of broadly familiar programming styles that Indian audiences are used to.

8. Global evangelism is a key objective and CBN's WorldReach, which was launched in 1995 and is viewed in 200 countries, is based on a combination of local production for terrestrial television and satellite and cable television. The regions of focus include USA,

Latin America, the Muslim World, Europe, India, Indonesia, South-east Asia, the Philippines, China and the Commonwealth of Independent States (CIS). Similarly, the UK-based GOD TV transmits programmes via 10 satellites and numerous cable outlets to 212 countries.

Christian broadcasting is an increasingly global project that is characterised by close correspondences with global mission agendas. These mission agendas often conflict with local traditions of consanguinity and the 'daily dialogue of life' that has remained a core feature of lived life in most parts of India. Fundamentalist Christian broadcasting legitimises a triumphalistic, exclusive version of Christianity on a daily basis. One can argue that in countries such as India where inter-religious tensions are on the rise, Christian broadcasting contributes to a reinforcement of existing inter-religious wedges.

Note

1. For an A–Z of televangelists in USA, see http://religiousbroadcasting.lib.virginia.edu/televangelists.html.

References

Asamoah-Gyadu, J.K. 2005. 'Anointing through the Screen: Neo-Pentecostalism and Televised Christianity in Ghana', *Studies in World Christianity*, 11(1): 9–28.

Babb, L.A. and S.S. Wadley. 1995. *Media and the Transformation of Religion in South Asia*. Pennsylvania: University of Pennsylvania Press.

Boerboom, S. 2006. 'Buying Videos to Save Souls: The Mobile Fundamentalist Commodity Form', paper presented at the International Conference on Fundamentalism and the Media, 10–12 October, Boulder, Colorado.

Brouwer, S., P. Gifford and S.D. Rose. 1996. *Exporting the American Gospel: Global Christian Fundamentalism*. NY, London: Routledge.

Christian Broadcasting Network (CBN). Available at http://www.cbn.com, accessed on 20 April 2006.

Committee for Accuracy in Middle East Reporting in America (CAMERA). 2006. 'Guardian Conceals Facts about Gaza Casualties'. Available at http://www.camera.org/index.asp, accessed on 20 April 2006.

De Witte, M. 2003. 'Altar Media's Living Word: Televised Charismatic Christianity in Ghana', *Journal of Religion in Africa*, 33(2): 172–202.

Frankl, R. 1998. 'Transformation of Televangelism: Repackaging Christian Family Values', in Linda Kintz and Julia Lesage (eds), *Media, Culture and the Religious Right*, pp. 163–89. Minnesota: University of Minnesota Press.

Giddens, A. 1999. 'Tradition', Lecture 3, BBC Reith Lectures.

GOD TV. 'Vision Statement'. Available at http://www.godnetwork.com, accessed on 16 April.

Hedlund, R.E. 2004. 'The Witness of New Christian Movements in India', paper presented at the IAMS Assembly in Malaysia, 31 July–7 August.

————. 2001. 'Previews of Christian Indigenity in India', *Journal of Asian Mission*, 3(2): 213–30.

Hoover, S. 2006. *Religion in the Media Age*. London and NY: Routledge.

Hoover, S.M. and K. Lundby. 1997. *Rethinking Media, Religion, and Culture*. Thousand Oaks, London, New Delhi: Sage Publications.

Horsfield, S. 1984. *Religious Television: The American Experience*. NY: Longman Press.

Hunt, S. 2002. 'Neither Here Nor There: The Construction of Identities and Boundary Maintenance of West African Pentecostals', *Sociology*, 36(1): 147–69.

Kintz, Linda and Julia Lesage. 1998. *Media, Culture and the Religious Right*. Minnesota: University of Minnesota Press.

Manuel, P. 1993. *Cassette Culture: Popular Music and Technology in North India*. Chicago: University of Chicago Press.

Phiri, I.A. 2003. 'President Frederick J.T. Chiluba of Zambia: The Christian Nation and Democracy', *Journal of Religion in Africa*, 33(4): 401–28.

Rajagopal, A. 2001. *Politics After Television: Hindu Nationalism and the Re-Shaping of the Public in India*. Delhi: Cambridge University Press.

Smith, D. and L.S. Campos. 2005. 'Christianity and Television in Guatemala and Brazil: The Pentecostal Experience', *Studies in World Christianity*, 11(1): 49–64.

Tawney, R. 1926. *Religion and the Rise of Capitalism*. NY: Harcourt, Brace and Co.

Thomas, P. 1999. 'Web Wars and Interfaith Futures in India', *Media Development*, XLVI(4): 39–46.

Thomas, S. and J.P. Mitchell. 2005. 'Understanding Television and Christianity in Marthoma Homes, South India', *Studies in World Christianity*, 11(1): 29–48.

Website

http://religiousbroadcasting.lib.virginia.edu/televangelists.html, accessed on 25 October 2006.

3

CHRISTIANITY IN INDIA

The official 2001 Indian Census figures available on the Internet do not include statistics related to the religious demography of people living in India. Its absence may be due to the bottlenecks that accompany data processing of such a large number of people (after all it is not often that one comes across a nation that boasts of more than a billion people). And yet, given the fact that the 2001 Census took place during the rule of the Bharatiya Janata Party (BJP)-led National Democratic Alliance (NDA) government, one is led to wonder whether this omission is linked with the 'real' and 'manufactured' sensitivities related to the growth of religious minorities in India, the Muslims in particular, but also Christians. The 1991 Census reveals that the population of Christians in India was in the region of 19,640,284, a mere 2.3 per cent of the then overall population, and figures available on the Internet on the 2001 Census reveal that the Christian population has remained at the level of 2.3 per cent. These figures have been persistently queried by the Sangh Parivar in the light of missionary-related activities in northeast, central and south India. In an article that refutes the projections of the Sangh Parivar, Sridhar (1999) observes that:

> The rate of growth of the Christian population in India was high between 1921 and 1971; in fact, between 1921 and 1971, the rate of growth of the Christian population was consistently higher than that of the total population, although the gap narrowed in successive rounds of the census. However, since 1981, this trend has been reversed. While

the population of India increased by almost 24 per cent between 1981 and 1991, the Christian population only grew by 17 per cent.

Beginnings

Despite the reality of majority–minority contestations in contemporary India, the fact remains that Christians have inhabited the Indian subcontinent for nearly two millennia. The historicity of the pre-colonial Indian church is a fact that most Indians including many Indian Christians are unaware of. There is a widely-held belief among the Syrian Christian community that the church in India was established by one of the Apostles, St. Thomas, who arrived in Kerala after the death of Christ and converted a few Brahmin families before being martyred in Mylapore, Chennai. While this tradition is part of the foundational mythology of the Syrian Christians, there is a strong evidence to suggest that trade-related movement of people between the Middle East and the Malabar Coast had been established well before the beginning of the Christian era. These traders, mainly from Syria, are thought to have been responsible for establishing the church in India, at least from the 3rd century onwards. There is evidence of two specific migrations—one in the 3rd century and the other in the 8th century. The former is evidenced by numerous references in historical writings of the patriarchs of the Eastern Church and the latter through the copper plates that contain records of grants given to Christians in Quilon (now Kollam) by the local Hindu king. These copper plates are kept at the Orthodox seminary in Kottayam and the Mar Thoma seminary in Thiruvalla.

The Christian population in India is often categorised in terms of their allegiance to:

1. The historical churches of India, Orthodox and Reformed, that belong to the St. Thomas tradition.
2. The churches that were established as a result of India's tryst with colonialism, beginning from the 15th century onwards. This includes the Catholic Church, on one hand, and Protestant denominations including the Anglican Church, the Lutherans and the Baptists, on the other.
3. The churches that were established in the post-Independence period. These include some of the Pentecostal churches and, in the recent past, a plethora of both indigenous and neo-Pentecostal

churches. The mainstream refers to the churches that were established at the turn of the 4th century—the Syrian Christians or the Thomas Christians—and the churches that were established during India's tryst with European colonialism (the Portuguese established the Catholic Church in the 1600s, and the Danes, Germans and English established various Protestant denominations).

The St. Thomas Tradition

This church tradition traces its history back to the mission of St. Thomas, who is popularly believed to have come to the Malabar Coast sometime during AD 52 and was martyred in present day Mylapore, Chennai. The story goes that St. Thomas came across some Nambudri Brahmins having their morning bath in a place called Palayur. Their morning ablutions involved taking a bath during which water was ritually thrown up in the air. St. Thomas asked them if their Gods had the power to suspend the water in the air to which they answered in the negative. Tradition maintains that the Apostle managed to perform the feat and that some of the Nambudris present at the event became the Apostle's first converts in India. That such legends continue to sustain the identity of a people is reflected in the central place given to miracles in contemporary forms of popular religiosity in India. Praying for miracles—on life's mundane issues such as passing a school exam to the big issues such as enjoying good health—remains a constant feature in all popular religious traditions in India. In that sense, both the charismatic Indian miracle-man Satya Sai Baba and the popular television evangelist Benny Hinn are remarkably similar, except that Sai Baba's miracles are directed towards a creation of the awe and power that is associated with the materialisation of goods out of thin air (magic) as opposed to Benny Hinn whose miracles are basically associated with 'faith healing', the healing of people suffering from one form or another of mental or physical illness.

Christianity as a religious tradition became established in the Malabar region of India primarily due to the adaptive nature of the Syrian Christians, their integration into the local political and economic systems, the gradual indigenisation of their rituals and practices, and the tolerance shown by Hindu rulers in that region. These Hindu rulers had been involved in trade with the Middle East and had, prior to the arrival of Apostle Thomas, welcomed a Jewish community whose ancestors (now reduced to a few stragglers) are found even today in the port city of Cochin. They had welcomed successive migrations of Persians fleeing persecution in their home country, including the documented arrival of a group of 400 Christian families headed by Thomas of Cana in AD 345 who landed in a place called Kodungallur on the Malabar Coast. Cheraman Perumal, the king of Malabar, granted these migrants privileges enjoyed by caste Hindus, together with land for their settlement. L.W. Brown (1956: 86) in a book called *The Indian Christians of St. Thomas* has this to say on the inscriptions on the copper plates given by the king to these Christians:

> The king not only gave Thomas (of Cana) this town (Mahadevappatanam) but also 'seven kinds of musical instruments' and all the honours, and to travel in a palanquin . . . to use sandals and to erect a pandal and to ride on elephants. And besides this he granted five taxes to Thomas and . . . to his associates both men and women, and for all his relatives and to followers of his faith for ever.

This was merely the beginning of a long history of minglings—Christian and Hindu. By the 13th and 14th centuries, the St. Thomas Christians had become thoroughly indigenised. Many had inter-married with the Hindu Nair community and the two communities had begun to share both social and ritual space. Christians had begun to take part in Hindu festivals such as Onam and Vishu (New Year)—a tradition that is still followed by some families today. Inter-faith relationships were destined to grow even stronger. Susan Bayly (1989: 253), in *Saints, Goddesses and Kings: Muslims and Christians in South Indian Society, 1700–1900*, has this to say on this golden age of inter-faith commensality:

> In many parts of Malabar, Nayars accepted Syrians as participants and donors in local temple rites and took part in turn in Syrian church festivals. The acknowledgement of the Syrian's right to share Hindu 'sacred space' was expressed in some centres by the construction of Syrian churches on sites virtually adjoining Hindu temples. Christians used Hindu-style torches, umbrellas and banners in their Cattam festivals, and in some localities had a single collection of processional regalia which was shared between both Church and Hindu temple. At least one Hindu temple regularly lent out its temple elephants to Syrian worshippers for use in their festival processions.

One or two churches built in the style of Hindu temples still exist in Kerala today. Umbrellas and palanquinned elephants continue to be used in the Syrian Orthodox Church processions in Kerala, although these symbols are not a part of a living tradition of inter-faith relationships as was the case in the past.

Colonialism and the Impact of Mission

Until the 15th century, the St. Thomas Church was the only church tradition in India. Its bishops were sourced from Syria despite the fact that the church itself had, to some extent, become indigenised. The arrival of Vasco de Gama in the 15th century on the Malabar Coast changed this equation. The Portuguese conquistadors were followed by missionaries and foot soldiers for the Catholic Church. Pope Leo X's Padroado effectively granted rights to the Portuguese over the Christians of the East. Their political and military power was systematically used to reinforce the doctrinal power of the Catholic Church. The St. Thomas Church was found wanting on doctrinal issues and on matters related to belief, and efforts were made to latinise this church. A blockade against the import of bishops from Syria was enforced. It led to the conversion of not only the Syrian Christians but also Hindus and Muslims and to the establishment of a Catholic bishopric in Goa. In 1599, the Synod of Diamper was called by the Archbishop of Goa, Alexcio de Menezes, for the purposes of persuading the Syrian Christians to confess their errors and change to the true faith of the Catholic Church. This was opposed by the Syrian Christian hierarchy and is symbolised most famously in the 1653 Koonen Kirusu Revolt in Mattancherry. These Syrian Christians swore to keep their faith and break free from Portuguese Catholic oppression.

The Inquisition had been introduced a century earlier and it was used as a powerful weapon to break the unity of the Thomas Christians. Francis Xavier, the founder of the Society of Jesus, who had arrived in India in the early part of the 15th century, played a key role in these forcible conversions and in convincing King Joao III of the need for the Inquisition. In a letter dated January 1545, written from Cochin, Francis Xavier describes the zeal of conversion:

When all are baptized I order the temples of their false gods to be destroyed and all the idols to be broken into pieces. I can give you an idea of the joy I feel in seeing this done, witnessing the destruction of the idols by the very people who but lately adored them (quoted from Kuriakose, 1999: 33).

51

The Portuguese, in effect, were the first to make strong links between imperialism and evangelism.

But this plan was thwarted by the British becoming the dominant power in India and their plans to colonise the country. Contact with the Antiochian Church in the late 16th century led to the adoption of the West Syrian liturgical tradition. For the next few decades and until the early part of the 19th century, bishops belonging to the Syrian Orthodox Church were routinely sent from Syria. It has been said that the city of Kottayam in Kerala has the distinction, dubious or otherwise, of hosting more bishops per square mile than any other city in the world! Today, there are far more Indian Syrian Christians belonging to the independent Malankara (Indian) Orthodox Church than to the Syrian Orthodox Church in Syria.

The coming of the Dutch in the 16th century and, more importantly, the English led to a reversal of the fortunes of the Syrian Christians. By then, however, the damage had been done. This church was in decline and large numbers had become Latin Catholics. The early bureaucrats involved with the East India Company were not especially keen on overseeing religious expansion, and the missionaries who arrived with the British were not encouraged in their mission.

The history of Protestant mission in India began with the arrival of two German Lutheran missionaries, Ziegenbalg and Plutschau, in Tranquebar in 1706. In 1813, following the renewal of the East India Company's charter, missionaries and sympathetic colonialists such as Thomas Babbington Macaulay began supporting the process of direct and indirect evangelisation, via education, training and support for the reformation of the Indian church. The Society for the Propagation of the Gospel (1701) was followed by the London Missionary Society (1795), the Church Missionary Society (1700) and other Christian organisations. Macualay's (1835) infamous Minute on Indian Education, which led to the institu-tionalisation of government support for English education, begins by rubbishing the worth of Hindu and Muslim literature and ends with the following words: 'We must at present do our best to form a class who may be interpreters between us and the millions whom we govern; a class of persons, Indian in blood and colour, but English in taste, in opinions, in morals and in intellect' (quoted from Kuriakose, 1999: 125). As a consequence of such deliberate efforts at identity-formation and strong links with the mother church, the church in India has been reluctant to indigenise, despite the efforts of a number of famous Indian Christian theologians and pastors inclusive of Sadhu Sunder Singh, Keshab Chandra Sen, Brahmabandhab Upadhyaya and, more recently, Swami Abhishiktananda,

Bede Griffiths and M.M. Thomas. Therefore, it is not surprising that contemporary Hindu nationalists view the church as a foreign entity—given its inability to root worship in an Indian ambience.

The involvement of the Christian Missionary Society (CMS) in Christian education and mission-related work in Travancore led to a desire by them to reform the Syrian Church (see Viswanathan, 1993). This directly led to the break-up of the Syrian Church and to the birth of the St. Thomas Reformed Church and the Mar Thoma Church (1889), which is based on a unique blend of Eastern rites along with reformed Protestant ideals. Missionaries were involved in establishing Anglican, Presbyterian, Methodist, Lutheran, Baptist, Pentecostal and other denominations in India.

One of the highlights in the history of the Protestant Church in India is the formation in 1947 of the ecumenical Christian council, the Church of South India, that brought together the Anglicans, Congregationalists, the Presbyterians and the Methodists. The Church of North India, made up of a similar group of churches, was formed in 1970. Today, the 25 million Christians in India owe allegiance to a variety of churches—Catholic, Orthodox and Protestant. These official census figures are contested by a number of Christian organisations—for instance, the World Christian Encyclopaedia that puts forward a figure of 33 million Pentecostals alone in India consisting of 1,253,041 classical Pentecostals, 5,032,741 charismatics and, what is by far the largest grouping, 27,234,219 neo-charismatics (see Burgess, 2001).

While Christian mission in the colonial era was responsible for ushering in India's tryst with modern Western thought, primarily through the extension of English education, social development and social reform, it can be argued that reform and development were the means to a larger end—the missionising of India. While there were individuals like Gandhi's close friend C.F. Andrews, who believed that Western, muscular Christianity could be redeemed by its encounter with Gandhi's humanism (see Nandy, 1983), for the most part, Christian missionaries were motivated by a desire to convert a heathen population to the true religion of Christianity. This objective was by no means fulfilled through the forcible conversion of Indians to Christianity that was one of the hallmarks of Portuguese colonialism. Rather, it was carried out primarily through the establishment of a discourse of texts and contexts, institutions and ideologies that furthered the project of Orientalism (see Gandhi, 1998). Gauri Viswanathan, in her book *Masks of Conquest* (1989: 85), has explored the uses and abuses of English education as a primary means by which Christianity was spread in India. She argues that the universalising of 'Christian sentiment' was a project that was taken forward by administrators influenced by 'outspoken missionaries like Alexander Duff, William Keane, and William Carey'. These administrators used

> English literature to maintain control of their subjects under the guise of liberal education. Though literature continued to be taught 'classically', with the emphasis on the history and structure of the langue, its potential usefulness in leading Indian youth to a knowledge and acceptance of Christianity quickly became apparent. For example, without once referring to the Bible, government institutions officially committed to secularism realized that they were in effect teaching Christianity through Milton (ibid.).

Indian Christians generally tend to agree with the view that fundamentalism is a Muslim and Hindu aberration and that it has nothing to do with Christians. Such a partial and myopic view of fundamentalism is based on a discounting of the fact that mission in the context of colonialism is partly responsible for the rise of Hindu fundamentalism in contemporary India. In fact, the presence and work of Christian missions provided part of the rationale for the establishment of Hindu missions such as the Vivekananada Mission and the more Hindu chauvinist Rashtriya Swayamsevak Sangh (RSS), the Hindu organisation that was founded in 1925 and which is the most powerful backer of Hindu revivalism in India today, along with movements such as the Arya Samaj and the Brahmo Samaj. Jacob Dharmaraj's (1993) far-reaching study *Colonialism and Christian Mission: Postcolonial Reflections* confronts the many glossed-over facts regarding the history of mission in India—for instance, the clear connections between economic colonisation, on the one hand, and educational and religious colonisation, on the other. His study is an analysis of the contributions made by the two best-known missionaries of the era of British colonialism in India, William Carey and Alexander Duff. Carey's connections with the colonial economic structure and Duff's with the cause of Western, English education are explored. While not discounting the positive contributions these missionaries made, Dharmaraj probes the deeper interests of the missionary as coloniser.

Christian mission in the post-colonial period has been strongly identified with health, education and development. Christian educational institutions, for instance, are found throughout India and it would not be far from the truth to claim that a large number of Indian political and economic elites have been educated in Catholic schools and Protestant colleges. However, post-colonial Christian mission in India was also strongly influenced by the ecumenical movement and Vatican II. This movement gathered momentum in the late 1960s and 1970s, and resulted in some churches and church-based non-governmental organisations (NGOs) opting for a more active, justice-oriented approach to mission. Liberation and feminist theologies, a conciliar approach to other religions and an appreciation of the need for inter-faith futures have influenced literally hundreds of initiatives oriented towards the extension of the 'Social Gospel'—Dalit liberation struggles, the liberation of children from bonded labour and women's struggles, to name just a few of the initiatives that the church in India is currently involved with. There have also been notable attempts by Christians to explore inter-faith dialogue, for example, Swami Abhishiktananda and Bede Griffiths, who tried to explore the Hindu–Christian meeting point. At the same time, mission has continued to extend the vision of Duff and Carey. In other words, mainstream churches in India today are involved in both types of mission—traditional and justice-oriented. Proclamation and conversion remain fundamental commitments of the Protestant and Catholic churches in India. In fact, in the context of the rise of Pentecostalism and neo-Pentecostalism, conservative, muscular approaches to mission have flourished throughout India. Some of these examples of aggressive mission have been highlighted in Chapter 7, which looks at web wars and inter-faith futures in India.

References

Bayly, S. 1989. *Saints, Goddesses and Kings: Muslims and Christians in South Indian Society, 1700–1900.* Cambridge: Cambridge South Asian Studies, Cambridge University Press.

Brown, L.W. 1956. *The Indian Christians of St. Thomas.* Unpublished.

Burgess, S.M. 2001. 'Pentecostalism in India: An Overview', *Asian Journal of Pentecostal Studies*, 4(1): 85–98.

Dharmaraj, J.S. 1993. *Colonialism and Christian Mission: Postcolonial Reflections.* New Delhi: ISPCK.

Gandhi, L. 1998. *Post-Colonial Theory: A Critical Introduction.* NY: Columbia University Press.

Kuriakose, M.K. 1999. *History of Christianity: Source Materials.* Delhi: ISPCK.

Nandy, A. 1983. *The Intimate Enemy: Loss and Recovery of Self Under Colonialism.* New Delhi: Oxford University Press.

Sridhar, V. 1999. 'A Numbers Game', *Frontline*, 16(25). Available at http://www.flonnet.com/fl1625/16250930.htm, accessed on 16 May 2006.

Viswanathan, S. 1993. *The Christians of Kerala: History, Beliefs and Ritual among the Yakoba.* Delhi: Oxford University Press.

———. 1989. *Masks of Conquest: Literary Studies and British Rule in India.* NY: Columbia University Press.

4

PENTECOSTALISM AND NEO-PENTECOSTALISM

The Global and the Local

Charlie Pye-Smith (1997: 52) in his travelogue *Rebels and Outcastes: A Journey through Christian India* writes about meeting up with one of the 'new church' pastors in Mumbai, Pastor de Souza. In the words of this pastor:

> The New Life Fellowship...had attracted a great deal of people: Hindus, Muslims, Catholics, Anglicans, Jains, Buddhists, high-caste and low-caste, rich and poor. Actors from the Bollywood film world had been drawn to the fellowship and a house church had even been established among a community of eunuchs. We are looking for India to become a Christian country.

That last sentence is enigmatic for many reasons. The intentionality of expansionism within a predominantly Hindu country, the expressed confidence, the audacity and matter of fact character of the statement, and the vehicle for this expansionism—Pentecostalism and its many variants—that Dempster et al. (1999) explicitly recognise as 'a religion made to travel' is today a South Asian reality. In an essential sense, the globalisation of Christianity is about the globalisation of Pentecostalism and its many variants and expressions—visual, textual and institutional. These include the charismatic churches that can be dependent on or independent of the mainstream churches, the tele-evangelists (local and foreign), who have a ubiquitous presence on Indian television, the indigenous churches and the numerous house churches that advertise their presence via neon crosses—the Full Life Church, the New Vision of God, the Church of God—from urban terraces and from within the urban sprawl of Chennai suburbs, jostling for attention between billboards, eating houses, hardware storeys and the paraphernalia of urbanity. While there are many differences as well as similarities between these groups in areas such as doctrine and belief, I would argue that an incipient fundamentalism of the type expressed by Pastor de Souza unites this movement. It is in this sense that I have argued that Christian fundamentalism can be ascribed to those who are involved in low-intensity and high-intensity struggles to spread the Gospel in India. While the mainstream churches fight a rearguard battle for survival, implode under the weight of their own contradictions or are forced to adapt the 'Full Gospel' in order to keep the flock, these new churches have begun to stitch themselves into the fabric of India to the extent that Chennai alone is home to 2,500 or more churches. Chennai, according to some observers, is the fastest growing hub of Christianity in South Asia. Numbers can of course be disputed, but the sheer numbers of churches listed in church directories available in Christian bookshops point to their growing presence. Raj and Selvasingh (2004: 10) have observed that 'Chennai is privileged to have the highest number of churches of all the cities in South Asia. In 1994 there were about 1,400 churches in Chennai...in 1999...1864 churches...small churches [formed] "by the influence of the Pentecostals".' While the New Life Assemblies of God (AOG) Church in Saidapet, Chennai, with its 35,000 members and seating capacity of 10,000 at a time, may not be much when compared with the Yoida Full Gospel Church in Seoul, South Korea, with its 900,000 strong congregation and seating capacity of 24,000 at a time, it nevertheless points to the extraordinary increase in the support base of these churches and indirectly to the decline in or stagnation of the growth of mainstream churches that have accommodated charismatic worship styles. We are, for better or for worse, living in the Pentecostal era. With its rates of global expansion, it is bound to surpass Catholicism to become the predominant form of Christianity in the 21st century—a process that is all too evident in Latin America, a once predominantly Catholic continent.

One of the interesting features of the new churches is their spatial presence in Chennai, their embrace of the official city and the unintended cities, the rural in the urban, and their being part of and catering to a globalising Chennai and Chennaites (Manokaran, 2005; Prakash, 2002). There is a real sense in which Pentecostalism intrinsically is a religion that was made to travel, for it is part of the flows of the global, at home in a crowded market area as in a gleaming mall (Cox, 1995; Dempster et al., 1999). Mendieta (2001: 20) observes that 'religion appears as a resource of images, concepts, traditions and practices that can allow individuals and communities to deal with a world that is changing around them', in the midst of places and shopping, leisure and recreation, production and consumption, an observation that captures the new church in changing Chennai. The cell church movement in India is an organic expression of church growth in the era of globalisation. Since church planting and the harvesting of souls are fundamental objectives of the new churches, members belonging to tightly-knit cell churches are required to facilitate a viral replication of these cells. A number of these new churches may be called indigenous churches responding to the fulfilment of local needs although as many are influenced by the Health and Wealth Gospel linked to the Faith movement. Stephen Hunt (2000: 344), in a perceptive essay on the Health and Wealth Gospel, observes that the success of this model relates to its value-addedness:

> Pentecostalism serves to develop attributes, motivations, and personalities adapted to the exigencies of the de-regulated global market...it has integrated the urban masses into a developing economy through the protestant work ethic and active citizenship. At the same time, the mobile new professionals and the educated in mega-cities carry a work ethic that *results* from a strict Pentecostal upbringing. The explanation for the success of the Faith movement is that it can adapt itself to such complexities. This makes it a global 'winner'.

Brouwer et al. (1996) in the book *Exporting the American Gospel: Global Christian Fundamentalism* provide a compelling narrative of the global spread of US-inspired Christian fundamentalism based on case studies from South Korea, the Philippines, Guatemala, Brazil and other parts of the world. They make the point that the political basis of this spread, rooted in the globalisation of the doctrine of 'Manifest Destiny', is integrally related to economic globalisation and the spread of global consumerism. The 'Prosperity Gospel' provides the moral basis for a political conservatism and legitimises individual wealth seeking, both of which are interpreted as the fundamental messages of the Bible. While they do recognise the presence of 'indigenous' churches, they are inclined to believe that the similarities and correspondences between these new churches far outweigh the differences.

Although primarily developed in the United States, Christian fundamentalism appears acultural or transcultural in the sense that it can be exported almost anywhere. Differences in emphasis, receptivity, and form exist. But what is striking is not so much the subtle variations among the new Christian churches both intra and inter-culturally, but rather the degree of similarity in...form, content and style that are strongly influenced by North American models. One can immediately recognize a 'Christian' service no matter whether the tongue is English, Tagalog, Spanish, Korean, or Swahili (Brouwer et al., 1996: 179).

This observation was borne out in my own research in Chennai where the evidence of superficial differences in worship styles were backed up by the much greater sense of consanguinity between these traditions of Christianity, particular in their sharing a sense of the inevitability of the global triumph of Christianity. While there are doctrinal and other differences between fundamentalists, evangelicals and indigenous Christians, and between traditional Pentecostals and neo-Pentecostals, I take the view that in the context of global Christian expansionism, the similarities far outweigh the differences. In other words, while these distinctions are useful from a heuristic point of view, they need to be seen as lesser than the reality of multiple correspondences. This discourse is especially evident in websites belonging to these groups. The strength of these new Christian witnesses has been quite significantly supported by a variety of para-church and mission agencies. Chennai, for example, is home to the Campus Crusade for Christ, which has, for years, been involved in dedicated screenings of the film *Jesus*, which is available in 852 languages including more than 25 Indian languages (Campus Crusade for Christ International). The ideology shared by these para-church organisations, inclusive of the Every Home Crusade and the Friends Missionary Prayer Band, often reinforces the ideology of the new churches. The international Christian mission World Vision that is avowedly involved in the business of development is home to some of the most fundamentalist Christians in India. In my interviews with Christians in India, it became clear that there is a natural reading of the necessary goodness and rightness of the US political and military hegemony and particularly its support for the Israeli government. The Indian public have never been overtly critical of television and this attitude is clearly displayed in their acceptance of contemporary Christian broadcasting. While there are those who cringe at the televised excesses of a Sarah Hughes and Benny Hinn, for the most part, Pat Robertson's seasonal ravings against a Hugo Chavez and the gay community, or for that matter the Biblical exegesis provided by Joyce Meyer, are accepted as a case of the 'anointed' proclaiming God's truth on television. Christian television, in turn, reinforces this view and this virtuous circle is reinforced on a daily basis. The very same mentality that justified Christian extermination of native populations in USA is now used to justify the proselytisation of 'non-Christians' throughout the world.

The great variety in global forms of Christianity today suggests that the church too has been deeply affected by the de-centring of grand narratives—in this case, the Biblical narrative that has spawned many interpretations, understandings and allegiances. Global forms of Pentecostalism have played a key role in this de-centring and in the reconstitution of the Christian message for a postmodern imaginary that is comfortable with an intuitive apprehending of reality, characterised best by the many exuberant celebrations of the Holy Spirit. This turn towards orality has been accompanied by the move away from a reliance on the written word—an essential condition of modernity. Pentecostalism in an essential sense is a harbinger of postmodernity. Its roots in the Methodist, Holiness and Evangelical movements; its origins in revivals that took place in Azusa Street, Los Angeles, in the 1910s, which were based on a mixture of African and Afro-American worship styles; and its invitation to de-centred worship based on the Gifts of the Spirit rather than textual exegesis resulted in the growth of an extraordinary variety of churches organised on dissimilar lines from the mainstream Protestant churches. As Peter Beyer (2003: 374) notes, this has led to an efflorescence of Pentecostal styles of worship:

> The typical Pentecostal church in say, Latin America, can in style, ritual practice, and emphasis be very different from Pentecostal churches in Sweden, Korea, Ghana, Ethiopia or Sri Lanka. And these all can in turn be quite different from each other. This 'internal' variety manifests itself again when the adherents of these different Pentecostalisms migrate to other parts of the world, thereby transplanting their particularized versions such that the different versions are not only aware of each other, but exist geographically in the same place and often belong to the same local umbrella organization.... The inter-relations, far from undermining the differences, actually are part of the process of constructing and preserving them, such that there seems to be no serious trend toward homogenisation as a result.

How to preserve unity in the midst of such diversity is bound to remain an issue for the ecumenical movement. This disjuncture was evident at the

World Council of Churches (WCC) Assembly in Harare in 1998, where the cerebrations of old style theologians was followed by a celebration by the African Independent Churches (AICs). This worship based on dance and song and the beat of drums seemed to suggest the continuity of 'primal' traditions, their reinvention and a bottom-up efflorescence of ways of connecting to the Almighty within a larger, primarily European understanding of the oikumene. Whether or not the WCC will be able to integrate the AICs within a council that includes those who value the primacy of doctrine and tradition (the Orthodox) as well as those with liberal understandings of the Social Gospel (mainstream Protestant churches) is anybody's guess. Unlike the old Gospel's cautionary tale of living in modernity—which is temporal, fleeting and incomplete when compared to riches in the afterlife—many variants of Pentecostalism celebrate consumption and the pursuit of prosperity in this life, while firmly believing that all those who are 'born again' will rank among the elect in Heaven. Sociologists of religion, surprisingly, have not explored the phenomenon of religion in a marketplace (Iannaccone, 1992; Percy, 2000), although the jury is still out on whether economic rationality is a sufficient reason for understanding the resurgence of religious growth and identifications in our contemporary world. According to Iannaccone (1992: 128):

> The working assumptions of economics imply that self-interest motivates clergy as it does secular producers; market forces constrain churches just as they do secular firms; and the benefits of competition, the burdens of monopoly, and the hazards of government regulation are as real for religion as for any other sector of society.

While Iannaccone's viewpoint certainly merits attention, this privileging of economic factors and economic rationality results in the undervaluation of the multiple factors and motivations—personal, cultural, social— that underlie the experience of religion as faith. Even Ferdinand Tönnies' *gemeinschaft–gesellschaft* typology and its subsequent elucidations by Durkheim and Weber offer contemporary sociologists of religion radical possibilities to explore the reinventions of community in a world that is resolutely defined along associational lines.

Global Features of Pentecostalism

How to apprehend and make sense of these new 'publics' and, in particular, the new cultures of publicness related to religion are yet to be explored.

The exploration of these new publics can only be based on a radical assessment of received notions of the bourgeois public sphere, which are based, for instance, on Habermas' ontology of the foundations of the public good based on communicative rationality and a politics of engagement committed to ensuring the universality of a public politics for the health of society. An understanding of the new publics of Pentecostalism, which does not 'have any necessary or predetermined relationship to formal politics, rational communicative action, print capitalism, or the dynamics of the emergence of a literate bourgeoisie' (Appadurai and Breckenridge, 1994: 5), remains an exercise yet to be explored.

Contemporary sociologists of religion (Martin, 1995; Stolz, 2006) have tried to explore the affinities of this expansionism with Weber's thesis of the role of the Calvinist Protestant ethic in the making of modern Western capitalism. There is, however, no conclusive proof that this is the case, given the sheer contextual diversity in the experiencing of Pentecostalism—from the Full Gospel Church in South Korea, which has built its success on an extant work ethic, to the many millions who see the basis for a better life in the Prosperity Gospel of the Word-Faith ministries. The sheer diversity of the Pentecostal experience, the accent on experience and not doctrine, its de-centred, non-territorial nature and its focus on bettering the personal morality of its individual members have undoubtedly led to its extraordinary outgrowth in every corner of the world. Despite this diversity, there are similarities in the global Pentecostal experience, and it is in this sense that one can put forward the view that this really is about a global *umma*. The key points of global identification and everyday practices include the following:

1. On the one hand, Pentecostalism been responsible for a turn around by the head of the household from a variety of practices such as domestic violence, alcoholism, drugs, gambling and neglect of the family—an extraordinarily powerful 'miracle' for those whose lives and families have been on the verge of decline. On the other hand, it also appeals to the middle classes, upper middle classes and the nouveau rich whose pursuit and celebration of wealth in the world of share trading, high salaries and real estate dealings is removed from the repressed Calvinist embarrassment of riches that the main-stream churches continue to exhibit. For Pentecostalism, to be pros-perous is a blessing from God and the more one gives to the church, the higher the returns. This ability to dissolve 'class' and structural inequity, and reach out to those who have made it—who are often

seen as exemplars of Christ's blessing—as well as those who aspire to wealth have enabled these new churches to recruit from across sectors in society. This stands in stark contrast with the mainstream churches that continue to remain hamstrung by questions related to caste, hierarchy and exclusion.

2. There is also emphasis given to the importance of each 'born-again' Christian as a child of God. In other words, each member is valued. This matters a great deal, especially for those who come from the margins of society and who have experienced neglect, social stigma, societal apathy and a lack of recognition. For the newcomer in a big city looking for work, these new churches provide the space for comfort, strength, emotional support and an environment that is suitable for the recuperation of spirits to deal with life's challenges. Christ is a personal Saviour who is present at every step of life's journey and who is there to give each person a helping hand in times of struggle.

3. Pentecostalist churches have contributed to creation of networks and solidarities that have been critical to the survival of people dispossessed by globalisation. Armet (2005: 319–20), in work carried out in Bogota, Colombia, makes note of the social dynamics of Pentecostalism and its strength in:

> small religious groups where members forge deep bonds of trust and commitment rooted in biblical values of fraternity and community. In many cases, church members act as surrogates for disappearing extended families and fictive kinship networks. The greatest benefit derived from their church affiliation...was 'a group of friends who help me in time of need (40%)'. To people who possess few material goods and live in modest functional housing, the church has become the community centre.

The role of the church in nurturing communities to become full participants in the consumer economy, beginning with their consumption of a commodified Christianity, provides each member the required strength to negotiate, take part in and benefit from exchanges in this consumer economy. This is an important reason for the success of these churches since they are intentionally and avowedly friends of the market. Unlike the mainstream churches who have a rather ambivalent, some would say hypocritical, relationship to 'mammon', the new churches accept economic prosperity as among the greatest of God's blessings, next to personal health. In this sense, we are seeing a renewed emphasis on the Protestant ethic, although the Calvinist piety that underpinned the rise of capitalism seems to have been replaced by a wholesale celebration of unabashed individualism and the unsaid belief in the market as a device perfected by God for the benefit of humankind. Unlike, say in the context of South Korea where Paul Yonggi Cho's Full Gospel Church and other manifestations of conservative Christianity can be implicated in the success of the South Korean economy, it is rather too early to hazard whether there is a similar relationship between the new churches in India and a rise in the prosperity of Indian Christians. Perhaps surveys of church membership and prosperity indices will need to be carried out to get a fuller picture of the ways in which the Protestant ethic is contributing to the development of the self-assured, prosperous Indian Christian consumer. While there is evidence that the liberalisation of worship has attracted young Indian Christians who are an essential part of the new, buoyant Indian economy—from information technology (IT) specialists to stockbrokers and real estate agents—the mainstream churches are yet to deal with this migration of affinity from the mainstream to the new churches. Paul Thangiah's ministry in Bangalore already caters to IT professionals on the lines of the Full Gospel Business Men's Fellowship International.

4. The freeing of worship from the strictures of received textual, doctrinal hegemony and the accent on a celebration of the individuality of worship and the legitimation of individual space have been responsible for the tolerance, indeed encouragement, of the expressive diversity of oralities in worship—from glossolia, to dancing, prophesying and other gifts of the spirit. The celebration of these oralities have, in a sense, been a powerful means by which new converts, particularly among indigenous communities in Latin America and India, have adapted their expressive cultures to Christian worship. At the Every Tongue, Every Tribe convention held in Chennai in early 2006, there were at least a hundred 'tribes' present—in their traditional costumes, singing and dancing. At the very same time, the many practices of culture deemed patently un-Christian have been excised. It is in this sense that one calls Pentecostalism a religion that expects, indeed enforces, radical discontinuities and ruptures of its converts. A frequent criticism of 'Christian conversion'

in India, particularly among tribal populations, is with regard to the expectation that the newly converted make a complete break with their past. This expectation and the pressures to confirm to the new codes of Pentecostal Christianity have caused a lot of individual distress and a break-down of the community. This is particularly acute in the context of tribal festivals, rituals and cultural mobilisations that often are ignored by new converts. The Pentecostal accent on conversion and the expectation that every convert will convert others to Christ reinforces conflict and division. In other words, while expressive genres have been adapted, the deep structures of tribal cosmologies have been radically altered to suit the evangelical agenda of Pentecostalism. Casanova (2001: 437–38), in an article on religion and globalisation, explores this apparent contradiction at the heart of Pentecostalism in the following terms:

> How can it be de-territorialised and local at the same time? Because it is an uprooted local culture engaged in spiritual warfare with its own roots. This is the paradox of the local character of Pentecostalism.... Pentecostalism is a not a translocal phenomenon which assumes the different forms of a local territorial culture. Nor is it a kind of syncretic symbiosis or symbiotic syncresis of the general and the local. Pentecostals are, for instance, everywhere leading an unabashed and uncompromising onslaught against their local cultures—against Afro-Brazilian spirit cults in Brazil; against Vodou in Haiti; against witchcraft in Africa; against shamanism in Korea. In this they are very different...from the traditional Catholic pattern of generous accommodation and condescending toleration of local folklore and popular magical beliefs and practices, so long as these assume their subordinate status within the Catholic hierarchic cosmos.... The Pentecostal attitude is neither compromise nor denial but frontal hand-to-hand combat, what they call 'spiritual warfare'.... It is in their very struggle against local culture that they prove how locally rooted they are.

This celebration of orality, 'primal speech' as Cox (1995: 82) describes it, is also, in a powerful sense, a celebration of the right of the repressed to speak. The silencing of the marginalised by the priest and prophet has been replaced by the right to ecstatic means of praise and worship—through Christian rock music or tribal dances.

5. There is a deep commitment to global evangelicalism and a millennial longing for a sowing and reaping of the fruits of the Great Commission. It is in this instance that the Pentecostal experience becomes perilously close to a form of Christian fundamentalism. While Harvey Cox (1995) and Joel Robbins (2004) insist on the need to analytically distinguish between Pentecostals and fundamentalists, given the latter's intent to preserve doctrinal purity and the accent by the former on the gifts of the spirit, this distinction, although necessary for heuristic purposes, is often blurred due to the routinised triumphalism that accompanies these discourses. During my research in Chennai, it was plain that Christian triumphalism is an essential element in the expansion of the church—conversion, proclamation to the Hindus and 'reaching the unreached' is at the core of this triumphalism. This was present in the more traditional Pentecostal AOG churches as well as the newer ministries such as PowerHouse. The fact that Pastor Paul Thangiah of the AOG Church backed Benny Hinn's convention in Bangalore, a convention that was fulsomely ratified by Pat Robertson on CBN's *The 700 Club*, does indicate that there are correspondences. While fundamentalism, in that traditional sense, is often used to describe those who ratify an unwavering, strict interpretation of the scriptures, today the term needs to be expanded to include all those who implicitly and explicitly ratify or are involved in robust, often exogenously-supported, forms of Christian expansionism.

6. Pentecostalism in its myriad varieties can in some ways be considered as Christianity for living in a globalised world, simply because it caters to people in a variety of contexts, rich–poor, black–white, urban–rural, and those working in the formal economy as well as the informal. Critically though, the allure of Pentecostalism is its ability to give a sense of certainty, incomplete although it may be, to people who are either the victims of globalisation or who are experiencing the 'blessings' of prosperity. It is a coping mechanism, a tool for survival. Interestingly enough, it proclaims the centrality and munificence of capitalism—in direct contrast to the anti-capitalist rhetoric of the 'Social Gospel' expressed in and through Asian and other variants of Liberation Theology. The market and individual enterprise are seen as natural end states, indeed, as inspired by God; therefore, the church is expected to make use of the market to its own advantage. Prosperity Gospels are perfectly suited for our times given the centrality of the market in the global imaginary.

This again is a far cry from the mainstream church that has often embraced ascetic values and lived in splendid isolation from the world inhabited by the majority of its congregation. Pentecostalists are at home with new technologies and are, of course, the premier supporters of mediated Christianity. And that really is not surprising given their strong emphasis on orality. Benny Hinn might open his Bible to read a verse or two, but the accent is on Benny Hinn making drama and the drama unfolding around him. While Christianity in India has always maintained its local–global links that were reinforced during the missionary enterprise and in the post-Independence era, in the era of globalisation and the Internet, the possibility for local–global links have become immense. The agenda of global Christianity, exemplified by the AD2000 Project, which is financially backed by a diverse range of mission and church groups in USA, has resulted in partnerships with literally hundreds of organisations based in Chennai and elsewhere. While there are numerous indigenous churches that are independent and do not receive funds from the outside, many of the major and minor Pentecostal churches receive funds from the outside. Many of these organisations run orphanages— support for which is mainly through funding received from USA and Europe.

7. Another reason for the success of Pentecostalism is its role in breaking of barriers between the expert, educated clergy and the lay person. Just like the happenings in the world of the media that are a consequence of new technologies and exemplified by the rise of 'citizen journalists', Pentecostal pastors often range from the 'unread' to those who have been to a Bible seminary. Since the accent is on experience and a handful of texts from the Bible, the scope for becoming a pastor is manifold today. Anyone with a certain amount of charisma can become a pastor. This has led to all sorts of interesting permutations. In Chennai, as is probably the case in the rest of India, the majority of the more prominent Pentecostal initiatives, inclusive of Brother Dhinakaran's ministry and Sam P. Chelladurai ministries, are family affairs. In the case of Brother Dhinakaran, his wife, son, daughter-in-law and grandchildren play key roles in the ministry. Sister Shanti Solomon plays a key role in Dr John Solomon's Miracle Ministry. The opportunity for leadership among women needs to be emphasised. Pentecostal ministries in Chennai include a number of women preachers, although an incipient patriarchy remains in place. Some have used the opportunity to be

schooled abroad—for instance, in Bible schools in USA—although most remain home-grown. Church planting can be organised by the schooled as well as the unschooled. One of the frequent concerns expressed in India is related to the lack of accountability. While mainstream clergy are accountable to their diocese, many of these new missions are not accountable to anyone creating possibilities for the misuse of funds. I was told of an incident involving the Joyce Meyer ministries. Her organisation had donated money to evangelists supposedly involved in 'tsunami relief', which was not used for the stated purpose.

8. Pentecostalism recognises and deals with the Devil and Satan. The accent on miracles and healing cannot be brushed off simply because the need for mental and physical healing and support is a felt reality everywhere in our world. South Indian Christians, as Caplan (1987) observed, believe in the effects of *suniam* (sorcery) and *peey* (evil spirits), very much like their Hindu neighbours. In fact, their belief in such extra-natural phenomena might well be a throwback to their pre-conversion days. The vanquishing of evil spirits is part of the repertoire of Pentecostalist preachers. In other word, evil spirits may have been banished by the rationalists and the intellectualised pastoral elite belonging to the Church of South India (CSI), but for ordinary people, their destructive presence is real enough. Caplan terms these preachers fundamentalists.

> [They] do not deny the reality of such (evil) forces which by intention, or otherwise, bring adversity. In this respect, they provide a strong contrast with the orthodox churches and their missionary predecessors. In South India, as in virtually every part of the missionised world, Protestant evangelists turned their backs on such concerns. The essential Christian doctrine of belief in the authenticity of miracles was suspended. Whereas Hindus had resort to a variety of deities and ritual specialists to protect them, the missionaries refuted and eliminated the agencies by means of which converts to Protestantism and their descendents sought protection from these dangerous powers (Caplan, 1991: 372).

Caplan further points out that in his conversations with CSI clergymen none 'could recall [an] occasion during their training or subsequently as ordained pastors when issues of this kind were even raised within orthodox circles' (ibid.: 373). Bayly (1994: 749), in her study of Christian fundamentalism in south India, observes that one of the objectives of these Christian groups is to show the superiority of Christian spirituality.

These believers want to reassert their primacy over the rich supernatural terrain of South India with its living pantheons of divinities, warrior heroes, and occult societies. For them Jesus, the Virgin, and the Christian saints must be made known to the wider world as fierce figures of power with the capacity to contend as warriors in the crowded and menacing supernatural landscape of contemporary South India (ibid.).

Pentecostalism in India

The history of Pentecostal revival in India predates the Azuza street revivals in USA that are often cited as the beginnings of modern-day Pentecostal revivalism. As Hedlund (2004: 18) observes:

The outpouring of the Holy Spirit at the Mukti Mission of Pandita Ramabhai in Pune, India, in 1905 is normally regarded as the origin of the Pentecostal revival in India. An earlier manifestation of tongues and other gifts had been reported in 1860 at a mission in Tirunelveli in Tamil Nadu. Revivals have been recorded in North-East India from as early as 1897. Manifestations such as unison dancing, were noted in the 1905 revival, whereas tongues, healing and prophecy were more recent phenomena, associated with the so-called Mizo high revival of 1935.

Organised Pentecostalism in India starts with the establishment of the Indian AOG (1918), the Pentecostal Mission (1923), Indian Pentecostal Church (1933) and the Church of God, Full Gospel (1936). The Church Missionary Society (CMS), the London Missionary Society (LMS), and the Methodist and Anglican churches experienced a wave of revivalism in the 1900s (Burgess, 1999).

Official versions of the history of the Protestant church in India often exclude the Pentecostal churches. This is not in hindsight surprising given the elitism, hierarchy, caste consciousness and high-caste hegemony of the mainstream Protestant church in India, on the one hand, and its general non-acceptance of traditions of worship based on the 'gifts of the spirit', on the other. Many of the early members of the Pentecostal churches in India, for instance, in the Punjab, Kerala and Tamil Nadu belonged to the lower caste and Dalit traditions. Bueno (1999), for instance, observes that studies of Pentecostalism ought to be based on the recognition of the historical fact that these churches were considered lesser than mainstream churches, an attitude that remains dominant even today. 'Pentecostal experiences should be examined and understood as specific historic formations, within unequal relations of power' (ibid.). Thomas (2003: 378–79) observes that the spread of Pentecostalism in Kerala among the Dalits was to an extent related to the liberation that they found in a worship style that legitimised their voice; 'speaking in tongues' liberated a people who had traditionally been silenced. Moreover, the cultural affinities that Pentecostalism allowed them to celebrate, such as 'the spirit-filled worship which has strong emotional elements, the transmuted elements of spirit possession in worship centred on the third person of the Trinity, the whole aspect of faith healing and exorcism which Pentecostalism offered', led to the affirmation of heart and emotion over the mind and the rational (ibid.). While lower-caste converts, for instance, the Dalits, have made a political bid to become recognised, the mainstream church in India is yet to fully integrate Dalit Christians within their midst. The Mar Thoma Church continues to have separate churches for the Dalits, while the elitism practised in the Catholic Church continues to alienate Dalits. While the church in north India, for instance, those of the Punjabi Christians, was drawn from the lower castes, the situation in the south was different. This elitism along with the need to cater to the needs of an industrial proletariat led to the growth of the Pentecostal churches in India.

While the legitimisation of these churches remains an 'ideological' challenge in many parts of the world, at a structural and global level, these churches have become powers in their own right and are in a position to exert influence on matters related to politics and society. The AOG in Chennai, Bengaluru and Kolkata are recognised for their congregational strength, which often runs into the thousands, along with their economic and political muscle. The demography of these congregations no longer coincides with lower income groups. In fact, throughout the world, the middle classes have become comfortable in their allegiance to various forms of Pentecostalism. The fact remains that different strands of Pentecostalism account for the greatest growth in church numbers in India in the recent past. Through their accent on church planting, mission and evangelism, these churches have spread throughout India and can be found in almost all parts of the country—in areas characterised by a deep distrust of Christian missions, such as Gujarat, Madhya Pradesh and Arunachal Pradesh, and in the more fertile Christian heartlands in south India, particularly in Tamil Nadu, Kerala and Andhra Pradesh.

While there have been attempts to define Pentecostalist churches on the basis of their specific beliefs and forms of worship, the term 'Pentecostalism' is used in a broad sense to denote all the churches that are not normally recognised as part of the mainstream. Pentecostalists, in turn, point out that such residual arrogance ought to be tempered in the light of the fact that they have effectively become the mainstream. Robbins (2003: 223) observes that the Pentecostal tradition is characterised by a set of 'hard practices' consisting of enduring links between values, meaning and practices that are common to all churches belonging to this tradition.

At the core of Pentecostalism understood as a hard form in this way is the set of charismatic practices that make it distinctive in the Protestant world: glossolalia (speaking in tongues), spirit possession, healing, etc. These practices seem to be similar wherever they are found, establishing a sort of global norm of Pentecostal Charismatic practice (ibid.).

Satyavarta (1999: 206–7) has attempted to categorise Pentecostals in India under the following headings:

1. Pentecostals with transnational organisational links
2. Pentecostal charismatics with a national and indigenous identity
3. Regional and local Pentecostal and charismatic churches
4. Catholic charismatics
5. Indigenous Pentecostal charismatic mission agencies
6. Non-denominational para-church charismatic networks

In reality, these categories are not as watertight as they would seem. Not only are there are correspondences in terms of worship styles and accents, but also in terms of their structures and linkages with global Christian organisations. While the key theoretician of the indigenous church movement in India, Roger Hedlund, does insist that there are local churches that are rooted in context and are successful primarily because they are independent of foreign influences, it would seem that this is a minority, given the rather obvious presence of foreign missionaries involved in church planting throughout India and the free flow of foreign funds. In a country as large as India, there are bound to be progressive variations in any given religious tradition. Among the thousands of house churches, independent churches and instances of communities such as the Mylapore Brahmins who have turned to Christ, there are certainly bound to be examples of a thoroughly indigenised Christianity. While Hedlund recognises 'Prosperity Theology' as a 'deadly American heresy' (personal interview), he is of the opinion that the indigenous churches have, by and large, kept these influences at bay. However, as Mathew (2004: 8) observes, the flow of foreign money has impacted on indigenous churches in India.

> The western churches are now collaborating directly with smaller churches providing financial support. 'Only a few indigenous groups are totally free from foreign aid and foreign control' (writes) Dr P.J. Titus evaluating the Pentecostal churches in Andhra Pradesh. 'Plenty of funds are drawn from the West.' The dependency of these churches make the sustainability of such churches difficult (ibid.).

Devi (2004) citing Foreign Contribution (Regulation) Act statistics for 2004 has observed that:

> Gospel for Asia with Rs 98.9 crore is the second highest recipient, while the World Vision of India with Rs 88.4 crore is in third place, according to data collated from the home ministry's latest annual report.... The bulk of the funding for Gospel for Asia in India comes from its parent organisation in the US, which heads the foreign donors list with Rs 111.2 crore.

One of the most accessible, informative texts on indigenous missions in India is the study by the Indian Christian artist and writer P. Solomon Raj. While his reading of indigenous mission in the book *The New Wine-Skins: The Story of the Indigenous Missions in Coastal Andhra Pradesh, India* (2003) is largely sympathetic to the larger Christian cause, he does recognise that, in reality, very few of these missions are financially independent of foreign money or are completely reliant on Indian leadership. As he points out, 'many of the 73 missions... studied in the survey do not fully qualify to be called indigenous or independent because many of them get money from the West and depend on foreign leadership.' He does tend to lump a variety of church groups in the indigenous category when, in reality, the Full Gospel Church, for example, is anything but indigenous. The clearest evidence, however, of church growth in Chennai is the Chennai Christian Directory (Albert, 2000) which lists 3000 churches and para-church organisations in this city inclusive of the Beulah Church (8 churches), End Time Zion (14 churches), Marantha Full Gospel Church (27 churches), Moving Jesus Mission (3 churches), Pillar of Fire Mission (6 churches), the Village Evangelism of Indian Mission (5 churches) and indigenous churches (645), among very many other churches in Chennai. It also lists 46 Bible colleges, 23 Christian media centres, 122 Christian magazines in English and Tamil, and 114 church planting missions. There is every reason to believe that there has been a further growth in these sectors to date.

Lionel Caplan (1987) remains among the first scholars of religion to have written about Protestant fundamentalism in India, and particularly in Chennai. He believes that the rise of Protestant fundamentalism in Chennai is an instance of what Foucault has termed the 'insurrection of subjugated knowledges'. According to Caplan, the poor belonging to the mainstream protestant church have always identified with the 'back to basics' approach of the 19th century conservative evangelical missionaries. 'Emphasis is placed on scriptural infallibility, Bible-centered sermons, piety, prayer and persistent evangelisation of the Hindus' (ibid.). The ecumenical agenda of the CSI and its emphasis on the 'Social Gospel' was seen essentially as an un-Biblical approach, not sanctioned by the Scriptures. Caplan's observations are important for the following reasons:

1. He explores Pentecostalism from within mainstream Protestant traditions and as a church on its own right. Pentecostalism has remained a residual force at the very heart of the Protestant Church in India. In other words, the Protestant Church's tryst with evangelism has never really been subjugated at the level of its congregations. The Mar Thoma Church's flagship evangelical Maramon convention was held in early March 2006 for the 111th time. The American Methodist Church in Chennai has had a strong conservative evangelical following. The evangelically-minded, therefore, have been among the first to transfer their allegiance to the new churches, although as many remain and are involved in multi-church attendance.

2. Caplan also refers to the influence of the charismatic prophets in Chennai and the congregation's tendency to see them as exemplars for Protestant ministers who are often seen as wanting in the area of preaching, healing and spirituality. Moreover, the charismatics include women who are routinely denied positions of authority in the Protestant Church in India.

The Mar Thoma Church's
Evangelism and Mission Strategy

This disjuncture is rooted in the ambivalence of the Christian mission in India. While the winds of Liberation Theology and the Social Gospel have blown through the windows of mainstream churches and have resulted in an accent on justice, empowerment and wholeness, these emphases themselves have become institutionalised. They have by no means become common currency, supported by the majority of people in the pew. The latter are, in all probability, more comfortable with traditional Biblical injunctions such as preaching and proclamation rather than the radical discontinuities offered by much of ecumenical thinking. More often than not, this has resulted in radical disjunctures between church hierarchies and theologians who are exposed to a variety of ecumenical discourses, on one hand, and the average member of a congregation who is comfortable with traditional teachings, on the other. The reformed Mar Thoma Church, which is part of mainstream Indian Christianity, continues to have a strong emphasis on proclamation and evangelism, a heritage of British church workers of the CMS.

> The first Anglican mission (CMS) started to work in Kerala in 1816. A number of Jacobites came under their influence and reforms were introduced on Anglican lines. Leadership for this reform group was provided by Palakunnath Abraham Malpan and Kaithayil Geevarghese Malpan, the two professors of the Syrian Seminary at Kottayam (The Mar Thoma Church in India).

The tension between personal faith and contextualised faith resulted in a schism in the Mar Thoma Church and the creation of the breakaway St. Thomas Evangelical Church in 1961. However, the Mar Thoma Church continues to keep its evangelical missionary zeal alive—not only through its social mission ministries organised through its support for educational institutions at a variety of levels, hospitals and development work, but also through its institutions such as the Maramon convention. The Mar Thoma Church's annual Maramon convention held on the banks of the Maramon River close to Thiruvalla, Kerala, is the oldest (1896) Christian convention in India. Its accent is on the proclamation of the Gospel, new birth, salvation and conversion. The Mar Thoma Church's mission strategy as a result cannot be distinguished from the strategies adopted by the new churches. While the Mar Thoma Church represents a unique blend of Eastern traditions and Western Protestantism, it would seem that in the present day, the influence of its reformed tradition is more pronounced than its Eastern tradition. How to sustain this blend, its Eastern traditions and at the same time indigenise the church is a challenge that the church is yet to face up to; where it is facing up to the challenge, it is not faring well.

While the traditions of the Mar Thoma Church certainly are unique, its emphasis on personal evangelism, the strategies adopted by it and its seeming inability to rein in its coterie of enthusiastic spreaders of the word does bring it uncomfortably close to some of the new churches. Take, for instance, this text from a book on the Mar Thoma Church written by K.T. Joy (1986: 94):

> Guruvayoor is [a] Hindu pilgrim centre where people from all over India come in large numbers. The mission centre is at Mukti mandiram where there is also a school. Efforts are being made to distribute gospels and tracts and personal evangelism is being carried about among the people under the leadership of Rev. C.S. Joseph, and Rev. Dr. P. Philip. The evangelists visit the nearby villages of Guruvayoor and Mukkola. At the Mukti mandiram chapel, Sunday worship, Sunday School, and Bible classes for student[s] are held. Open air meetings are arranged for preaching the gospel at various places such as Trichur, Guruvayoor, Mukkola and Tirunavai.

These four localities are distinguished by the fact that they are important Hindu pilgrimage centres. Guravayoor, for instance, is no ordinary place but one of the most sacred sites for Hindus from Kerala and the rest of India. Its long history is shrouded in myth and includes desecration at the hands of the Dutch in the 17th century and later on by the southern India Muslim rulers, Haider Ali and Tipu Sultan. It is, in the words of one website:

> The fourth biggest temple in India in terms of the number of devotees per day, Guruvayoor Temple dedicated to Lord Krishna.... Being one of the most sacred and important pilgrim centres of Kerala, it is probably the only temple in the state that hosts the maximum number of marriages and rice feeding ceremony, the ritual first meal for infants (Pilgrimage India).

To target pilgrims visiting these religious sites for conversion seems extraordinarily intolerant.

This accent on personal evangelism, while broadly supported by the church, is nevertheless contested by many from within the church, not least by the outspoken head of the Mar Thoma Church, Metropolitan Philipose Mar Chrysostam Mar Thoma, who is inclined towards a version of transformative mission that is concerned with 'wholeness' rather than with the personalised, born-again form of evangelism. As he observes in an interview recorded in the book by Athyal and Thatamanil (2002: 40):

> The missionary preachers, who organised massive evangelistic campaigns in Kerala during the last century, were not loyal to any mainline church tradition. Owing to their influence, therefore, many left the church and joined various sects. Sadhu Kochukunju Upadesi, as part of his evangelistic work, addressed the social needs of the people, but this was not the core of his message. Upadesi's approach, like most of ours, was one of disaster management or mere charity work. That is good Samaritan service but cannot be a substitute for sustained developmental work aimed at the total transformation of the society.... Even today, most of our itinerant preachers do not have a theological understanding of the place of the church in the redemption of the world; neither do they have a deep concern for the society. Their preaching can be a positive danger to the church.

In this sense, the specific field of the Mar Thoma Church is a field of struggles, over power and different types of capital. These struggles are influenced as much by the exigencies and imperatives of tradition, as by the pressures generated by competitors in the field such as K.P Yohanan's Thiruvalla-based Gospel for Asia Ministry (with an income of US$ 30 million in 2004) and, to a lesser extent, by pressure from new theological thinking from fraternal bodies such as the WCC and other organisations linked to the ecumenical movement.

However, these struggles over meaning, identity, power and capital are also played out at the microcosmic level of all churches, mainstream or otherwise. The Catholic hierarchy, for instance, still considers the Catholic Church as the only legitimate expression of authentic Christian witness. Internecine struggles within the Orthodox Church has led to the emergence of two factions—the Syrian Jacobite Church and the indigenous Malankara Orthodox Church. The unity of the conciliar body, the CSI, is plagued by inter-denominational tensions. However, the challenge posed by neo-Pentecostalism and charismatic Christianity are potentially more divisive than the intra- and inter-church struggles within the main-stream churches. The challenge is addressed at the level of the very identity of these churches, their specific traditions, structures, theologies, and ways of comprehending the fit between church and society, inclusive of their attitude towards other faiths. The Pentecostals place a premium on 'inner experience' and this stands diametrically opposed to the mainstream church emphasis on hierarchies of mediation of the religious experience and inherited, formalised styles of worship. From a Pentecostal perspective, there is a perceived lack of spirituality in the mainstream church. This has become part of public knowledge—litigation, factional infighting, the indiscretions of bishops and priests, and violent clashes between rival groups that even results in death. This struggle to establish primacy is also being played out over satellite and cable channels, although, given the near complete control of these channels by those who favour Pentecostalism, the mainstream churches are yet to work out an ecumenical media strategy in response. The lack of a united response is in itself a reflection of the real divides that exist between the mainstream churches, which are also expressed at a global level. While there is ongoing dialogue between the Vatican and the WCC, and there are certain affirmations of church unity, real possibilities for church unity within the mainstream church are a distant prospect.

References

Albert, S.V. 2000. *Chennai Christian Directory*. Chennai: Church Growth Association of India.

Appadurai, A. and C.A. Breckenridge. 1994. 'Public Modernity in India', in C.A. Breckenridge (ed.), *Consuming Modernity: Public Culture in Contemporary India*, pp. 1–20. New Delhi: Oxford University Press.

Armet, S. 2005. 'Controlling the Means of Production: The Urban Poor in an Age of Globalisation', *Culture and Religion*, 6(2): 309–26.

Athyal, J.M. and J.J Thatamanil. 2002. *Chrysostam on Mission in the Market Place*. Tiruvalla: Christava Sahitya Samithi.

Bayly, S. 1994. 'Christians and Competing Fundamentalisms in South Indian Society', in M.E. Marty and R.S. Appleby (eds), *Accounting for Fundamentalisms: The Dynamic Character of Movement*, pp. 726–69. Chicago & London: The University of Chicago Press.

Beyer, P. 2003. 'De-centring Religious Singularity: The Globalisation of Christianity as a Case in Point', *Numen*, 50(4): 358–86.

Brouwer, S., P. Gifford and S.D. Rose. 1996. *Exporting the American Gospel: Global Christian Fundamentalism*. NY & London: Routledge.

Bueno, R.N. 1999. 'Listening to the Margins: Re-historicising Pentecostal Experiences and Identities', in M.W. Dempster, B.D. Klaus and D. Petersen (eds), *The Globalisation of Pentecostalism: A Religion Made to Travel*, pp. 268–88. Carlisle: Regnum.

Burgess, S.M. 2001. 'Pentecostalism in India: An Overview', *Asian Journal of Pentecostal Studies*, 4(1): 85–98.

Campus Crusade for Christ International. Available at http://www.ccci.org/locations/asia/india/jesus-on-film-seeing-is-believing.aspx, accessed on 15 May 2006.

Caplan, L. 1991. 'Christian Fundamentalism as Counter Culture', in T.N. Madan (ed.), *Religion in India*, pp. 366–81. New Delhi: Oxford University Press.

————. 1987. 'Fundamentalism as a Counter-Culture: Protestants in Urban South India, in L. Caplan (ed.), *Studies in Religious Fundamentalism*, pp. 156–76. Basingstoke/London: Macmillan Press.

Casanova, J. 2001. 'Religion, the New Millennium, and Globalisation', *Sociology of Religion*, 62(4): 415–41.

Cox, H. 1995. *Fire from Heaven: The Rise of Pentecostal Spirituality and the Reshaping of Religion in the Twenty-first Century*. Cambridge, Mass.: De Capo Press.

Dempster, M.W., B.D. Klaus and D. Petersen (eds). 1999. *The Globalisation of Pentecostalism: A Religion Made to Travel*. Carlisle: Regnum.

Devi, Y. 2004. 'NGOs Hit Pay Dirt on Dollar Trail', *The Economic Times*, 20 January.

Hedlund, R. 2004. 'The Witness of New Christian Movements in India', paper presented at the IAMS Assembly in Malaysia, 31 July to 7 August. Available at http://www.missionstudies.org/conference/1papers/fp/Roger_Hedlund_Full_Paper.pdf, accessed on 21 March 2006.

Hunt, S. 2000. '"Winning Ways": Globalisation and the Impact of the Health and Wealth Gospel', *Journal of Contemporary Religion*, 15(3): 331–47.

Iannaccone, L.R. 1992. 'Religious Markets and the Economics of Religion', *Social Compass*, 39(1): 123–31.

Joy, K.T. 1986. *The Mar Thoma Church: A Study of its Growth and Contribution*. Kottayam: Mar Thoma Sabha.

Manokaran, J.N. 2005. *Christ and Cities: Transformation of Urban Centres*. Chennai: Mission Educational Books.

Martin, B. 1995. 'New Mutations of the Protestant Ethic among Latin American Pentecostals', *Religion*, 25(2): 101–17.

Mathew, S.K. 2004. 'The Church in India: Status, Trends and Challenges', *Ethne*, 3(8): 5–9.

Mendieta, E. 2001. '*Invisible Cities: A Phenomenology of Globalisation from Below*', City, 5(1): 7–26.

Percy, M. 2000. 'The Church in the Marketplace: Advertising and Religion in a Secular Age', *Journal of Contemporary Religion*, 15(1): 97–119.

Pilgrimage India. Available at http://www.pilgrimage-india.com/south-india-pilgrimage/guruvayoor-temple.html, accessed on 26 June 2006.

Prakash, G. 2002. 'The Urban Turn', in *Sarai Reader*. Available at http://www.sarai.net/publications/readers/02-the-cities-of-everyday-life/02urban_turn.pdf, accessed on 15 May 2006.

Pye-Smith, C. 1997. *Rebels and Outcastes: A Journey Through Christian India*. London: Viking, Penguin.

Raj, P.S. 2003. *The New Wine-Skins: The Story of the Indigenous Mission in Coastal Andhra Pradesh, India*. Delhi: ISPCK.

Raj, V.S. and J.W. Selvasingh. 2004. 'Churches in Chennai: Characteristics of Churches in Chennai', *Ethne*, 3(8): 10.

Robbins, J. 2004. 'The Globalisation of Pentecostal and Charismatic Christianity', *Annual Review of Anthropology*, 33: 117–43.

————. 2003. 'On the Paradoxes of Global Pentecostalism and the Perils of Continuity Thinking', *Religion*, 33(3): 221–31.

Satyavarta, I.M. 1999. 'Contextual Perspectives on Pentecostalism: A South Asian View', in M.W. Dempster, B.D. Klaus and D. Petersen (eds), *The Globalisation of Pentecostalism: A Religion Made to Travel*, pp. 203–21. Carlyle: Regnum.

Stolz, J. 2006. 'Salvation Goods and Religious Markets: Integrating Rational Choice and Weberian Perspectives', *Social Compass*, 53(1): 13–32.

The Mar Thoma Church in India. Available at http://members.tripod.com/ ~ Berchmans/ marthoma.html, accessed on 15 May 2006.

Thomas, V.V. 2003. *Pentecostalism among the Dalits in Kerala from 1909 to the Present: A Subaltern Reading*, Doctoral Thesis, Union Biblical Seminary, Pune.

THEORY AND CONCEPTS

5

BOURDIEU, CHRISTIANITY AND
MEDIATED CHRISTIANITY IN INDIA

The advent of global satellite broadcasting in South Asia that began with CNN during the first Gulf War paved the way for a series of transformations to the mediascape in India (see Page and Crawley, 2001). The 'illegal' cabling of India and the availability of Indian language satellite channels uplinked from Hong Kong, Singapore and other countries rapidly led to the establishment of a national alternative to the state monopoly broadcaster Doordarshan. India's turn towards and advocacy of economic liberalisation that gathered speed in the early 1990s, after decades of following a strictly dirigiste model of development, was to some extent legitimised by satellite and cable channels. Zee TV, SUN TV, ASIANET and NDTV, along with many others channels, celebrated models of progress and prosperity in the business and finance sectors and legitimised the pursuit of capital accumulation. Serials and other popular entertainment programmes that explored the changing cultures, roles, expectations and desires of the Indian middle classes, amply supported by advertising, played key roles in spreading the message of consumerism, leading to a fuelling of the demand for consumer goods and services. Indian language versions (for instance, in Hindi and Tamil) of *Who Wants to be a Millionaire* are examples of this unabashed celebration of 'making it', while copycat versions of *Big Brother* indicate a change in mores and a willingness to explore new boundaries for public morality. This new-found celebration of cultural, even sexual, freedom is complemented by other freedoms related to the pursuit of individualism—investments in the stock market, conspicuous consumption, a rise in salaries of people working in sectors closely linked to economic globalisation and a rapacious appetite for real estate.

Until 1990, the popular entertainment in India was, for all practical purposes, synonymous with the Indian film industry. Today, cinema continues to be the key source for popular culture, although it is now complemented with other types of popular culture. While cable and satellite channels continue to extend India's film culture, these have also become the source of a thriving, independent entertainment industry in its own right. Not only have a variety of film spin-offs—song and dance, comedy excerpts—been turned into televised entertainment, but also the intentional exploration of existing sub-culture fuelled desires has resulted in the creation of new tele-visual genres hitherto unexplored in the Indian context, from situation comedies, to documentaries, to hard-hitting current affairs programmes. Television has become the barometer of changing India, and it is in this sense that one can affirm the centrality of mediation in the negotiation of cultural, social and national identities in India. Television's many discourses have begun to deal with lived life, especially as it is lived in urban India and, this in turn, has led to people recognising television's 'local' nature. This is a far cry from the typical experience of monopoly television in India that was authoritarian, removed and remote.

Satellite and cable channels are critically involved in the mediation of globalisation and globalised religion. Religion on television has become a staple cultural commodity available throughout the country. While these channels certainly inform and educate audiences on aspects related to religion, draw the faithful together and offer them an opportunity to reinforce belief, they have also provided the space for negotiating religion as national identity. Arvind Rajagopal (2001) has assessed the ways in which the serialisation of the Indian epics *Mahabharat* and *Ramayan* by the state broadcaster Doordarshan in the mid-1980s contributed to the popularisation of a Hindu national identity that was turned to political advantage by the right-wing Bharatiya Janata Party (BJP) and its allies. While Rajagopal suggests that the transmission of these two serials on Doordarshan violated the taboo against religious partisanship in broadcasting, it can be argued that this transmission merely routinised Indian broadcasting's incipient favouring of high culture, which in India is synonymous with Brahminic culture. All India Radio (AIR), for instance, continues to be partial to Indian classical music and Doordarshan to traditional, classical Indian dance, over other traditions. However, the state broadcaster no longer has a monopoly over the transmission or mediation of religious programmes. The accentuated liberalisation of television has led to any number of opportunities for religious broadcasting and, consequently, possibilities for the communication of any number of religious identities. Just as the Hindu epics were used to create an essentialised version of the Indian identity, local and global Christian channels, today, routinely claim the Indian nation for Christ.

Mediation

The Colombian media scholar Jesus Martin-Barbero (1993: 185), in his classic study *Communication, Culture and Hegemony: From the Media to Mediations*, explains the emergence of social sectors in Latin American as a consequence of mediation:

> Over the last few years a Latin American movement, dissolving pseudotheoretical issues and cutting through ideological inertias, has opened up a new way of thinking about the constitution of mass society, namely, from the perspective of transformations in sub-alternate cultures. Communication in Latin America has been profoundly affected by external transnationalisation but also by the emergence of new social actors and new cultural identities. Thus communication has become a strategic arena for the analysis of the obstacles and contradictions that move these societies, now at the crossroads between accelerated underdevelopment and compulsive modernisation. Because communication is the meeting point of so many conflicting and integrating forces, the centre of the debate has shifted from media to mediations.

Martin-Barbero's insights are important precisely because these deal with mediation in both a narrow sense as media-specific audience negotiations of meaning and in that wider sense of our everyday negotiations with institutions, cultures and processes that, in turn, shape our individual habitus within the multiple identity groups that we belong to. In the former sense, mediation is consonant with the experience of millions of Indians who have, over the last decade, begun to consciously or otherwise negotiate tele-visually mediated meanings on subjects ranging from patriotism (for example, Kargil), to the economy (the 'India Shining' campaign that backfired on the National Democratic Alliance [NDA] coalition), to changing mores in India. The heterogeneity of television in India, offers spaces for celebrating the essentialised 'nation' (flags, *Vande Mataram*, cricket matches) as well as its obverse, the multiple identifications of a heterogeneous population differentiated along class, caste, gender, language, religion and other markers of identity. Television acts like a prism, refracting the multiple stories that make up the epistemic story of globalisation and India's futures within the real and imagined embrace of globalisation.

The Mediation of Religion

Religious fundamentalism today is mediated via a variety of genres on television—news and features, music and talk shows, and the coverage of crusades and celebrations. While there are Islamic and Hindu channels that support exclusive views, Christian channels account for more religion on global television than any other faith-based channels. From Fiji to Ghana, USA to Russia, Christian channels such as Pat Robertson's Christian Broadcasting Network (CBN) and Paul Crouch's Trinity Broadcasting Network (TBN) are available over cable, satellite and terrestrial channels. Even nationally-owned television channels reserve time for a variety of tele-evangelists. Typically, their stories are defined by a series of exclusions of the 'other' that in the case of Christian fundamentalists in India consist of the 'heathen Hindu', their repertoire of rites and rituals, gods and goddesses, cultures and ways of life. Stolow (2005: 125) urges us to get away from instrumentalist approaches to understand religion and media and to explore

> how the media and mediation constitute inherently unstable and ambiguous conditions of possibility for religious signifying practices, as well as their articulation with broader public realms of religious belonging, to say nothing of the incorporation of religious regimes of discipline, virtuous conduct and ecstatic performance in embodied everyday life contexts, and in the cultivation of the self.

While the negotiation of symbolic meaning by active audiences makes sense in the context of the negotiation of everyday information and knowledge, one can argue that in the context of India, ordinary viewers are less likely to confront or negotiate mediated religion precisely because a culture of dissent or confrontational attitude towards religion is not a culture that people are familiar with. While I did come across Christians in Chennai who were, for instance, critical of Benny Hinn on television, this group was certainly a minority when compared to those who valued tele-evangelists and the programmes offered by Christian broadcasting in India today. I met Hindus who had adopted a more Catholic approach to the religions in India and who were quite content with Christian broad-casting precisely because all 'God talk', in their way of thinking, was valuable since it dealt with the same universal God. Christian television does have a niche audience predominantly among Christians, but also among Hindus. These channels are involved in the maintenance of audi-ences through direct marketing mail order contact. I did come across the *God TV Christmas Edition Guide to Programming* (Asia/Middle East) in numerous homes that I had visited in Chennai.

From the perspective of political economy, this extensive investment in broadcasting's symbolic capital needs to be theorised in relation to the extraordinarily important economic and political role played by the cultural industries in our world today. The Fox Network is not just a purveyor of global news and entertainment but is integrally related to the extension of a neo-conservative political and economic world order. Similarly, in the context of India, the Chennai-based Sun TV network's offerings, while certainly extending choice and the breadth of popular south Indian culture, also need to be seen from the perspective of media ownership and of the ways in which politics and economics have shaped the empire it is today. In other words, television is both culture and economics and, in this sense, the symbolic and the material need to be accounted for in any serious analysis of television's role in society today. The global satellite channel GOD TV is a purveyor of conservative Christianity and is quite open about its support for a Christian century, US geo-politics and Zionism.

In this sense, Christianity and mediated Christianity in India are, at a fundamental level, about institutions that are shaped by continuity and change, and ideologies of practice, and that are involved in the exercise of power aimed at system maintenance and system expansion. The Church of South India's (CSI) real estate is a formidable asset and the processes involved in maintaining offices and officers entail dealings with mammon. The maintenance of church property is a fraught process and church properties throughout India are high on the list of real estate de-velopers. Christianity and mediated Christianity are integrally and intensely related to the symbolic in theory and practice. In the context of the church in India and, in particular, the competition for the true faith and followers between the mainstream churches and new churches, the cultural and symbolic legitimacy of the 'true' church is being contested.

At the same time, economic and symbolic capital is being separately marshalled by competing church groups in the pursuit of their own claims and interests. While a number of social and cultural theorists including Raymond Williams, Stuart Hall and Graham Murdock have explored the links between the symbolic *and* the material, and the symbolic *in* the material, Pierre Bourdieu's contributions to the analysis of culture and the economy is framed by a desire to both understand the relationship between the ideational and the material as well as the involved linkages between agency and structure. This intent squares with my own objective to explore the economics and culture of mediated Christianity in India. Hence, we next turn to a brief assessment of Bourdieu's key concepts.

Using Bourdieu to Illumine Mediated Christianity in India

The French sociologist Pierre Bourdieu's analysis of the role played by culture in social domination and the specific concepts he invokes to study the links between ideational and material power can be applied to understanding a variety of societal fields, including that of religion. Bourdieu's project of *constructivist structuralism* attempted to bridge the differences between the objective and the subjective, between agency and structure, between cultural idealism and historical materialism, and was an attempt to theorise the mutually constitutive connectivities between social structures and actors. Central to Bourdieu's arguments are his use of terms such as *habitus*, *field*, *symbolic capital* and *distinction*. The following section will include an explanation of these terms and the relationships between these terms. Central to Bourdieu's explication of social theory is the term habitus. This refers to the interpretive schemas and cultural dispositions that lead individuals to evaluate, organise, categorise, think and act. The guidelines that shape every individual's habitus are not fixed but instead a permeable, changeable set of unconscious rules that help individuals strategise and negotiate structures and practices. The habitus itself is a product of the specific social, structural conditions and the position of the individual in society, although Bourdieu suggests that this relationship between agency and structure is not determining but relational. As Siedman (2004: 148) explains:

The habitus is a product of an individual's social structural conditions and yet structures his or her social practices in ways that reproduce the agent's objective conditions of social existence. This process of social reproduction...does not imply an instrumental, mechanistic view of social practice...the relationship between social structure, habitus, and social practice is not a simple, linear, causal and mechanistic one.

In this sense, the habitus is not fixed for all time but is elastic and can be stretched or for that matter compressed. The specificities of each individual's habitus are influenced by his/her relationship to, membership of and status within a range of different social fields that include academia, religion, the economy and politics. Each field values certain types of capital—for instance, in the context of religion, social and symbolic capital are perhaps more revered than other types of capital, although televised religion may attach importance to other types of capital. As Jenkins (1992: 85) explains, Bourdieu's concept of the field:

is a structured system of social positions—occupied either by individuals or institutions—the nature of which defines the situation for their occupants. It is also a system of forces which exist between these positions; a field is structured internally in terms of power relations. Positions stand in relationships of domination, subordination or equivalence (homology) to each other by virtue of the access they afford to the goods or resources (capital) which are at stake in the field. These goods can be principally differentiated into four categories— economic capital, social capital...cultural capital...and symbolic capital.

The field plays an important role in shaping the habitus—the logic of practice followed by individuals and the groups that they belong to.

Bourdieu, like Weber, Durkheim and Marx, was of the opinion that religion was a declining institution. Bourdieu did not value religion as anything more than an aspect of false consciousness. While Bourdieu's interest in religion is not as developed as that of his other concerns including art and culture, a number of his key concepts, inclusive of 'belief', 'distinction', 'field' and 'habitus' are derived from his readings of Max Weber or based on his observations of the culture of Catholicism in France (Dianteill, 2003). His relatively less known study 'Genesis and Structures of the Religious Field' (Bourdieu, 1991: 9) is one of his rare studies that is explicitly concerned with the relationship between the religious field, symbolic capital and religious power. Unlike Max Weber who suggested that 'charisma' was an inherent quality, a gift of nature, Bourdieu explicitly connects charisma to the exercise of symbolic violence linked to the creation of 'misrecognition'.

> Inasmuch as it is the result of the monopolisation of the administration of the goods of salvation by a body of religious specialists, socially recognised as the exclusive holders of the specific competence necessary for the production of or reproduction of a deliberately organised corpus of secret (and therefore rare) knowledge, the constitution of a religious field goes hand in hand with the objective dispossession of those who are excluded from it and who thereby find themselves constituted as the laity...dispossessed of religious capital...and recognising the legitimacy of that dispossession from the mere fact that they misrecognise it as such (ibid.).

The misrecognition of the 'goods of salvation' reminds us of Gramsci's notion of hegemony as the means by which people end up consenting to their own domination.

The Cultivation of 'Distinction'

Bourdieu's (1984) emphasis on the cultural basis for 'distinction' seems particularly apt to understanding mediated forms of Christianity in India today. There is a nationwide platform (tele-visual) for the mediation of 'distinctiveness'—and it is being mobilised to create distinctions between the old and the new, the old church and the new church, new doctrine as opposed to old doctrine, new sources of Biblical authority as against traditional sources and interpretations, new understandings of the qualities of a pastor as against conventional understandings, as well as new understandings of the objectives of Christian ministry and the individual's relationship with God as against standard understandings of the objectives of Christian ministry and the individual's relationship with God. This distinctiveness is not only reflected in the personal grooming and rhetorical styles adopted by evangelists and tele-evangelists, but also in his or her complete symbolic repertoire. Tele-evangelists, such as Benny Hinn and others, have, in an elemental sense, reclaimed a belief in religion as fundamentally about using magical powers to effect healing, restoration and reconciliation. In Weber's way of thinking, magic was the basis for early forms of religion that depended on a magician's coercion of the divine for human ends. The advent of organised religion led to the superseding of magic and the magician, and to the establishment of an extensive meta-physics of religion. As Weber (1963: 30) has pointed out: 'The full devel-opment of both a metaphysical rationalisation and a religious ethic requires an independent and professionally trained priesthood, permanently occu-pied with the cult and with the practical problems involved in the cure of souls.' However, despite the institutionalisation of organised religion, the reliance on magic as the basis for delivery from the chains of the devil has remained a potent sub-text in all the major religions and in the many religious cultures and traditions found throughout the world. Mainstream Protestant Christianity's overt rationalisation of its faith, its denial of alternative, popular expressions of healing and its inability to deal with the 'unexplainable' has been exposed as wanting and out of touch, par-ticularly so, in the context of the rise of tele-evangelists, who have, by their reliance on magic, contributed to what one might call the 're-enchantment' of Christianity. One can argue that 'healing' is among the most distinctive features shared by the tele-evangelists and neo-Pentecos-tal preachers; this makes their ministry different from that followed by other ministries. Healing connects to the spirit world, to malevolent forces that play a significant role in the lives of people living in globalised contexts throughout the world. The recognition of evil in the world of the everyday allows for a continuation of belief in the presence of evil—the principalities and powers that are graphically described in the lan-guage of the Bible. It connects to the belief in the supernatural that remains a residual element in the lives of Hindu converts to Christianity. The power to heal is a powerful draw and especially so in a globalised world where access to healing is mediated by professionals. In the Indian context, there has always been space for faith-based healing and healers, although Christian evangelists are responsible for making faith healing a public spectacle.

In Bourdieu's way of thinking, these elements of distinctiveness are implicated in a politics of power that works through a 'misrecognition of [their] material interests' (Swartz, 1996:3). Tele-evangelists such as Benny Hinn, Kenneth Copeland, Sarah and Peter Hughes, Sam Chelladurai and Brother Dhinakaran communicate themselves as persons chosen by God to do God's command, often through a highly personalised repertoire of unique, oftentimes idiosyncratic, symbolic capital that is communicated via expressive styles and methods of audience identification (Rey, 2004). Such attempts at identification are often highlighted at the expense of the oftentimes intense materiality of these enterprises. This disconnect is powerfully visible in the living histories of numerous evangelists and tele-evangelists in India today, whose self-interest has been made invisible by many layers of mediated pietistic purposefulness. Television has been used to cultivate 'disinterestedness' as, for instance, Benny Hinn's frequent confirmations that God is the healer not him or the more disingenuous advertisements on GOD TV fronted by Indians who claim that the funds are required solely for the greater glory of God's ministry and plan for India. This misrecognition is reflected in what is a common subtext shared among many Christians and people of other faiths in India that Benny Hinn and other tele-evangelists, whatever their shortcomings, are God's representatives on earth. They have been blessed. There is a misrecognition of the real connections between the other-worldly metaphysics of these preachers and the very real-world materiality of their ministries. What Weber and Bourdieu have tried to stress are the correspondences between the exercise of religion and the exercise of power, the exercise of ritual power as an exercise of material power.

Bourdieu also draws useful parallels between the priest, who is involved in the extension of established religion, and the prophet whose 'added value'—for instance, through his or her penchant for faith healing and or charisma—contests the power of the priest and the control over religious capital. This contestation between old and new purveyors of religion affects all religions, although the rise of Pentecostalism and neo-Pentecostalism in the context of Christianity has brought this contestation into sharp relief. Engler (2003: 447) makes the point that: 'For Bourdieu, the priest plays a conservative role, attempting to maintain control over religious capital, and the prophet is an innovator producing a new variant of religious goods, attempting to share a share of the market.' The Pentecostalist preacher is a representative of global Christianity and is perfectly adapted to the needs of Christians who long to be part of a faith community that validates their involvement in and experience of globalisation, both as victims and winners. The prophet plays a major role in legitimising 'prosperity' theology against the other-worldly theology of the established church and their accent on deferred rewards. The prophet advocates the centrality of the market and church growth as a project that is intimately involved with the market. And as part of that project, the prophet claims and adapts new technologies and the media as 'anointed' instruments that have been given by God for the purpose of advancing God's reign all over the world. This melding of faith with practice is reflected in the synergies between habitus and field, a meshing of the individual's practical belief with the larger objectives of Pentecostal Christianity. There is little space for irony or for a critique of technology. The prophet is involved in spreading faith in global futures.

The Processes of Misrecognition

For the older generation of Christians in India, the advent of Christian television has certainly provided the space and opportunity to explore Biblical meanings throughout the day, although early mornings and late evenings seem to be the preferred time for watching such programmes. These times coincide with the availability of programmes by the evangelist Joyce Meyer, whose programmes are popular throughout India and available in numerous languages. As I heard on a number of occasions, her sermons are different not only because they are well constructed and delivered, but also because she deals with topics that are of an everyday human nature—marriage, money matters, conflict, compassion, and the like. In this sense, mediation offers an opportunity for the reinforcement of Biblical doctrine, for seven days a week Biblical instruction and for larger identifications with a global community of believers.

However, these televised programmes offered the opportunity for viewers to review the inadequacy of Christian worship and the remoteness of priests and church structures. The order and clarity of these televised programmes was often contrasted with the quality of locally-made Christian programmes and the lack of clarity and order in the local church. In other words, it is clear that many viewers use the same yardstick to judge the manufactured world of televised Christianity as the institutional church and religious institutions in general in the real world that often are embroiled in messy processes and the politics of survival, which are far from the vocations of 'spirituality'. This inability to differentiate often translates into demands for slick, choreographed real church services, for better sermons and for sermon delivery based on global styles. In other words, mediated religion is contributing to the creation of a self-critical Christian public, which not only tolerates new forms of conservative Christianity but also projects these desires on to its existing church in real time. Mediation, in other words, does lead to an unsettling of the habitus and to demands on the field. At the same time, my path did cross with viewers who were selective in who and what they watch. There were those who were unimpressed with Benny Hinn's Prosperity Theology and the antics of local evangelists, and who were worried of the impact of such programmes on the Indian church. There were those who were critical of the tele-evangelists and the political positions that they take, although, given the daily presence of Pat Robertson on *The 700 Club* on channels such as GOD TV, it is difficult to not be exposed to such interpretations. What was perhaps most disquieting was the tendency for viewers exposed to some of these programmes to reiterate stereotypical, dominant views on Muslims, accept the rightness of the war in Iraq, affirm the rightness of the Zionist Israeli nation, critique idol-worshipping Hindus and acknowledge that God has especially blessed USA to lead other nations to Christ. When such affirmations are reinforced in local neo-Pentecostal churches, for instance, the Assemblies of God (AOG), there is always the possibility that members of the congregation assign credence to such ways of understanding.

Such programming—inclusive of its theology, Christian understanding of church and society, and Biblical doctrine—fits in squarely with the theology popularised by the Pentecostal and neo-Pentecostal churches in Chennai and elsewhere. It is this identification, bolstered by the presence of many of these local pastors on satellite and cable channels, that has led to a greater visibility and to the legitimacy of these new churches. Younger viewers, at least the ones that I had interviewed, seemed to be eclectic in their viewing habits. Rather typically, they enjoyed Gospel rock and Christian music in general but were less likely to sit through a sermon by a tele-evangelist. They tended to be far more critical of the perceived shortcomings of many of these tele-evangelists, particularly the local ones, with their foreign wives, the manufactured programmes, and the gaps between their professed love for God in heaven and orphans on earth, on one hand, and the 'material' lives that they led, on the other. The strange disjunctures, cultural gaps and perceived insincerity of the Sarah Hughes ministry (Miracle Net) were a conversation piece in many contexts. At the same time, they see such programmes as liberating, given the obvious generational affinities with GOD TV's programming style that is playful, postmodern and oriented towards the 'Y' generation.

While Bourdieu's notion of 'misrecognition' has been critiqued for its one-dimensionality (see Dillon, 2001), I believe that the issue at stake is not whether there are contestations within mainstream religion but whether these contestations have led to qualitative changes in relationships, processes and practices. Dillon suggests that the presence of reformist movements within the Catholic Church indicates that the project of misrecognition is contested from within. While reformist movements certainly play a key role in religion, the very fact that the Catholic Church continues to resist the ordination of women and that it elected a Pope whose credentials for conservatism weighed in his favour during the electoral process would seem to indicate that, for all the presence and activities of reformist-minded Catholics, it continues to have the power to privilege and maintain its essential doxa from change.

Symbolic Violence

The material and political interests of the tele-evangelists are hidden by their apparent concern for the spiritual welfare of people, their seeming altruism, their explicit hankering after transcendental rather than earthly rewards—in Benny Hinn's words, 'It is God working miracles, not me' (Evangelical Church for Financial Accountability). In Bourdieu's (1992: 127) words, such statements reflect symbolic violence: 'that gentle, invisible violence, unrecognised as such, chosen as much as undergone, that of trust, obligation, personal loyalty, hospitality, gifts, debts, piety, in a word, all of the virtues honoured by the ethic of honour.' The field of Christianity in India is an arena of competition in which churches and missions are involved in the production, reproduction, control, expansion, and legitimisation of specific religious experiences and religious capital. While Bourdieu's class-based analysis predisposes it towards a certain rigidity, he does recognise the fact that in the pursuit of religious capital, the most unlikely of alliances and correspondences occur. This is certainly true in the Indian context in which Pentecostalism has broken through the class, caste, gender barriers and even religious barriers. The very fact that right-wing Hindu groups such as the Shiv Sena in Mumbai allow a Benny Hinn extravaganza to take place indicates that there are points of correspondence between these faiths. The exchange of money in return for political support and security is one among many points of correspondence. I was, at least on a couple of occasions, privy to conversations with church leaders who explained the reality of realpolitik and the most unusual of correspondences between highly-placed public figures of the Hindu right wing and Christian groups. The appeal of blessings from a 'powerful' Christian healer would seem an enticing prospect for the most ardent of Hindu nationalists.

The Field and the Habitus in the Context of Conversion

While there are ontological correspondences between the habitus and the field, in the context of a globalised world constituted by the fracturing of identity and possibilities for many identifications, the correspondences between the field and the habitus is not straightforward. Globalisation does not encourage essentialised identifications and the globalised religious market offers competing claims on individual identities. Even the 'tradition' of the historical churches in India no longer provides sufficient markers of distinction that can be mobilised for thier growth today. In fact, the new churches blame 'tradition' for the non-growth of the church in India today, and for their perceived accommodations with the principalities and powers. However, and despite challenges to the historical church, its institutional culture continues to provide the terms of identification for its members. The caste conscious Syrian Christian does attend 'casteless' Christian conventions and prayer meetings, although this suspension of a marker of identity does not extend to the personal and ritual domains—for example, marriage, where caste, family and status continue to play a pivotal role.

Mediation is a continual process of negotiations between 'fields' and the individual/group habitus, for instance, between the religious field and one's personal/familial/class disposition towards religion, the pulls and pressures of identification, which are ultimately related to the individual/family coming to some sort of equilibrium/certainty with respect to some of life's large existential issues. This negotiation is by no means an effortless or straightforward process. The claims made by a variety of Christian denominations through overt proselytisation and covert offerings of a better life, expressed through routine, everyday ways and novel, dramatic means, towards influencing the logic of individual/group practice is an example of the pressure by the field on the habitus. This process, however, is never complete and is by no means a one-way process. There is resistance, rupture, re-negotiation, partial adaptation and, in the context of a religious market, possibilities for a constant search by individuals for transcendental forms of security and certainty.

The 'field' of Indian Christianity is currently a space for low-intensity struggles over symbolic, economic and political capital, a struggle that is essentially between mainstream Christianity, on one hand, and the many versions of indigenous Christianity and imported versions of neo-Pentecostalism, on the other. The struggle at a very elemental sense is over the frameworks of understanding, 'practical belief' that is moulded in the intersections of habitus (everyday ways of living, relating and thinking, and individual dispositions), and over the very nature of the habitus itself. 'Conversion' is an attempt to translate a new framework for knowing the world onto a pre-existing set of dispositions. It is a process that is grounded in and results in radical discontinuities, given that conversion is aimed primarily at adherents from other religious traditions—the Hindus, indigenous people, and the like. Conversion is almost always backed up by a denomination, sect or cult. The fact that conversions do occur seems to indicate that the acquired set of dispositions that make up the habitus are by no means fixed for eternity but can be changed and are transposable. Conversion can lead to a change in the classificatory principles and in the organising principles of action in a given habitus. While there is a case to be made for voluntary conversion given the basic need to respect the exercise of free will, more often than not, the conversion of an individual is based on real and imagined inducements—life in this world and the other. This process arguably involves the exercise of symbolic violence and quite often the misrecognition of the 'goods of salvation'. Conversion is a messy process and whatever theological, social justification that one can marshal in support of one's case for conversion, the very fact that it results in radical discontinuities between one's received culture, belief and habitus, on one hand, and a new orientation, on the other, requires us to treat it with the necessary circumspection. In this aspect, critics of conversion in India and, in particular, public figures such as Arun Shourie are right in their condemnation of Christian conversion, although their own silence with respect to Hindu conversion of indigenous people remains problematic. However, our moral indignation at conversion needs to be mindful of the larger context of conversion in India. In spite of the fact that conversion most often is not based on mutually agreed inter-subjectivities, it does place in relief real divides and blind spots within Hinduism—for example, that of the Dalits. Conversion offers an alternative system of identification for those who have been denied dignity or recognition. Anthony Copley (1997: 255), in a largely sympathetic study of conversion in late colonial India, observes key shifts in the field of evangelism on the realisation of its own failures: 'Having set its heart on the conversion of Brahmins, it found, instead, that its future lay in the conversion of the outcastes and the tribals, exiled communities as they themselves were, fellow outsider's in India's society.' While Copley's analogy can be questioned—after all an exiled missionary with his servants and bungalow did not exactly live a life of perpetual penury, in hock to moneylenders—the fact remains that the conversion of lower castes and Dalits remains key to the numbers game being played in India today.

This Gramscian 'war of position' that is an aspect of 'ferments within the field' of Indian Christianity has resulted in significant repercussions at the level of practical belief. The claims on practical belief are often made from two distinct traditions of practice. The inherited traditions, rules, rites, rituals and hierarchy that are characteristic features of established mainstream church traditions and denominations stand in contrast to the accent on personal experience, the spirit-filled sermon, the charismatic preacher, free forms of worship, glossolia and the universal Christ. As Howell (2003: 239) points out, in the latter tradition:

> in a far more explicit way, the Bible, Christian history, and the Jesus narrative are always understood to exist 'outside' any specific cultural, social or historic context, creating a 'totalising discourse', which encompasses the world prior to any ritual or community activity.... Preaching and Preachers [are] experienced as 'emplaced in a non-local transcendental context connecting these local congregations with the global, non-culturally specific, and a-historical'.

In other words, there is an attempt to explicitly identify Christian mission as a home for all foot-soldiers of Christ irrespective of where they come from or their specific beliefs. Time and time again, during field work in India, I heard the sentiment expressed that despite theological differences and ways of carrying out the Christianity ministry, the very fact that they were involved in proclaiming the Gospel—the common cause—was the determining factor. Everything else was secondary. This attempt to collapse the specificity of approaches, identities and motivations that exist in real life Christianity into a concept of brotherhood and sisterhood in the universal Christ is an attempt to create an *umma*, a global fraternity of believers in Christ. This stance allows many of the Pentecostal churches to create fluid relationships and correspondences with preachers, church bodies and networks located outside of India, especially in USA. And so, in the churches belonging to the AOG, 'white' pastors are reverentially acknowledged as somehow being representative of the real Christianity—an attitude that denies local Christian authenticity and the fact that Indian Christianity is nearly as old as Christianity itself.

There is a lighter side to such correspondences—for just as call centre workers in India mimic a variety of foreign accents in their many daily conversations with consumers situated in USA, UK, Australia, and elsewhere, the local Indian evangelical pastor has adopted an unmistakably US accent, which is most pronounced among indigenous tele-evangelists. The extraordinary incongruity between rhetoric and context is no longer a point of conversation, although the personal mannerisms of tele-evangelists still are. This suggests that the ubiquitous, global, US accent of evangelists in India is accepted even if it often results in incongruous situations such as the frequent drifts and slip-ups between vernacular translations of sermons in English. Even sermons in vernacular languages are delivered largely in a US American rhetorical style, complete with the required emphasis but also with an accent! I witnessed the same accented form of worship at the PowerHouse, a rock-based ministry in Chennai, where the songs in particular were sung in a style that reminded me of popular US Christian rock and Gospel. The Americanisation of the worship experience has spread throughout the church in India—and in fact many mainstream churches including the Mar Thoma Church have begun to incorporate 'praise and worship' sessions that mimic American-style worship, in particular the accent on popular Gospel songs. As a Mar Thoma priest told me, this move towards establishing space for praise and worship every fourth Sunday is an attempt to provide youth with a worship experience of their liking. The youth are free to invite preachers from outside of the Mar Thoma fold to sing contemporary Christian songs and to witness through testimonials and personal stories. While this, on one level, is an attempt by the Mar Thoma Church to accommodate a youth Christian culture, it is also, on another level, an attempt to keep the youth, who would otherwise drift to the new churches, within the Mar Thoma fold. This is in many ways a classic form of accommodation—for this kind of evening worship is on the margins and does not affect the constancy of traditional Mar Thoma worship.

The strategy does have its risks though, for the youth of today might well become the church leaders of tomorrow. What is perhaps most telling is that neither the new churches nor the mainstream churches offer praise and worship based on the styles of *bhajans* (popular Hindu devotional hymns) or for that matter include traditional Indian instrumentation (the tabla, the harmonium, and so on). While the tradition of the 17th century Tamil Christian poet Vedanayaga Sastriar, who composed many devotional Christian songs in traditional Indian classical Carnatic style, continues to be kept alive by descendants of his family, the Tamil Christian mainstream is yet to embrace this style of worship (Angustine, 2004). When the mainstream churches offer such fare, these are often in the context of rarefied environments—progressive seminaries like the United Theological College in Bengaluru and the Tamil Nadu Theological Seminary in Madurai—and on special, commemorative occasions. This obvious disjuncture and the unwillingness of church traditions to accommodate such forms of worship is an indication that indigenisation has its limits in India. While new church traditions consider anything remotely connected to 'heathen' faiths, including their instrumentation, as properties of the devil, there is no excuse for mainstream churches to not embrace such local traditions. It would seem the case that the conservative 'field' of Christianity in India just does not have the resources or the will to provide the means for an indigenous Christian identity based on new practices and new conditions for the habitus.

However, indigenisation itself can be viewed as a hegemonic device/impulse that denies multiplicity. There is an issue related to a consideration of what is 'authentically indigenous' given that, for the most part, the indigenisation of Christian worship has primarily meant the embrace of hymns sung in the popular Hindu bhakti tradition, the use of symbolic goods such as the 'lamp', hymns set to Carnatic music and, particularly among Catholics, the adaptation of classical Indian dance forms such as the south Indian Bharatanatyam. Even the basis for Hindu–Christian dialogue, for instance, the venerable tradition that can be traced back to Bede Griffiths and Swami Abhishiktananda is a predominantly Sanskritic, Vedic tradition. This then is the Christianity that Hindu nationalists would like Christians to adopt. While there certainly is a case for Indian Christianity to adapt to Indian culture, we are no nearer to an understanding of what this ought to mean in practice. Ideally, the church should reflect locality in all its diversity, although this might be a case of wishful thinking.

One could of course look at this dilemma from a totally apposite perspective. For if, as Indian history textbooks proudly proclaim, India has been a melting place for religions from time immemorial, then it would necessarily be right and proper for it to accept new religions, new traditions, new styles of worship and new ways of apprehending the Ultimate, just as it had in the past. After all Islam, Christianity and Buddhism, despite their flirtations with the dominant culture—the experiments of Akbar in the 15th century and the close correspondence that Syrian Christians forged with Hindus in Kerala—did not radically alter their core principles, despite many centuries of consanguinity with Hindu India. One can argue that what is needed is less of the cerebral, intentional indigenisation of Christianity in India, but a continuation of spaces for traditions that celebrate life in all its multiplicity. Susan Visvanathan's (1993: 238) description of the Peryannal (feast day) at the Kurisu Palli, the Church of St. Thomas in Puthenangadi, Kerala, stands as an evocative reminder of that daily dialogue of life that continues despite the ravages of inter-religious schisms.

The festival, which goes on for three days begins with the *sandhya namaskaram* (evening prayer) with everyone gathering at dusk.... The drummers are of the Izhava caste, and have been given this privilege for generations.... The streets are festooned with palm leaves.... There are no paper streamers; instead rows and rows of light green leaves are strung on coir rope. In the backyard of the church, a *nella villaku* (bronze lamp)... has been filled with oil... Around this, in a semicircle, the drummers stand in white *mundu* (sarongs), bare-chested, their *chendas* (drums) tied obliquely across their shoulders and chest with a sash (ibid.).

References

Augustine, C. 2004. 'In Pursuit of a Divine Calling', *The Hindu Online*, 24 September. Available at http://www.hindu.com/fr/2004/09/24/stories/2004092402750600.htm, accessed on 21 October 2006.

Bourdieu, P. 1992. *The Logic of Practice*. Stanford, CA: Stanford University Press.

—————. 1991. 'Genesis and Structures of the Religious Field', *Comparative Social Research*, 13: 1–43.

—————. 1984. *Distinction: A Social Critique of the Judgement of Taste*. London: Routledge & Kegan Paul.

Copley, A. 1997. *Religions in Conflict: Ideology, Cultural Contact and Conversion in Late Colonial India*. New Delhi: Oxford University Press.

Dianteill, E. 2003. 'Pierre Bourdieu and the Sociology of Religion: A Central and Peripheral Concern, *Theory and Society*, 32(5–6): 529–49.

Dillon, M. 2001. 'Pierre Bourdieu, Religion and Cultural Production', *Cultural Studies↔ Critical Methodologies*, 1(4): 411–29.

Engler, S. 2003. 'Modern Times: Religion, Consecration and the State in Bourdieu', *Cultural Studies*, 17(3–4): 445–67.

Evangelical Council for Financial Accountability. Information on GFA's Income. Available at http://www.ecfa.org/ContentEngine.aspx?PageType=Control&PageName=MemberProfile&MemberID=5294, accessed on 15 October 2006.

Howell, B. 2003. 'Practical Belief and the Localisation of Christianity: Pentecostals and Denominational Christianity in Global/Local Perspective', *Religion*, 33(3): 233–48.

Jenkins, R. 1992. *Pierre Bourdieu*. London & NY: Routledge.

Martin-Barbero, M. 1993. *Communication, Culture and Hegemony: From the Media to Mediations*. London, Newbury, New Delhi: Sage Publications.

Page, D. and W. Crawley. 2001. *Satellites over South Asia: Broadcasting, Culture and the Public Interest*. New Delhi: Sage Publications.

Rajagopal, A. 2001. *Politics After Television: Hindu Nationalism and the Re-Shaping of the Public in India*. Delhi: Cambridge University Press.

Rey, T. 2004. 'Marketing the Goods of Salvation: Bourdieu on Religion', *Religion*, 34(4): 331–43.

Siedman, A. 2004. *Contested Knowledge: Social Theory Today*. Malden, USA; Oxford, UK; Carleton, Australia: Blackwell Publishing.

Stolow, J. 2005. 'Religion and/as Media', *Theory, Culture and Society*, 22(4): 119–45.

Swartz, D. 1996. 'Bridging the Study of Culture and Religion: Pierre Bourdieu's Political Economy of Symbolic Power', *Sociology of Religion*, 57(1): 71–85.

The Mar Thoma Church. Available at http://www.indianchristianity.org/marthoma.html, accessed on 16 October 2006.

Visvanathan, S. 1993. *The Christians of Kerala: History, Belief and Ritual Among the Yakoba*. Madras: Oxford University Press.

Weber, M. 1963. *The Sociology of Religion*. Boston: Beacon Press.

THE CULTURAL/MEDIA PRACTICES OF CHRISTIAN FUNDAMENTALISM

6

THE CHANGING NATURE OF
CHRISTIAN BROADCASTING IN INDIA

As David Lelyveld (1990: 42) has observed, 'broadcasting can stand as one of the last instances of a long history of British efforts to transfer their own institutions—armies and police, bibles and churches, tax collectors and judges...to India.' Although the foundations for broadcasting in India were laid by the British in the mid-1930s, there is little evidence to suggest that it was used by them specifically for the purpose of spreading Christianity in the subcontinent. That was a task that was eagerly pursued through indirect means such as the project of 'Christian Education' in India, via schools and colleges established by English and Scottish missionaries (Viswanathan, 1989) and the support for the reform of Christian traditions in India. There were Christians who were interested in using broadcasting to spread the Word, for example, the Jesuit Michael DeLisle Lyons. As MacQueen (2003) observes:

[his grand uncle] Mike wrote an article in the January–February 1927 Physics Bulletin entitled: *Plan to Utilize Radio to Hasten the Conversion of Asia*. Mike's article had received notice at many levels throughout the Jesuits and the Catholic Church hierarchy. Mike proposed setting up radio stations in three locations in India, two in China, one in Japan and one in the Philippines at a cost not to exceed $ 25,000 per station. His idea was to utilize these stations to broadcast their messages to the masses, and even into the palaces of the maharajahs in the hopes of speedier conversion into the Catholic faith.

While the BBC did, during the inter-war years, broadcast programmes such as Missionary Talks on its national programme, it had far more important objectives, given the need to reinforce the fast shrinking ideal of Empire (Nicholas, 2003). However, this reluctance to explicitly support missionary work was, in hindsight, compensated by that grand, patrician imperial project of employing educational broadcasting to create Indian subjects in line with Macaulay's famous Minute on Education. A description of the use of broadcasting carried in *The Times* (1937) evokes this grand project:

> Three hundred million people live in villages in India. 'Village' in England means...thatched cottages and rustic seclusion; it does not mean 2,000 underfed human beings crowded into a barren circle of window-less mud huts, with little or no contact with the outside world, living as they doubtless lived 2,000 years ago, intent on two things only—avoiding taxes and dragging sufficient harvest from the dusty land. Among such you do not find purchasers of wireless sets.... The influence of wireless as a subtle moulder of thought and opinion need not be stressed.

It was in the immediate post-Independence years that this objective of explicitly employing Christian broadcasting was carried forward by conservative Christian groups, although it is the period coinciding with India's tryst with the global satellite and cable revolution that has seen the greatest expansion of Christian broadcasting in India. While the state continues to control the extent and nature of religious programming on its public broadcasting systems, the liberalisation of the airwaves and the entry of private cable and satellite television in particular has led to the profusion of specifically 'made in India' religious channels along with a host of transnational, religious satellite channels that are mainly Christian in content.

The *World Christian Trends AD 30–AD 2200: Interpreting the Christian Megacensus* (2001)—a project that offers a comprehensive overview of the historical, contemporary and projected growth of evangelical Christianity—claims that there are 4,000 Christian radio and television stations worldwide, 1,050 national and international Christian broadcasting agencies and 120,000 full-time personnel in Christian broadcasting, figures that probably are in need of revision given the enormous resources invested in Christian broadcasting in countries like India (Barrett and Johnson, 2001). K.P. Yohanan's Dallas-based Gospel for Asia (GFA) radio alone broadcasts in 92 Indian languages including many tribal languages. Along with the GFA, there are literally hundreds of Christian radio broadcasts into India inclusive of Radio Veritas Asia, Vatican Radio, Far Eastern Broadcasting Association (FEBA) Radio, Sri Lanka Broadcasting Corporation (SLBC), Adventist World Radio, Bible Voice Broadcast Network, Christian Vision/Voice, KWHR Hawaii, Trans World Radio, WFYR Family Radio, along with numerous others.

These broadcasts into India effectively bypass what is popularly seen as the Indian government's taboo on support for religious programming. While Article 25 in the Constitution of India supports the 'Freedom of Conscience, Practice and Propagation of Religion', the Prasar Bharati (Broadcasting Corporation of India) Act, 1990 does not even mention the word 'religion'. This taboo, however, is open to interpretation given the continued belief in the universality of a single Indian (Hindu) culture and the professed need for broadcasting to support Indian culture. A recent news report 'PHDCCI to Implement Broadcasting Code' carried in the *The Hindu Business Line* illustrates this position. The report is on the PHD Chamber of Commerce and Industry's (PHDCCI) request to the Broadcasting Council to ensure that broadcasting does not support the 'exploitation of religious susceptibilities and offence to the religious views and beliefs of those belonging to a particular religion', although it concludes on the following note, 'Due emphasis should be given to promote Indian culture, religion and beliefs.' In other words, Indian broadcasting policy's unspoken support for majoritarian culture has acted as a conduit for the spread of Hindu high culture. For example, All India Radio's (AIR) support for Carnatic music at the expense of other types of popular or folk music in the early years and, in the late 1980s, Doordarshan's support for Hindu mythologicals played no small role in the re-enchantment of Hinduism and the emergence of Hindu nationalism in India. It is quite extraordinary that Doordarshan's Citizen Charter mentions that Doordarshan 'Undertakes at regular intervals auditions for classical dances' (http://www.ddindia.gov.in/Information/Citizen + Charter). These levels of confusion remain. The Phase II tender for FM radio broadcasting services under Section 3 'disqualifications' point (d) explicitly disallows a company controlled by or associated with a religious body from owning an FM radio station. However, policy documents related to the opening up of the community broadcasting sector indicate that religious bodies will be allowed to operate such stations: ' Religious bodies engaged in socio-economic developmental activities should be allowed to apply provided the station is used to promote development of the community' (*The Hindu Business Line*, 2004).

This confusion, along with the latent aspirations of the Hindu elite seem to be leftovers from an age that did not offer the possibilities for bypassing a singular national and religious identity. It is clear, however, that this inability to frame a single code is by no means exclusive to broadcasting. It is also reflected in the shaky framework of 'secularism' that India adopted as part of its Constitution in 1950. As Chatterjee (1995: 24) has pointed out, the Indian state's ambivalent approach to matters related to religion has been a primary cause for the distrust of the principle of secularism among majority and minority communities. While the state deliberately entangled itself in the overseeing of Hindu institutions and the reform of 'Hindu' practices, it kept away from involvement in the religious affairs of other faith communities. 'If it was accepted that the state could inter- vene in religious institutions or practices in order to protect other social and economic rights, then what was the ground for intervening only in the affairs of one religious community and not of others?' (ibid.).

This loose framework of secularism in India provided the scope for numerous low and high-intensity contestations that periodically shook the very foundations of democracy in India, most recently, during the early years of the ascent of Hindutva as a political force. I argue that this loose framework of secularism, along with the globalisation of religion, has provided a perfect opportunity for a renewal of the Christian project, this time aided by transnational and national Christian broadcasting.

The Beginnings of Christian Broadcasting in India

Bringing Christ to India was among the first Christian radio programmes broadcast to India. It was produced in USA by the Lutheran Layman's League and beamed into India on Radio Ceylon and Radio Goa. This organisation started producing radio programmes in 1955 in Tamil and Malayalam that were broadcast over Radio Ceylon. The Lutheran Layman's League was directly involved in establishing the Christian Arts and Communication Service (CACS) in Madras (now Chennai) in 1967. This organisation was involved in supporting a range of Christian com- munication initiatives—from dance drama to broadcasting—in order to fulfil its objective of 'Every man, woman and child in South India con- fronted effectively with Jesus Christ'. Whereas CACS, which boasted state of the art studios in the 1970s, was a prominent Christian communica- tion centre, it was embroiled in labour and financial scandals that led to its demise and its replacement by the Christian Media Centre (CMC) that was established in 1984. The Lutherans continue to be involved in radio broadcasting, through the Lutheran Church Hour Ministries, out of the CMC. They are involved in recording material in Tamil, Malayalam, Telugu, Hindi and English, and in broadcasting these through FEBA out of Seychelles and the SLBC. The Lutheran Church Hour Ministries Area Director for India and Sri Lanka Herb Hoefer describes his task as follows:

> What is important, then, is that we begin developing methods of outreach and of church life that reflect our vision for the vast majority of India. The dalit church has plenty to do to reach out to their fellow dalits with the Gospel, and they will feel comfortable in joining the church. What has been needed is to partner with Indian Christians and foreign missionaries on culturally-rooted forms of Indian Christianity. We have needed approaches to evangelism and nurture that move beyond church walls.

The CMC is also involved in the production of tracts, audio-visuals and Christian magazines.

> Since more than 70% of our radio listeners are non-christians, the programmes contain songs, short dialogues and dramas, Biblical stories and other interesting material which would attract the attention of the people. An average of 40,000 letters are received every year and more than 70% of them are from Hindus who ask for literature about Jesus Christ (CMC, India).

If this is the broadcasting agenda of what admittedly is a conservative faction of the mainstream Lutheran Church, which incidentally does have a reputation for supporting the 'Social Gospel', it would seem that the Indian government's explicit policy to restrict religious broadcasting on AIR and Doordarshan to key festivals such as Christmas for the Christians is wholly justified. The line between using broadcasting for explicit evangelism as against plain moral uplift has been a thin one indeed. AIR's explicit support for Hindu high culture led to the migration of many thousands of listeners to Radio Ceylon in the 1960s, a broadcast institution that in hindsight was appreciative of the audience's potential for popular Indian culture—Hindi, Tamil and Malayalam film music.

The stance taken by AIR and Doordarshan stands in sharp contrast to that taken by the SBLC that provides equal space for all religions along with free broadcasting time. However, despite the fact that SBLC has been a faithful supporter of numerous Christian broadcasting initiatives into India, it would seem that that policy has less to do with an enlightened policy as with the potential for regular streams of income support. In fact, the obvious lack of regulatory control over religious broadcasting by SLBC is highlighted in the following observations:

> Many Christian broadcasters in Sri Lanka use the free broadcasting time to conduct studio services, with songs, prayers and sermons. Others use the time with the motive of converting people of other faiths to Christianity. Only very few use the media with the realization that they were broadcasting to the 18 million people in Sri Lanka and to some parts of South India (Jebanesan, 1998: 359).

While the Government of India continues to regulate radio broadcasting in India, it is powerless to regulate exogenously-transmitted broadcasts. Today, there are literally hundreds of Christian organisations in India broadcasting Christian radio programmes over the SLBC, the FEBA, Trans World Radio, the Manila-based Radio Veritas, and other transnational radio stations. The Far Eastern Broadcasting Corporation (FEBC) was set up in 1945 by two US ex-servicemen John Broger and Bob Bowman to specifically proclaim the Gospel in China. They established a short-lived station in Shanghai that had to move out after Mao's clampdown on missionary activity; FEBC then established its ministry in Manila in 1948 and resumed broadcasting to China in 1949. The FEBC set up FEBA to broadcast to Asia, Africa and the Middle East. Today, the FEBC is involved in a global radio ministry in 158 languages, with a total per day broadcast output of 627 hours transmitted via 147 stations. It has established stations in what it considers to be high population, strategic cities—Manila, Moscow, Seoul and Jakarta—and plans to set up stations in Pnomh Penh, Ulaan Bataar and Bangkok. As its statement of faith attests:

> FEBC's mission is to develop radio programming and deliver it to listeners in Asia so that they move toward Jesus Christ and into his kingdom, they know him as their Lord and Kind, follow his teaching, and live in obedience to Him as his servants and as a local body of believers (FEBC).

For instance, Brother Dhinakaran's Jesus Calls Ministries started broadcasting over FEBA in 1972 and the evangelism department of the

Chennai-based Hindustan Bible Institute (HBI) started broadcasting over SLBC in 1975.

Voice of Love: The HBI, Chennai

The HBI, a Christian organisation committed to mission, evangelism and Christian education, started radio broadcast in 1969 over the SLBC and FEBA. Starting with a weekly programme in Telugu, by 1994 they were broadcasting nine weekly programmes in seven languages including Lambadi (see Table 6.1).

Table 6.1 Voice of Love (Prema Vani) Schedule

Language	Title	Meter	Day	Time
Telugu	Prema Vani	25.41 SLBC	Saturday	2.45 to 3.00 PM
Hindi	Prema Vani	25.41 SLBC	Tuesday	7.15 to 7.30 AM
Gujarathi	Prema Vani	19 FEBA	Friday	7.00 to 7.15 PM
Marathi	Prema Vani	19 FEBA	Sunday	6.15 to 6.30 PM

Their radio ministry is located within the evangelism and follow-up department. They have a full fledged studio involved in producing an average of 250 programmes per year. This positioning of radio within their evangelism and follow-up department is significant given that the major objective is to reach the unreached in order to make disciples of them. As Table 6.2 illustrates, radio is a key tool in evangelism efforts. The director of this department, a committed Christian, was candid in her views related to her role in the expansion of the Great Commission. Radio was a personal medium and it could be used with great effect. It was particularly suited to 'fishing' for Christ and for connecting to 'seekers' of the Word. She pointed out that in remote areas where there were no churches or prayer groups, radio had become the focus for worship. They get on an average 40–50 letters per day, mainly from people living in Andhra Pradesh, although they occasionally get letters from north India from 'idol-worshippers'. The receipt of a letter is the beginning of a process aimed at bringing that person to Christ. A personal letter is sent to them and the committed are enrolled in a correspondence course and given a certificate at the end of it. These disciples are expected to convert other people—family and friends. Their radio ministry has been used to establish 27 worship centres in Andhra Pradesh. In the early days, key playback singers from the film industry inclusive of P. Susheela and S.P. Balasubramaniam were involved in recording songs at the HBI. The involvement of Hindu singers was contested but accepted as one strategy to reach people of other faiths who were familiar with film-based music. Today, the HBI's radio ministry is one among numerous ministries from Chennai. In 1999, HBI started a television ministry although it had to be discontinued given the costs of production involved. These television programmes were produced by Good News TV and aired over Raj TV. The department has a Gospel songs archive. A favoured radio format is the use of the traditional Burrakatha as a means of communicating the story of Christ. The costs of production and telecasting are raised from USA.

Table 6.2 HBI Statistics on the Impact of Radio and
Other Types of Evangelism

Language	Total Response	Hindu	Christians	Muslims	Saved
Telugu	34,476	25,857	8,274	345	1,929
Tamil	2,964	2,223	445	296	266
Hindi	1,242	932	298	12	99
Marathi	528	396	127	5	68
Gujarati	264	198	63	3	34
Kannada	120	90	28	2	11
Total	39,594	29,696	9,236	662	2,407

The presentation of inflated figures related to conversions, reaching the unreached, and audiences are a stock characteristic of many conservative Christian organisations operating in India. These figures, freely available on their websites and publicity material, must be treated with caution. In the context of contestations over religious identity, such figures are used as ammunition by both sides—by the proponents of Hindutva who cite figures to prove their case and by conservative Christian groups who are impatient to sow the seeds of the Great Commission.

Christian Television

The only time given for faith communities on India's national television station, Doordarshan, has been during specific religious festivals—in the case of Christians this was during Christmas. That programme was in itself bounded by various do's and don'ts. Prominent members of the Christian church, like the Catholic Archbishop, were invited to give a message. This was followed by a few Gospel songs. Then, as is the case now, the mainstream churches were not enamoured by the project of broadcasting. In fact, the Chennai-based evangelist Dhinakaran (Jesus Calls) was one of the first Christian leaders in India who appreciated the potential and possibilities of Christian television. His presence on national television during Christmas was made possible by the support of Christian broadcasters within Doordarshan. This small group of producers, cameramen, script writers and technical staff played an important role in training Christian leaders like Dhinakaran in television. To most conservative Christians in India, television was synonymous with India's film industry and it therefore had a reputation for the same moral laxity. This distrust of popular culture continues to be a barrier to the entry of the mainstream church in television. However, evangelical churches, taking their cue from USA, have been at the forefront of religious broadcasting, in radio first and now on television.

Without a doubt, the advent of satellite and cable television in the early 1990s began the renewal of religious broadcasting in India, in particular Christian broadcasting. David Page and William Crawley's (2001) classic *Satellites over South Asia: Broadcasting, Culture and the Public Interest* remains the best introduction to what continues to be an evolving phenomenon, although their emphasis was its impact on popular culture and public interest, and had little to do with specific television genres.

There are, broadly speaking, five avenues for Christian broadcasting in India (see Table 6.3):

1. The occasional space on the national broadcaster Doordarshan for Christian programmes.
2. Transnational satellite channels including GOD TV, Christian Broadcasting Network (CBN), Trinity Broadcasting Network (TBN), MiracleNet and Daystar TV that are available via cable.
3. Christian programming on a variety of secular cable channels available throughout the country on Raj TV, Zee TV, Vijay TV, and others channels.
4. Stand-alone indigenous Christian cable channels such as Blessing TV, Angel TV, Shalom TV, Jeevan TV, and others.
5. Web-based telecasting, for instance, *Jesus Calls* on Num.TV. Webcasting remains an evolving reality in India with limited audiences.

Table 6.3 Christian Television in India

Indian Christian Channels	Transnational Christian Broadcasters	Secular Channels that Feature Christian Programming
Angel TV	GOD Channel/TV	Teja TV
Blessing TV	Daystar	Maa TV
Jesus TV	Miracle TV	Z Marathi
Shalom TV	CBN (Audiences unknown)	Vijay TV
Jeevan TV	TBN (Audience figures unknown)	Podhigai
New Hope TV	TCT World	Tamilan TV
Grace TV	EWTN	AsiaNet
Manna Channel		Raj TV
Tamil TV		Alpha One
		Win TV
		ETV-2
		Namma Cable
		Star Vijay
		Raj Digital Plus
		ETC TV
		Star News
		SAB TV
		Sony YV
		Jaya TV
		DD1
		SS Music
		Sakthi TV
		Zee Kannada
		Namma Cable TV
		Alpha Bengali
		Nayuma Cable TV

There are also a host of Christian channels that are yet to be launched, such as Yathra TV, Good News TV, Power TV and Sathyavani TV.

The liberalisation of the airwaves, in particular the satellite and cable revolution played a major role in the expansion of Christian broadcasting in India. However, the Indian government's evolving attitude towards the regulation of cable and satellite televisions, inclusive of

Direct-to-Home (DTH) television and uplinking, has meant that satellite broadcasters have had little choice but to comply with national regulations (Singh, 2001). At the very same time, they have had to also work with local cable operators, particularly the monopoly providers, Hathaway, Sumangali, IndusInd Media and RPG Netcom, and other multiservice operators (MSOs). These cable operators are on top of the cable hierarchy and they distribute these satellite signals, in turn, to many thousands of smaller access cable operators (ACOs) who operate at local levels. In Chennai, Tamil Nadu, the monopoly MSO is Sumangali. All existing and prospective cable channels have to negotiate carrier fees with the MSO as well as the signal-uplinking fees that are paid to the Videsh Sanchar Nigam Ltd, the publicly-listed company that is part-owned by the Tata Group of companies and which is the principle provider of public international telecommunications in India. Thus, GOD TV, for instance, pays Rs 700,000 per month as uplinking fees alone. The Government of India's 'Guidelines for Uplinking from India' (December 2005) stipulates that all television satellite broadcasting services uplinked from other countries to viewers in India must be through a registered company in India, which has the exclusive marketing/distribution rights of the channel in India. This requirement has already been met by a number of Christian companies. GOD TV's Asia and Middle East distribution office, for instance, operates out of West Anna Nagar, a suburb in Chennai, while MiracleNet operates from Teynampet, Chennai.

GOD TV's syndicated programmes are also available on some of the channels featured on DishTV (owned by the Zee TV group), one of two operational DTH networks in India, and there are plans to launch the channel on Doordarshan's DTH service. Three more DTH services, Sun Direct TV, Space TV (Tata Sky) and Reliance, were launched in 2006–07 and a number of new entrants including Bharti Airtel Ltd and Reliance Entertainment are expected to offer services in 2008. The fact that the owners of Sun TV, who also own the monopoly MSO Sumangali, are priming themselves for a slice of the DTH action is disquieting, given the potential for abuse of what already is a monopoly situation. The intense rivalry between the incumbent chief minister, of the All India Anna Dravida Munnetra Kazhagam (AIADMK), and the patriarchs of the rival Dravida Munnetra Kazhagam (DMK), inclusive of the Maran family that owns the Sun network, also involves turf wars over control of cable and satellite televisions in Chennai and the rest of Tamil Nadu. This has resulted in the government of Tamil Nadu's promulgation of the Tamil Nadu Acquisition, Transfer and Taking Over of the Administration of

Cable Television Network (Including Multiple Service Optical Transport System) Bill, 2006 that is ostensibly aimed at all MSOs, although it is widely seen as an attempt to curb the power of the Sun network prior to the advent of local elections. These local wars often destabilise power relations and offer new opportunities for a re-arrangement of these relations. However, it does affect cable and satellite operators who will have no choice but to negotiate access with a state government. To make matters more complicated for cable and satellite operators, the ability of transnational Christian channels to operate DTH services in India is restricted for the following reason:

> Under India's present regulatory regime, any company wishing to provide a subscription based television service to customers in India must uplink from Indian territory, and further must use either an Indian satellite, *or a satellite system approved by India's Department of Space ('DOS')*. The approval process for using non Indian satellites involves DOS, the Wireless Planning Committee ('WPC') and the Information Broadcasting Ministry ('MIB'). Preference is given to Insat satellites, operated by ISRO (Loft Communications, 2006: 3–4, emphasis original).

New television in India, like its old self, is at one level about structures, power, influence, profits, the lowest common denominator, closures and silences. If mediation essentially relates to culture, structures relate to political economy, and, in that sense, it is extraordinarily important that both aspects of television in India are adequately theorised. Today, both cable and satellite television in India are part of empires in the making. If Doordarshan was the empire then, today, in spite of its continuing national audience reach, it is the Sun group and Zee TV. The Sun group, controlled by the powerful, DMK-based Maran family is an example of a media empire that has, on one level, catered to the regional interests of its mainly Tamil-speaking audience and, on the other, turned itself into a manufacturer of mainstream Tamil opinion, tinged with a predictable bias against the DMK's traditional rivals, the incumbent AIADMK government. Kalanidhi Maran, founder and managing director of the Sun group, is, indirectly and otherwise, helped by his connections to brother Dayanidhi Maran—member of parliament (MP) and former minister of Communications and Information Technology in the Union Cabinet. The Sun group presently owns four Tamil channels, two Malayalam channels, along with Gemini TV, Teja, Aditya, the Telugu channel Visaka and three Kannada channels—Udaya, Udaya News and Ushe. The group also owns the monopoly MSO in Chennai, Sumangali Cable Vision, three FM radio stations in Tamil and a 5,000 strong film library; it puchases 90 per cent of all Tamil films released in any given year and has substantial print interests including Kungumum Publications, the Tamil daily *Dinakaran* and the evening paper *Tamizh Murasu*. Govardan (2006: 3) describes the reach and power of the Sun TV empire:

> Launched on April 14, 1994, SUN TV controls almost 75% of the audience share in Tamil Nadu which accounts for a television advertising spend of Rs 350–400 crores. While Sun accounts for the top 100 slots among all channels in Tamil, it also accounts for over 30 slots out of the top 100 among all channels in India.

The monopoly power of its MSO Sumangali Cable Vision, which controls cable transmission, is used for rent-seeking purposes. In the context of intense rivalries between the DMK and AIADMK, the current moves by the government of Tamil Nadu to take over MSOs in the state is an attempt to break the power of the Maran empire and to use it to the incumbent government's electoral advantage (*The Hindu*, 2006).

In the course of my research in Chennai, it became clear that among English-speaking middle classes, GOD TV and Daystar TV were the two transnational Christian channels that had audiences in Chennai. However, these audiences remain small. GOD TV maintains that it is available in 216 major and minor cities in India—from Aizawl, Mizoram, in northeast India to Trivandrum, Kerala, which is located close to the tip of south India—having a total audience reach of 21 million. However, the Nielsen-owned audience rating company TAM Media Research India's February 2006 viewing figures for GOD TV reveal that it has a total reach of 3.9 million homes (4.6 per cent) out of an all-India market of 85 million cabled homes. GOD TV's audience figures of 150,000 viewers (3.53 per cent) for Chennai, out of an estimated 4.2 million cabled homes are not exactly flattering. Daystar TV's Chennai figures of 270,000 viewers are only marginally better. A third transnational channel Miracle TV, whose offices are situated in Chennai, fared even worse on TAM ratings. While they have no presence in Chennai, their all-India reach for the said period was 600,000 (0.7 per cent). A number of Christians involved in this industry were of the opinion that for the purpose of 'reaching the unreached', a standalone Christian channel's chances of recruiting audiences was severely limited because: (*a*) there are literally hundreds of channels vying for audiences; (b) in a primarily 'Hindu' country, an explicit channel devoted to furthering the project of global Christianity has limitations; and (c) English-only programmes have a restricted reach. It is for this reason that many independent Christian producers such as Good News TV and Jesus Calls produce Indian-language based programmes for premier local channels. While Jesus Calls programmes are available on GOD TV in English, five days a week, the bulk of their programmes are on a host of local channels in local languages—Sahara One TV, Star Vijay, Win TV, Raj TV, Surya TV, Asianet TV, Namma Cable, Alpha Bengali, ETV-2, and others. No wonder, Raj TV's 2006 viewership figures for Chennai are 3.6 million (85.3 per cent).

GOD TV in Chennai

GOD TV was established by a UK-based South African couple, Rory and Wendy Alec, in 1995. In 2004, they moved their broadcast office to Israel and today it is a 24-hour, global channel available throughout the world, as their tag line states, 'broadcasting from the Holy Land to the ends of the earth'. With seven separate feeds, carried on 12 satellites, plus three non-contracted satellites, the GOD Channel is currently broadcast around the world 24-hours a day, reaching 275 million people in more than 200 nations and territories. The founders exult in Armageddon-speak (W. Alec, 2005: 20):

> The darkness across the heavenlies of Britain and Europe had been pierced and the first bastion taken—the years 1995–2005 were to be a death blow to the devil's hold on the media, opening up the airways for the Gospel and sending the forces of darkness reeling.

Endorsed by Pat Robertson, Joyce Meyer, Crefilo Dollar, Dhinakaran, Benny Hinn, and other 'healing' and 'prosperity' evangelists, the GOD Channel is a slick Christian channel that features 21 ministries of recognised tele-evangelists including Kenneth and Gloria Copeland, Jesse Duplantis, Billy Graham and Benny Hinn; praise and worship programmes that include Christian rock and Gospel (on the channel Dream On TV) and the Australia-based *Hillsong TV*; magazine programmes; news and current affairs programmes; counselling programmes; celebrity interviews; review of the arts; and programmes for children, including the *Bed Bug*

Bible Gang and the *Story Keepers*. All this in order to extend their vision: 'With a servant's heart we will equip His Body to reach the lost through media. This ministry exists to enable every television household to hear the gospel of Jesus Christ so that they may believe in Him, call upon His name, and be saved.' There are a handful of Indian evangelists on the GOD Channel including Sam Chelladurai (Apostolic Fellowship Tabernacle, Chennai), Paul Thangiah (Full Gospel Assembly of God, Bengaluru) and Dhinakaran (Jesus Calls, Chennai), although the majority are US-based. Apart from these Indian evangelists, the only Indian presence is the regular evening solicitation for funds that is presented by Indians. As the Regional Director for Asia, Middle East and Australasia explains, 'as more channels crop up and crowd the limited bandwidth in India, cable operators have hiked prices and are unwilling to negotiate.... Our needs are great...thank you for your assurance of partnering us on a monthly basis' (quoted in *The GOD TV Guide*, 2005).

In its upfront approach to creating a financial base, GOD TV created what it calls 'Angels' and 'Business Angels'—corporations and individuals who are willing to back up this enterprise. In GOD TV speak:

These are modern day media missionaries with a passion to reclaim the airwaves, for Christ. The call has not changed though the methods may be different. By giving towards Christian Television, you put yourself right at the forefront of today's media mission field! Will you answer this call by supporting the evangelistic outreaches of the GOD Channel world-wide?(http://us.god.tv/Group/Group.aspx?id= 1000028035).

The request to the Angels is for a one-off gift of $ 750 or for $ 63 per month and to the Business Angels a one-off $ 5,000 or a precise $ 417 per month. One could also become a plain partner[1] and help GOD TV produce the programmes that have been blessed. 'Your gift of Rs 500/HK$300 or more per month enables us to create anointed, supernatural programming and to distribute this in Asia across the globe, into every nation'[2] (http:// uk.god.tv/Group/Group.aspx?id=1000013647). The GOD TV shop offers a number of religious products for sale—books, music, videos, copies of the Bible, software and products from the featured ministries. It even features a currency converter that is meant to ease transactions from around the world. Sadhu Sundar Selvaraj, the founder of the Chennai-based Angel TV, supported by Jesus Ministries, is even more upfront with his solicitation of funds (Angel TV).

The Lord has amazingly helped us trim our budget bringing some amazing contacts.

We need $ 1 million more.

I am sure there is someone reading this, Oh, saints of God, who could write a check for this amount. Your check is not just for another ordinary work of God. No!, it is for an end-time work of God. Your generous giving will enable God to speak to this whole world calling the people to fear God; informing the people that Babylon has fallen; and to warn the world of the mark of the beast. For your giving unto God you shall be blessed as: He who receives a prophet in the name of a prophet shall receive a prophet's reward (Matthew 10:41) (*Healing Love Newsletter*).

Some of the salient features of this channel and others like Daystar TV and the CBN are as follows:

1. These channels, backed up by Christian organisations, agencies and conventions, represent a type of muscular Christianity based on a promise of health and wealth for all those who are Christian. At the same time, it offers an uncertain future for those who either do not belong to the Christian faith or are opposed to it. This agenda is, for instance, foreground in Pat Robertson's *The 700 Club* as well as through Alec and Wendy's current affairs round-up. Frameworks for understanding global politics, the war in Iraq, global terrorism and democracy are frequently drawn, and the boundaries clearly delineated. For a Christian audience in Chennai, not previously exposed to Biblical justifications for right-wing politics, such programmes, sandwiched between Joyce Meyer's homily on 'familial strife' and Sam Chelladurai's 'Prosperity Theology', offer justifications for a range of issues from Christian Zionism to easy understandings of the causes and nature of evil in contemporary societies. The truth of these stories have been revealed to God's anointed and, therefore, have been blessed by God. In a situation characterised by the mainstream church's distance from interrogations of global and national politics, the primary Christian version of politics on public display is that advocated by tele-evangelists. The average Christian in India has a very conservative understanding of politics in the Middle East—and these channels, CBN and

GOD TV in particular, routinely privilege and sanction the right-wing politics of the Israeli government and reinforce stereotypes of Muslims and people of other faiths. The fact that GOD TV's operations are Jerusalem-based and thus 'anointed' is frequently alluded to. Pat Robertson's open critique of Hindus and Hinduism on his syndicated programmes has contributed to a generalised Christian baiting by any number of Hindu nationalists. The de-centring and fragmentation of Christianity in India today provides a perfect opportunity for the project of re-centring Christianity along conservative lines by the global Christian right supported by its foot-soldiers in India.

2. These channels tap into and are sustained by the core message of economic globalisation that the pursuit of wealth and profit-making are premier virtues, over and above the pursuit of communitarian, inclusive futures. Chennai, today, with its call centres, salaried professionals and the rising spending power of its youth, has the space to celebrate the religions of globalisation. Sam Chelladurai's ministry, the Assemblies of God (AOG) churches, Brother Dhinakaran's ministry, that of PowerHouse and numerous others ministries celebrate the Health and Wealth Gospel. The MTV style Gospel rock music on GOD TV with its bland and repetitive lyrics is also on offer at the PowerHouse and the Vineyard, where young information technology (IT) professionals and stock brokers rock to an anodyne version of Christianity. The lyrics may be modern, but, in essence, are a throwback to the triumphalist hymns of yore that celebrated the primacy of the Christian God.

3. These channels have reinforced evangelism as a family business proposition. Like the Dhinakarans and most other evangelists in Chennai, inclusive of Dr Manickam Prakash (the founder of South India Soul Winner's Association [SISWA]), who involve their entire family in the business, Christian television networks like GOD TV and Daystar TV as well as Christian production houses such as Good News TV are also all family concerns. There are Rory and Wendy on GOD TV, Sarah and Michael Hughes on Miracle TV, Marcus and Joni Lamb of Daystar TV, the Crouches of TBN and, of course, assorted tele-evangelists such as the Copelands, the Dollars and the Robertsons, among very many other family-based missions. Mission initiatives that are not answerable to a board of directors have had a history of problems to do with accountability, best exemplified by the history of many infamous tele-evangelists

including the contemporary Benny Hinn. Problems related to accountability are legion in the new churches. While the Church of South India (CSI) and the Catholic Church in India have had their share of financial scandals, there are checks and balances in place that act as a deterrent to a cleric who has his eye on the parish finances. Such a system of accountability is just not there in many of these new church circles. As a travel agent in Chennai, who books tickets for a stable of evangelists confided, 'There is a lot of fraud and first class travel'.

4. While Pat Robertson, Paul Crouch, and others, are not involved directly in influencing politics in India, they do act as lobbies in the US. Their Indian counterparts are very involved in local politics. While Ezra Sarguman who organised the Every Tribe, Every Tongue convention is associated with the opposition party DMK (hence the presence of DMK and Congress heavyweights at the convention), Dr Prakash of the SISWA Trust, which acts as the distribution arm of TBN, is a strong supporter of the AIADMK and was the chairperson of the State Minorities Commission. Political connections are necessary for the expansion of neo-Pentecostal churches in India and also necessary for the permission to stage religious crusades and conventions by evangelists such as Benny Hinn who is opposed by sections in India (Rediff.com, 2005).

5. These organisations, in turn, act as a conduit for vast amounts of funds, from USA in particular, which, in the political context of India, is necessary for the organisation of mega-events such as a Benny Hinn crusade. Money is the common denominator in politics in India and its exchange results in permissions to stage a Benny Hinn convention, even in cities like Mumbai, where the right-wing Hindu political organisation Shiv Sena plays a dominant role ensuring the security of public spectacles. In fact, the Shiv Sena supremo Bal Thackeray, who otherwise is a scourge of the minorities in India, attended the crusade.

6. While most Christian channels avoid any direct criticism of Hinduism, unlike websites where the most disrespectful descriptions of other religions are on display, there is an implicit message that Hinduism is a lesser religion, mired in superstition and destined to be marginalised by the Christian message. There is an endless circulation of persecution stories of Christian missionaries in India, noticeably on K.P. Yohanan's GFA radio broadcasts and Pat Robertson's CBN. Benny Hinn's video of the crusade held in Bengaluru in

November 2005 begins with God's miraculous delivery of the crusade from anti-Christians who tried to get the government of India to ban the evangelist from entering the country. While there has been persecution of Christians in India, one rarely comes across information on what these missionaries were doing in the heartland of Hindu India in the first place. Missionaries who deem it a virtue to topple deities in a Hindu temple can be expected to be persecuted. Persecution and the battle of these evangelists against Satan add to the allure and the mythos of these modern day crusaders riding into battle against heathen hordes. Praying for a secular government in India is also rather widespread on these channels. At the Every Tongue, Every Tribe conference, which was held in Chennai in January 2006, God was exhorted to change governments in numerous Bharatiya Janata Party (BJP) governed states. There is a strong belief in the power of prayer to change lives and situations. The fact that India had become Congress-led was directly attributed to the 'hand of God' and the power of prayer.

7. It is also interesting to note that the US State Department monitors the state of religious freedom in countries like India. Its 2005 report notes that:

> A number of cable television networks dedicated to religious programming operate in the country and propagate their beliefs. In January, the Government permitted the US-based evangelical leader Benny Hinn to hold a rally in Bangalore attended by thousands. The Government stipulated that the event must not disturb the peace and that no one should perform 'divine healing'. One online news service reported that Hinn carried out 'divine healing', but the Government took no action. A few Hindu groups protested the event, resulting in minor damage to property and vehicles in the area. Another U.S.-based Christian evangelist, Pat Robertson, spoke at a prayer meeting in Delhi on May 13 attended by dignitaries such as Congress leader Subodh Kant Sahay.

Such reports reinforce a variety of stories sourced from evangelical groups working in India.

8. Many of these channels are involved in supporting local development efforts. The 2004 Asian tsunami was the basis for a variety of

fund-raising initiatives. And it continues to be a money spinner for these ministries. Joyce Meyer, for instance, has adopted fishing villages in Villipuram district, Tamil Nadu, affected by the tsunami, and those involved in PowerHouse and other ministries have devoted resources to the rehabilitation and 'conversion' of the tsunami-affected (see David, 2005). Orphanages are a key source of income generation. In fact, many Christian ministries in Chennai are registered orphanages. CBN India has a humanitarian arm called Operation Blessing that is involved in 'developmental' work, although, given the uncompromising neo-Christian agenda of Pat Robertson, it is more than likely that such activities are a front for the Christianising of India. In CBN's case, their Indian operations are yet to be transmitted through a dedicated CBN channel. Given the new laws related to uplinking and DTH, particularly as they relate to channels that have a news/current affairs component, it would seem that a programme such as *The 700 Club* will be unable to get transmitted over a dedicated channel, unless it gets a licence to do so. TBN has the 'Smile of a Child' campaign that involves distributing toys to children in India and elsewhere.

9. There is an endless recycling of programmes given that the better-known tele-evangelists are shown on most channels. Joyce Meyer, for example, is available on a GOD TV along with numerous lip-synced versions in a variety of regional language channels. Flicking channels on 17 December, 6.30 AM in Bengaluru, I observed that Joyce Meyer was on Maa TV (Telugu), Z (Marathi), and Vijay TV (Tamil). The popular US-based televangelist Joyce Meyer's programmes are 'dubbed' into a variety of Indian languages and are available not only on dedicated global Christian channels such as GOD TV and Daystar, but also on secular channels such as Raj TV and Zee, and indigenous Christian channels such as Angel TV and Blessing TV. Benny Hinn's conventions are a staple fair given that he does a couple of conventions a year that are in turn sold as DVDs and as syndi-cated programming on numerous channels. Given the average daily of a maximum of eight hours of 'original' programming, the rest of the time is filled with repeats, old favourites and freebies. This culture gives ample opportunities for mutual reinforcement of min-istries, with Pat Robertson endorsing Alec and Wendy, and Brother Dhinakaran endorsing Benny Hinn. Unlike mainstream Christian denominations that often speak from a variety of scripts, these tele-evangelists, by and large, speak from a single script.

---

10. The advent of Christian broadcasting in India, transnational as well as local channels, offers the space for identification with a Christian *umma* far beyond the boundaries of the territorialised nation-state. This thriving space for religion on contemporary Indian television does, in hindsight, reveal the short-sightedness of the post-Independence broadcasting policy that kept minority religions in India at a distance. Despite India's many trysts with socialism at the federal and state levels, religion has been a defining factor in the lives of its people. This, more than any other reality, suggests that the active recognition of, space for and presence of religion in broadcasting were simply a matter of time. That time is now.

11. Despite the information and broadcasting ministry's involvement in licensing and regulation, in a highly competitive market, the key determinant is finance. The ability to pay the licence and carrier fees are primary requisites. It is interesting to note that many of the Christian channels first appeared on the scene during the rule of the BJP and they continue to flourish during the reign of the Congress government. Local channels give space and breaks to any number of budding tele-evangelists. Any pastor who has the requisite finances can get a broadcast-quality sermon produced by local Christian production houses, such as Good News TV, which have the necessary contracts with Raj TV and Tamilan TV to broadcast the programme. While this may be seen as an opportunity for a 'citizen clergy' to 'dis-intermediate local hierarchies' (Martelli and Cappello, 2005: 253), it also provides the space for fundamentalist preachers to advocate Christian separatism.

12. While production standards at Good News TV and Jesus Calls are above average, many of the programmes produced for local channels are made in-house and on a shoestring budget. Such productions are now part of a thriving cottage industry, run by independent evangelists and small Christian production houses. Given the decreasing costs of camera and recording equipment, many productions are done at makeshift home studios. Given this bottom line, there are a number of local channels such as Blessing TV, Angel TV and Jesus TV whose programmes are of a consistently poor quality, based on poor production standards. Given the sub-standard production quality of many products, it is not surprising that many of these channels have poor viewing figures. The fact remains that there are very few Christians who have a thorough knowledge of production skills. Paul Dhinakaran, the son of Brother Dhinakaran of Jesus Calls, Prabhu

from Daystar and a few of those at Good News TV are among a handful of Christian media professionals in Chennai who have the requisite background in Christian television production.

13. Given the demand for Christian television and the need for professional programming, established musicians and production staff from the Tamil film industry, including playback singers, sound technicians and camera persons, do get involved in the creation of Christian programmes. An example of a Bollywood singer turned 'Born Again' Christian is the playback singer Vijay Benedict who is a regular on Christian television and is a crowd puller at evangelical conventions such as those organised by Benny Hinn and the Every Tribe, Every Tongue conference. Benedict and other singers have played an important role in adapting Bollywood and MTV music styles and in the creation of cross-over styles of Indian Christian popular music. Given the extraordinary influence of film music in India, such personalities are crowd pullers who have demonstrated a market for contemporary Indian Christian popular music. In Benedict's case, the songs are often couched in an 'India for Christ' thematic, and the sessions include flag-waving patriotism. The spectacle often includes the appropriation of the tri-coloured Indian flag by Christians, a symbolic wresting of the flag from the Hindu nationalists and its anointing for a Christian nation. The theme 'Saving the Nation for Christ' is featured at numerous revivals and crusades and includes the ritual reclamation of the Indian tri-colour for Christ and, by extension, the Indian nation for Christ.

14. There are many opportunities for cross-media synergies today, given numerous media outfits located in India and outside that are involved in the production of Christian video, films, music and books. These are sold in Christian bookshops in Chennai—for example, at the Hebron bookstore and the Evangelical Literature Society bookshops. The *Left Behind* series of books, for example, were available at the Hebron bookstore. There are a number of online stories that specialise in the sale of Christian products, although I suspect that sales figures are not high. These productions are also featured on cable channels. Featured products are made by a number of organisations including CD Films, Cephas Cine/Tele Communications (Pvt) Ltd, Galilean International Films and TV Services of India, Good Shepard Videos and mission outreach ministries. The mission outreach ministries include Harvest Ministries, India Campus Crusade for Christ, Jesus Ministries and Jesus Redeem Ministries, among many others.

The Campus Crusade film *Jesus* that is reputedly one of the most watched films in the world has been translated into numerous Indian languages and is often featured on cable television.

15. The reception of these programmes varies. The interviews that I had carried out do suggest that the closer the involvement of audiences with Pentecostal churches, the greater the possibility of identification with some of these programmes and what they stood for. However, I came across a variety of attitudes in some of the interviews. There were those who were thoroughly sceptical, that is, those who watched these programmes specifically because they seemed ludicrous—roaring like lions, the routine of being 'slain by the Spirit', the rather histrionic environment of healing that is regular stock in trade of Sarah Hughes on Miracle TV. Then there were those who were selective in what they watched—there were those who liked Joyce Meyer for the practical advice that she gave, while there were others who were of the opinion that she was lesser than others because she did not have the power to heal. Also, there were those, especially among older Christians, who watched these channels because they were a moral alternative to the immoral fare on offer on most cable and satellite channels. To those who are of the opinion that the Sunday service offers limited opportunity for an interpretation of the Scriptures, the 24-hour availability of Biblical interpretation is a blessing. It is interesting that a couple of people mentioned the case of infirm family members who were not in a position to get to a Sunday service and hence were grateful for the tele-visual experience of worship.

16. Irrespective of their personal likes and dislikes, and the personal foibles of tele-evangelists, the majority of those I interviewed believed that since they were doing God's work, they were in an exceptional, 'called', 'anointed' ministry that was above reproach.

17. The fact remains that there is already more than adequate availability and choice of Christian programming on offer in Chennai and it would seem that, in this light, maintaining a regular audience is going to be a difficult prospect in the years to come. So while these texts are negotiated in different ways, the lack of countervailing Christian or, for that matter, inter-faith discourses on television poses a problem, given that the only shows on offer are from conservative perspectives. Even the Catholic-run channel from Kerala Shalom TV is in the 'charismatic' tradition and its fare includes relay programmes from the US Catholic broadcaster, Mother

Angelica's Eternal Word Television Network (EWTN). The audience for these programmes belong to mainstream, Pentecostal and indigenous churches.

18. A number of those interviewed believed that the best way to reach out to non-Christians was through channels based on 'family values'. For instance, the production house Good News TV had plans to launch such a channel in 2007, though this has not, to date, been achieved. This intent is based on the belief that in the context of a profusion of programmes that are now available to all age groups over a variety of media, there is a need for channels that are family-friendly and that reinforce traditional family values. There seems to be a clear division between those like the TBN whose programmes are entirely foreign in origin and those like CBN and GOD TV who have opted for Indian language-based programmes featuring Indian evangelists.

19. These programmes are integrally and synergistically linked to the agenda of the Pentecostal and neo-Pentecostal churches. I had attended an evening worship at the AOG mega church in Saidapet, Chennai, where there was a special segment devoted to the project 'My Hope Campaign', supported by the Billy and Franklin Graham Ministries (*Mathew and Sons Manual*, 2005). Representatives from this organisation presented the project. The project consisted of a series of the 30-minute long television programme *Mathew and Son* that was to be shown on channels in Chennai during the Christmas season. The objective of this exercise was to recruit as many people as possible to organise an event around these programmes. The congregation was asked to invite non-Christians in particular to watch these programmes:

> If you have a television, invite unbelievers to your home. You could call them for tea or dinner and while they are at your home, you could ask them to watch the *My Hope* television broadcast on various channels on primetime, in different Indian languages (*Mathew and Sons Manual*, 2005).

Each of them was asked to each invite 10 people to watch the programme, present a testimony and follow up with those who expressed an interest in 'Christ'. The representatives were on a whirlwind tour of Chennai churches that day. A 'how to' video was shown that took the congregation one step at a time through this process.

Similarly, Pastor Thangiah of the AOG Church in Bengaluru, provides the logistics and support for Benny Hinn's campaigns; he frequently endorses such campaigns and is often on GOD TV. It is in this sense that one can conclude, that despite the complexity that characterises the new church environment in Chennai, it remains a receiving city of global imports of conservative Christianity. As Rory Alec of GOD TV concluded after a recent visit to the Chennai regional headquarters of GOD TV:

> It is an extraordinary hour for India and more now than ever, we have a power and authority and responsibility, indeed I could add the word 'urgent', that Christians and particularly our viewer's work with the God channel to get it to every household as quick as we can.

Conclusion

While it is necessary for us to understand the distinctive expressions of 'primal piety', there is also a need for us to understand the reasons for the making of a common ground between these expressions of Christianity and the mainstream expressions of Christianity. Why is it the case that the message of conservative Christianity has greater inter-denominational acceptability today? One reason could be the need for a united Christian identity, a united front in the face of imagined and real persecution.

While the mainstream churches are in no immediate danger of being 'left behind', there is a shift in the relationship between politics and the church, with a definite movement towards political alignments with the Pentecostal churches for the vote banks that they represent. In exchange for such support, their leaders have begun to play a prominent role in the representation of Indian Christians and Indian Christianity.

Given the relative absence of mainstream churches on Christian television in Chennai, the only channels present are aligned in one way or the other with the more conservative Christian churches, national and transnational. A large part of the content available on these channels can be considered conservative, narrow and inimical to the project of interfaith understandings and futures. The attempt to take over public space in Chennai by the new churches is a phenomenon that needs to be studied on its own right. Their presence in malls, the Christian paraphernalia market, rallies and conventions, posters and banners, broadcasting and the new spaces of globalising Chennai is very distinct from the spaces occupied by the mainstream church.

One of the strengths of the new churches is their keen understanding of the traumas faced by people in a globalising city and, in particular, the presence and manifestations of 'evil' (*pèy*), be it expressed through ill-health, bad luck or unemployment. The healing of broken people and ritualised triumphs of good over evil is a staple fare on Christian television and in rallies and conventions. Healing is also directed at idol worshippers who are possessed by evil spirits.

While this study has not explored audience mediations of meaning to any great extent, I think that there is a case for such explorations in the context of increasing multi-denominational attendance. However, I think that from the perspective of political economy, the key need is for extensive studies on the export of conservative Christianity, its local manifestations and the roles played by global Christian broadcasting in creating a worldwide Christian *umma*.

Notes

1. A plain partner refers to an ordinary partner who sponsors a programme or covers a part of the programme costs.
2. Lewis-Smith's (2002) critique of GOD TV reveals that the new generation of television evangelists continue to operate on the lines of the old evangelists such as Jerry Falwell, the Bakers, and others:

> Founded by Rory and Wendy Alec, both channels (God Channel & God Revival) broadcast hour upon hour of hate-filled, rabble-rousing, homophobic bigotry, much of it featuring (and funded by) right-wing American evangelists. Before the ITC lost its few remaining teeth, it roundly condemned The God Channel for its denigration of other beliefs, and fined it £ 20,000 for its denunciations of homosexuality as an abomination. But nowadays, it is allowed to broadcast without official reproach, while its sister channel, God Revival, preaches explicitly about God's prophetic agenda for Israel, and its plans to reposition the European Church to enable it to fulfil its significant end-time role in Europe and the Middle East. A few minutes spent listening to some of these US preachers (whose influence on the Republican Party is as profound as their theology is shallow) gives a sobering insight into the mindset that is currently determining American foreign policy.

References

Alec, Rory. 'Partner Connect India', *GOD TV South Asia Magazine*. Available at http://uk.god.tv/Publisher/Article.aspx?ID=1000026177, accessed on 24 March 2008.

Alec, Wendy. 2005. 'Great Britain Land of End Time Destiny'. Available at http://www.ourchurch. com/view/?pageID=228994, accessed on 16 May 2006. Also available in *The GOD TV Guide* (August–September 2005).

Angel TV. 'A Prophet of God'. Available at: http://www.jesusministries.org/healinglove3.html, accessed on 17 May 2006.

Barrett, D. and T. Johnson. 2001. *World Christian Trends AD 30–AD 2200: Interpreting the Christian Megacensus*. Pasadena: William Carey Library.

Chatterjee, P. 1995. 'Religious Minorities and the Secular State: Reflections on an Indian Impasse', *Public Culture*, 8(Fall): 11–39.

Christian Media Centre (CMC), India. Available at http://www.christianmedia.in/cmci/component/option,com_frontpage/Itemid, accessed on 15 May 2006.

David, S. 2005. *Report on Relief and Rehabilitation Activities carried out by District Administration and NGOs in Villupuram District*, August. Available at http://www.tntrc.org/downloads/RnRActivities_VilllupuramDt.doc, accessed on 18 May 2006.

Far Eastern Broadcasting Company (FEBC). Available at http://www.febc.org/about/core_values.html, accessed on 15 May 2006.

Govardan, D. 2006. 'Sun TV Mega IPO in Feb', *The Economic Times*, 10 January.

Government of India. 2005. Ministry of Information and Broadcasting Invitation for Pre-Qualification Bids for Expansion of FM Radio Broadcasting Services through Private Agencies (Phase II), Tender No. 212/14/2005—FM, Guidelines for Uplinking From India: File No. 1501/2/2002-TV(1)(Pt.), 2 December.

Healing Love Newsletter. Available at http://www.jesusministries.org/HEALING%20LOVE%202007%20English_WEB.pdf, accessed on 17 May 2006.

Hoefer, H. 'Faith beyond the Church'. Available at http://faculty.cu-portland.edu/herbhoefer/articles/FaithBeyondChurch.htm, accessed on 12 January 2006. http://www.ddindia.gov.in/Information/Citizen+Charter, accessed on 17 May 2006.

Jebanesan, A.W. 1998. ' Religious Broadcasting in a Multi-Faith situation: A Model for Sri Lanka', *Asian Journal of Theology*, 12(2): 358–69.

Lelyveld, D. 1990. 'Transmitters and Culture: The Colonial Roots of Indian Broadcasting', *South Asian Research*, 10(1): 41–52.

Lewis-Smith, V. 2002. 'God in the Box'. Available at http://www.newhumanist.org.uk/printarticle.php?id=224_0_12_0_C, accessed on 11 April 2006.

Loft Communications. 2006. *India Satellite Services and Regulatory Overview*. Prepared by the Cable and Satellite Broadcasting Association of India & GVF, 14 February. Available at http://www.casbaa.com/upload/India_Satellite_Services_Reg_Overview.pdf, accessed on 17 May 2006.

MacQueen, J. 2003. 'WWJ, a Jesuit and the Bomb'. Available at http://www.oldradio.com/archives/stations/wwj1.htm, accessed on 17 May 2006.

Martelli, S. and G. Cappello. 2005. 'Religion in the Television-mediated Public Sphere: Transformations and Paradoxes, *International Review of Sociology*, 15(2): 243–57.

Mathew and Sons Manual. 2005. Secunderabad: My Hope India.

Nicholas, S. 2003. 'Brushing Up Your Empire: Dominion and Colonial Propaganda on the BBC's Home Services, 1939-45', *Journal of Imperial and Colonial History*, 31(2): 207–30.

Page, D. and W. Crawley 2001. *Satellites over South Asia: Broadcasting, Culture and the Public Interest*. New Delhi: Sage Publications.

Prasar Bharati Act. 1990. Available at: http://www.ddindia.gov.in/Information/Acts+And+Guidelines, accessed on 18 May 2006.

Rediff.com. 2005. 'CM attends Benny Hinn's Meeting', 21 January. Available at http://in.rediff.com/news/2005/jan/21bang2.htm, accessed on 18 May 2006.

Singh, S. 2001. 'Cable vs. DTH', 3 January. Available at http://www.indiainfoline.com/nevi/cabl.html, accessed on 17 May 2006.

The GOD TV Guide. 2005. August–September.

The Hindu. 2006. 'State to Take Over Cable Network', 22 January. Available at http://www.thehindu.com/2006/01/22/stories/2006012209440100.htm, accessed on 16 May 2006.

The Hindu Business Line. 2004. 'TRAI Widens Eligibility Norms for Community Radio', *The Hindu Business Line*, 9 December. Available at http://www.blonnet.com/2004/12/10/stories/2004121003060300.htm, accessed on 17 May 2006.

———. 'PHDCCI to Implement Broadcasting Code'. Available at http://www.thehindubusinessline.com/2006/01/30/stories/2006013001820500.htm, accessed on 17 May.

The Times. 1937. 'Broadcasting in India: II-The Villager, If He Can Be Made to Laugh', *The Times*, 28 July.

US State Report. 'India—International Religious Freedom Report 2005'. Released by the Bureau of Democracy, Human Rights, and Labor. Available at http://www.state.gov/g/drl/rls/irf/2005/51618.htm, accessed on 18 May 2006.

Viswanathan, G. 1989. *Masks of Conquest: Literary Study and British Rule in India.* London: Faber and Faber.

Websites

http://www.ddindia.gov.in/Information/Citizen+Charter, accessed on 17 May 2006.

http://us.god.tv/Group/Group.aspx?id=1000028035, accessed 16 April 2006.

http://uk.god.tv/Group/Group.aspx?id=1000013647, accessed 24 March 2008.

7

CYBER-CONTESTATIONS

Christian and Hindu Fundamentalisms on the Web*

The reports of an upsurge in inter-religious conflicts in India—that peaked in December 1998 in the state of Gujarat—and of sporadic violence against religious minorities and missionaries in the Indian states of Orissa, Bihar, Karnataka and Kerala during the first half of 1999, once again brought into sharp relief some of the tensions besetting democracy in India (see Dasgupta, 1999; Engineer, 1999a, 1999b; Shah, 1999; Vyas, 1998a, 1998b).

While Hindus, Muslims and Sikhs have suffered the consequences of planned and random inter-religious, 'communal' violence for years, it is only recently that the Christian minority has become a target of such violence. According to some newspaper reports, particularly the vernacular press in the Hindi belt, the issue of 'conversion' was the primary reason for the violence. Other newspapers, especially sections of the moderate English press, were of the opinion that the violence was premeditated and orchestrated by the Hindu nationalist network, collectively known as the Sangh Parivar, with the tacit encouragement of one of its members, the Bharatiya Janata Party (BJP) that was a key partner in the coalitional National Democratic Alliance (NDA) that was in power between 1999–2004. Members of the Sangh Parivar include the Rashtriya Swayamsevak Sangh (RSS), the Vishwa Hindu Parishad (VHP), the Shiv Sena and the

---

* An earlier version of this paper 'Web-wars and Inter-faith Futures in India' appeared in *Media Development*, 1999, Vol. 4, pp. 39–46.

Bajrang Dal, among others. The gradual but deliberate ascendance of the RSS network—from relative obscurity in the 1920s and its marginalisation after an ex-member Nathuram Godse was found guilty of assassinating Mahatma Gandhi in 1948, to becoming the power behind the throne recently—is, according to some observers (see Basu et al., 1993; Vanaik, 1994), very similar to the rise of National Socialism in Germany in the 1930s. While there are differences, the continuities between these two types of nationalisms run deep, and RSS stalwarts like D. Savarkar, M.S. Golwalkar and K B. Hedgewar, and, in particular, the Shiv Sena leader Bal Thackeray have publicly admired Hitler and the ideology of Nazism.

The politics of religious nationalism in India has been fuelled by a variety of fears and interests—imagined, manufactured, resurrected, real— that have coalesced to form part of the national imaginary of a large section of people belonging to the majority community, that is, the Hindus. It has also correspondingly affected the worldview of minorities, in particular Muslims and Christians in India today. The Hindutva version of this story is made up of many strands supplied by certain groups of people, for example:

1. Disaffected Hindu priests and *mahant*s (Hindu religious officiants), mainly Brahmins, whose ritual and sacral powers have been marginalised in the context of secular India.

2. Hindu nationalists and their intellectual supporters who are: (*a*) keen to restore the physical and spiritual unity as well as the Hindu ethos of India, through righting the wrongs inflicted by countless Mughal rulers on India in the past, (*b*) united in their efforts to counter the perceived hegemony of socialists and secularists in present-day India in education and opinion making, (*c*) committed to resisting the expansionist zeal of adherents belonging to the Semitic religions in India and their allies abroad, (*d*) united in deploying the symbol of a militant and virile Lord Rama in their efforts to mobilise Hindus against the enemies of the nation within, particularly non-Hindu minorities, and without, for example, mobilising against the geo-political aspirations of China and Pakistan in particular, the threat from the immediate West, the hard-line Taliban in Afghanistan and, in the East, the Sino-Myanmarese axis, and (*e*) wedded to the project of institutionalising and centralising an all-India version of Hinduism.

3. Hindu traders who have had to compete with their Muslim counterparts in the retail of brassware, handicrafts, textiles, and other goods.

4. The diasporic Hindu community from USA, Europe and elsewhere, with their many fears and grievances against exclusionary policies in their adopted country, and with articulated transnational longings and pan-Hindu desires via movements such as the World Council of Hindus.

5. High caste Hindus who are against the practice of positive discrimination in favour of the 'Scheduled Castes' in government, educational institutions and employment in general, and the perceived pandering to minority interests, and who blame Christian missions and non-governmental organisations (NGOs) for the empowerment of the lower castes and tribals.

6. The many Hindus living in north India, who had been the victims of the Partition and have not reconciled themselves to memories of the loss of family, friends and property during that violent episode in Indian history.

The strands represented by these groups of people, along with others, form a complex web of longings, fears, aspirations and counter-aspirations that has been over-simplified for popular consumption by nationalist Hindu politicians. Popular sound bites such as that India is a Hindu nation, that Indian identity is co-terminus with Hindu identity and that minorities must recognise the primacy of the Hindu state or face being alienated are some of the popular slogans that were given an extensive all-India legitimacy, particularly so in the Hindi Hindu heartland. In a context characterised by widespread economic and political insecurities, the exploitation of such primary fears through the naming of enemies, the emphasis on identity and the framing of exclusive Hindutva futures were guaranteed to secure certainty and hope for some sections of society at the expense of others.

The key beneficiaries of this project have undoubtedly been the BJP and its Hindutva allies who wielded power until May 2004. While they are currently in the Opposition today and continue to hold power in a few state governments, fratricidal politics seems to have weakened their once invincible aura. Nevertheless, the BJP continues to be an influential political force. This party had assiduously built a platform of ideas and action based on the failure of previous governments to privilege the interests and ethos of the majority nation, created alliances with other nationalist groups and organisations, manipulated popular religious sentiments based on an exclusive version of identity-speak and exploited religious symbolism to great effect through spectacles like the *Rath Yatra*,[1] televised mythologies and a variety of information/communication channels.

The use of symbols—expressed through a blurring of distinctions between everyday language and ritual language based on a common body of myth— was a powerful means by which a pan-Indian national identity was formed. The BJP gave new meaning to the term patriotism in India—valorisations of the Indian flag, the re-signification of the patriotic song 'Vande Mataram' in the national imaginary, and determined efforts to communicate a re-surgent, militarily strong India via nuclear tests in 1998 and a near war with Pakistan in 1999 were all aspects of the BJP's brand of Hindu nation-alism. In fact, the BJP is, by a long shot, the first thoroughly modern political party in India. Its image was assiduously created and promoted by the media. It employed a wide array of spin doctors, academics and technocrats, and enjoyed extensive electronic coverage.

Against the Grain: Inter-faith Relationships in India

The BJP's selective manufacture of reality inevitably failed to account for the many lived correspondences between the majority and minority communities, even in the heart of the Hindi belt, where Muslims and Hindus continue to live side by side in the most unlikely places. Nandy et al. (1997: 2–3), in a study of the Ram Janmabhumi Movement that led to the destruction of the Babri Masjid in Ayodhya nearly a decade ago, allude to lived realities in this city. They have observed that:

> Even today, despite the bitterness of the last eight years, the flowers offered for worship in the Ayodhya temples are almost all grown by Muslims. The Muslims still weave the garlands used in the temple and produce everything necessary for dressing the icons preparatory to worship.

They also add that:

> Until some years ago, the making of the crowns of the gods was the near monopoly of Muslim master craftsmen such as Rahmat Sonar and Nannu Sonar; the thrones for the gods are even today made by the likes of Balam Mistri, a highly respected Muslim carpenter.

Writing of the development of Hindustani music in north India, Manuel (1996: 122) notes its emergence in creative collaborations between Hindu and Muslim artists and patrons in colonial India. Even in south India, where the classical tradition of Carnatic music is dominated by the Brahmins, the discerning ear can still hear the 'Other' as one of 'Us'—like the late Sheik Moula Sahib's nageswaram-based rendition of the song, *Mahaganapathim* (Venkatasubramaniam, 1998).[2] A great many Christians too have contributed to an inclusive vision of India— from the Gandhian S.K. George, to the theologian and ex-Governor of Nagaland M.M. Thomas, to numerous individuals who are involved in exploring inter-faith futures, along with those involved in a variety of service institutions—notably education and the medical field. But by far the most significant witness to inter-faith life in India is what one may term the 'daily dialogue of life', which characterises living in many parts of India. These countless instances of intricate inter-community weavings, both formal and informal, are rarely, if ever, highlighted by the media. On the contrary, local media in the Hindi belt, in particular Hindi newspapers such as *Aaj* and *Dainik Jagran*, have on innumerable occasions (see Gupta and Sharma, 1990; Nandy et al., 1997) been accused of misinforming the public, misinterpreting events, adding a communal twist to reporting and generally supporting the cause of Hindutva.

Counter Fundamentalism

It is tempting to place the entire blame for the breakdown of inter-faith relationships on the Sangh Parivar, but that would be far from the truth. Their role in the many acts of violence against minorities, the complicity of BJP-run state governments and the tacit support given by the previous government to the initiators of violence cannot be denied. The prevarication shown by the BJP government and its unwillingness to condemn violence on numerous occasions, especially that carried out by members belonging to the Sangh Parivar, have been cited as examples of their inherent anti-minoritism (see Vyas, 1998a).

However, religious conflict in India has also been fuelled by groups from within minority religions. For instance, in their zeal to convert all non-Christians, in particular tribals and Hindus, certain Christian groups have antagonised many by their insensitivity, narrow-mindedness and disrespect for local belief systems and cultures. It can be argued that fundamentalist evangelical Christian groups, by their actions, have often contributed to the undermining of the development, relief, dialogue and social justice work carried out by mainstream Christian groups in India, such as the Catholics, mainline Protestants and the Orthodox, over many years.

137

While critics of Christian mission in India, notably Arun Shourie, have critiqued the Catholic mission in development as a means to a larger end, that is, conversion, there are many who would agree with Shourie's intent but disagree with the larger objectives of his analysis. While one may or may not agree with Shourie's objective, the all-India growth of Christian revivalism; the proliferation of literally hundreds of independent Pentecostal and neo-Pentecostal churches, church movements and para-church organisations throughout the country; the presence of Indian evangelists on transnational Christian broadcasting platforms that are openly fundamentalist as well on indigenous Christian broadcasting—radio and television that are primarily involved in taking the message of the Gospel to the unreached in order to convert them; the charismatic movement within the mainstream churches; and the Christian presence in the cities of India—in the malls, on banners, Bible schools and public spectacles such as a Benny Hinn extravaganza, have contributed to a rise in inter-faith tensions. Mainstream churches, concerned over the exodus of their flock to evangelical churches, have increasingly begun to accept multi-church attendance and seem unwilling to antagonise members who entertain narrow views on inter-faith matters.

There is also a widely held feeling among the majority community that minorities have benefited from their position as a convenient vote bank for political parties, the Congress in particular, in exchange for the protection of their religious rights and institutions from state interference (see Chatterjee, 1995). This stands in marked contrast to the situation of the majority community, whose religious institutions, such as temples, fall under the purview of state-run boards and who, therefore, have had to contend with occasional state interference. Such an example of a perceived bias in favour of minorities has become a matter of controversy. Minorities tend to invoke the Constitution as the basis for their right to practise religious freedom, but as contemporary events in Indonesia have borne out, the text of the *Pancasila*[3] is not necessarily upheld by its implementation in real life—an implementation rendered difficult by the micro-politics of innumerable identity negotiations which involve the state, religious organisations, personalities and ordinary people. In other words, the negotiations of daily life are, despite constitutional guarantees, necessarily fragile—a fact that is made even more complex in pluralist societies. It would seem that unless the concept of a multi-faith society becomes institutionalised as a practical norm, plural societies like India are bound to remain in thrall to dominant 'interpretive' communities and to their visions and versions of religious futures.

The South Asia correspondent for *Le Figaro,* Francois Gautier, in an article that appeared in *Himal* (1999) has criticised the warped, non-objective, pro-Christian bias shown by many reporters in their coverage of communal conflicts, in contrast to their reticence to highlight the plight of Hindu victims of such violence, as an example of their captivity to colonial frames of mind—a view that must have been welcomed by the then beleaguered government. The article also refers to 'the aggressive methods of the Pentecostal and Seventh Day Adventist missionaries' and 'their muscular ways of converting' as contributing factors in the rise of inter-faith tension in parts of north India, a view also echoed by William Dalrymple (1999) in *The Guardian Weekend.* Dalrymple refers to the new-wave Pentecostalist movements spreading through India, their connections with a variety of fundamentalist Christian missions located in the Bible belt in USA and to their overtly anti-Hindu websites. While Gautier's inference that journalists in India are captive to colonial frames of mind is misplaced, given that journalists in India are recognised for their independent reporting standards—a tradition that stands vindicated in contrast with the coverage by the Western press of the war in the Balkans—his comments on insensitive Christian evangelism in India remains a fair critique.

Such robustly critical and provocative pieces of journalism stand in marked contrast to communiqués from the ecumenical Christian community in India, which has in general opted for a defensive, rather than self-critical, position on the tensions in Gujarat and elsewhere (see Akkara, 1999a, 1999b; Doogue, 1999; *People's Reporter,* 1999). While it is necessary to condemn violence against any given community, it is, as far as I can see, equally important that the ecumenical community responds by opening up spaces for reconciliation and dialogue, on the one hand, while simultaneously using such opportunities, on the other hand, to rein in the zealots in the Christian fold. I would argue that the articulation of a merely generalist response will, given the present level of ignorance on religious issues, precipitate a general backlash against all Christians in India, who are by no means united in their understandings of mission, Christian identity and presence in a pluralist context. Lest this be interpreted as a strategy to 'save one's own skin', I expect the response from the church in India to be articulated from within a conscious conviction of Christian rights and responsibilities, leading to what one might term a covenantal approach to reconciliation.

There are, of course, obvious benefits to be gained by a movement for religious rights and responsibilities in a country like India. In addition,

such responses would prepare mainstream churches to deal with potential challenges to inter-faith relationships in India such as that posed by
global religious satellite broadcasting, which is presently controlled primarily by fundamentalist evangelical Christian interests. The Rupert
Murdoch owned News Corporation's channel International Family
Entertainment (IFE), which until very recently was part of the US tele-
evangelist Pat Robertson's Christian Broadcasting Network (CBN), can,
without too many technical difficulties, be offered for general availability
in South Asia through Direct-to-Home (DTH) satellite broadcasts. In
the event that it does become available, will it further erode inter-faith
relationships in India? Will the ecumenical community in India be in a
position to take a stand on such issues or will it back off from confronting
the indigenous Christian right whose allies in USA have, for instance,
used broadcasting as a key weapon in their strategy for evangelisation?
While fear is a legitimate human response to the prospect of an uncertain
future, the cultivation of a nationwide fear psychosis restricts self-
criticism and reinforces escapist withdrawal, which, in turn, precludes
possibilities for a meaningful search for long-term solutions.

The following section will address issues related to the new media and
the politics of fundamentalism and revivalism in India. It will, in particular, deal with the use of the new media by Christian groups in India, who,
for all practical purposes, are an extension of their counterparts in USA,
and contrast this use of the Internet with its use by the Hindu right. It
will point to the ways in which this 'transcendent' agenda is pursued
through an aggressive fronting of websites maintained by rival supporters
who are generally located outside the subcontinent. It will conclude with
a section on appropriate information policies for a pluralist society.

Web Wars

Instant communication has its uses and abuses. In this chapter, I argue
that, in the cyber era, the website has become an extended space for inter-
faith net wars fought by, among others, the religious right for the minds,
allegiances and purses of people. The Internet largely remains an unregu-
lated domain in terms of content, used by all manner of people and communities in their pursuit of interactivity, identity and association. While
the Indian government's Computer Emergency Response Team has on
occasionally censored blogs deemed to have the potential to incite communal hatred, for instance, in the immediate aftermath of the Mumbai

train blasts that occurred in mid-2006, such moves are rare given its potential to backfire against the government's support for religious freedom and the freedom of expression. Mitra and Cohen (1999: 199) refer to what they term the unique characteristics of the web texts: 'its inherent intertextuality, its lack of centre, its volume, its multimedianess, its international scope, its impermanence, and the resulting altered sense of authorship'. It would however seem the case that its uniqueness lies not so much in its technological features per se, but in the many ways in which these features are used by people to appropriate and interact with web texts for particular ends. It is in this sense that I agree with Christiane Brosius (2004: 139), namely, that the Internet offers:

> access for its users to the shared production of affect on a transnational basis, the feeling of participation and empowerment in the making and dissemination of shared myths, identities and histories, as well as fears and desires between various locally-based groups and individuals by means of an imagined networked community.

Religious websites communicate global, transnational identities that signify particular, exclusive intent. Some of these sites afford opportunities to understand the 'other' and to network. But since the Internet traffic is not determined by its content and is not policed except through self-regulation, it also provides limitless space for all manner of sites, including those fronted by organisations that have no desire to understand the 'other', and who are in fact committed to the negation of 'others'—be they Muslims, Christians, Jews, the UN,[4] people of colour or sexual minorities (Whine, 1997). The promise of limitless space accompanied by a widely subscribed to freedom of access ethic has led to sites on the World Wide Web playing an active role in national and transnational virtual inter-religious information wars, which often complement inter-religious strife in real time, often resulting in serious human consequences. While naming and shaming the medical fraternity working at abortion clinics, and encouraging anti-abortionists to physically harm those involved in aiding and abetting abortion has led to violence, even death, in the context of US-based web and real wars between the pro- and anti-life lobbies, the blacklisting of people on religious sites have yet to result in such vendettas. That however is not for a lack of religious websites blacklisting people. The website hinduunity.org, for instance, under an image dripping blood, names a variety of people for committing crimes against the Hindu nation—inclusive of Pervez Musharraf, Sonia Gandhi,

Romila Thapar and M.F. Husain. It gives people the option to right the wrongs inflicted on Hindus with the words:

> This page exposes the evil forces that are against the hindu people. Each of these persons and or organization have been found guilty of leading efforts against our movement through their actions or otherwise. Their crimes are crimes against the hindu people. Know your enemies! Know who will be responsible for the downfall of Bharat... and prepare yourselves for the duty towards your religion and nation (http://www.hinduunity.org/hitlist.html).

Information wars fought between rival newsgroups on the Internet were the precursors of present day web wars (Tepper, 1997). Web wars merely extend this phenomenon by reinforcing positions, although from within a protective space that is less vulnerable to 'flaming' and 'cross-postings'. Granted that net access is denied to the majority of people in India, such wars can, even if only tangentially, heighten insecurities among diasporic Indian communities and provide ammunition to ultra-nationalist politicians, leading to tensions between faiths and to the breakdown of the remains of an already fragile consensus. Evelyn Kallen (1998), in a paper entitled 'Hate on the Web: A Question of Rights/A Question of Power', describes three ways in which the 'other' is transmogrified into a figure of hate:

1. **Invalidation myth** (prejudice): definition of target group as inferior and/or dangerous
2. **Invalidation ideology**: development of theory of vilification and provision of supporting arguments and 'evidence' to 'justify' denial of fundamental human rights
3. **Platform for action**: incitement to hatred and harm (discriminatory action); denial of human rights.

www.Mission.India

Even a cursory monitoring of religion-based websites, in this case with the Yahoo search engine, yielded 153 sites on the subject of mission (http://div.yahoo.com/society_and_culture/Religion_and_Spirituality/Faiths_and_Missions). This list included all manner of mainly Christian missions from the mainstream Protestant, Catholic and Evangelical churches. However, sites belonging to evangelical organisations predominate. Most of these organisations originate from USA, subscribe to the Lausanne Covenant on World Evangelisation and are involved in mission work in different parts of the world, including India. India is located in what they refer to as the '10/40 Window', that is, 'the unevangelised and unreached belt between 10 degrees north and 40 degrees north of the equator, from West Africa to East Asia' (http://www.ad2000.org/uterpeop.htm). The year 2000 is obviously significant for many of these groups, and organisations such as AD2000 and their Joshua Project 2000 have targeted 1,700 communities globally for church-planting efforts, including 200 in north India (see Box 7.1). The north Indian Hindi-belt is also the primary location for contemporary forms of Hindu nationalist resurgence.

One of the striking features of these websites is the language and imagery used. Like Joshua, who sent spies to survey the land the Israelites were to inhabit, God is helping to 'spy out the land' that we (meaning Christians) 'might go in and claim both it and its inhabitants for Him'(http://www.ad2000). The Sam P. Chelladurai Outreach Mission web page describes India as 'a land of opportunity', 'a free country' that allows 'the right to preach and propagate the Gospel', a country where one 'can preach,

---

Box 7.1 The Joshua Project: Purpose and Mission

Joshua   *Project*

Our   *Purpose*   ...

to spread a passion for the supremacy of God among all unreached peoples.

Our   *Mission*   ...

to highlight the people groups of the world that have the least Christian presence in their midst and to encourage pioneer church-planting movements among every ethnic people group.

Our   *Rationale*   ...

'This gospel of the Kingdom shall be preached in the whole world as a testimony to all the nations and then the end will come'

(Matthew 24:14).

Source: http://www.joshuaproject.net/

---

make disciples, baptize and add people to the church' (http://www.
samindia.org/html/greetings.htm). Dr Roger Houtsma's World Outreach
Ministries website refers to his work in Vyara and Songadh, cities in north-
western Gujarat, the state which incidentally experienced a number of
religious conflicts in late 1998—'India is experiencing the greatest harvest
in its history. Now is the time that we must reap' (http://www.wo.org/
crusade.asp?sub = VY). The Accelerating International Mission Strategies
(AIMS) (http://www.aims.org/index.html) home page refers to the Caleb
Declaration (http://www.calebproject.org/cdecl/htm) and to people sign-
ing it becoming 'part of a movement of Christians who are zealous for
God's glory and for seeing His Kingdom advanced and His name pro-
claimed among all nations!' Their priority 'Gateway Cities' include Jaipur
in Rajasthan, Patna in Bihar and Varanasi in Uttar Pradesh. Believers are
asked to pray for the sublime—'that the millions of pilgrims visiting the
Ganges River...find the living water given by Jesus'—and the ludicrous:
'Worship of rats produces conditions that foster pneumonic plague. Pray
that the idolatry underlying this health hazard would be bound.' And
then, the most zealous prayer of all 'Pray that the strife between Muslims
and Hindus would cause disillusionment, leading them to the true Prince
of Peace' (http://www.aims.org/jaipur/html).

What is perhaps most regrettable in many of these websites is the disrespect with which they describe Hindus, their Gods, Goddesses and practices. In the AD2000 series sign #4 'Why North India', Varanasi, the seat
of Hindu faith, is described in the following manner:

> Varanasi in the state of Uttar Pradesh is Hinduism's holiest city, with
> thousands of temples cantering on the worship of Shiva, an idol whose
> symbol is a phallus. Many consider this city the very seat of Satan.
> Hindus believe that bathing in the Ganges River at Varanasi washes
> away all sins (http://www.ad2000.org/uters 4.htm).

In the same vein it adds that: 'A number of Christian workers took up the
burden of prayer for this city and in prayer walks boldly declared before
the idols, "you are not a living god"' (ibid.). The same fervour is exhibited
in the Gospel for Asia web page (http://www.gfa.org/SEND/index.htm)
that informs the world that 6 million tracts were distributed to Hindu
pilgrims at the Kumbh Mela, an important Hindu festival. These are
examples of, what may be described as, zealotry run riot.

The contents of these websites reflect the typical narrative structure
of fundamentalist churches in USA—their belief in global 'evangelism,

biblical inerrancy, pre-millennialism and separatism' (Ammerman, 1998). A striking feature is the call to activist foot-soldiers who have a responsibility to not merely wait for the Kingdom, but to usher it in—exemplified by the subtle and not so subtle work carried out by evangelical teams in India. These websites are also totally in character with the well-funded communication strategies employed by the religious right in USA that employ a variety of rhetorical devices to communicate a fusion of interests between the this-wordly and the eschatological. What is evident is a strategic plan for global evangelism that may not in the end amount to much, but the separatist intent of which can be interpreted as a call to arms. It is clear that the rhetoric of Christian mission websites employ the three stages identified by Kallen (1998): invalidation myths, invalidation ideologies and a platform for action.

These US-based missions fund a network of national and local organisations in India, which are involved in mission work.[5] These include the India Missions Association, the Evangelical Fellowship of India, the North India Harvest Network, the Evangelical Church of India and New Life Assemblies of God among literally hundreds of other institutions. Communication is critical to the work of these missions and a variety of means are employed—innumerable print ministries such as those undertaken by the Gospel Missions of India; radio ministries through Trans-World Radio, Good News Broadcasting Society, the Far East Broadcasting Association (FEBA) and Gospel for Asia Radio Ministries; Bible translation ministries such as the Indian Institute of Cross Cultural Communication, India Bible Translators, New Life Computers and the Friends Missionary Prayer Band; and a variety of seminaries and Bible training schools, which in turn churn out hundreds of evangelists and pastors. South Indian Christians, primarily from the states of Kerala and Tamil Nadu, form the bulk of recruits for these missionary organisations, the foot-soldiers for the Cross in north India. Given the money, resource power and media-savvy character of North American evangelical groups, their presence on the web is only to be expected. They have historically been adept at exploiting the technologies of mass communications for their own ends. The conviction that every new advance in communications technology is a gift from God and should be exploited for the cause of the Kingdom is also a view that resonates in mainstream Christian circles in India, even though, perhaps fortunately, their involvement has been minimal.

Evangelism and conversion are of course integral to the Christian faith but their meanings vary widely, from the absolutist positions taken by fundamentalist Christians to the risky openness of conversion subscribed to by some in the ecumenical movement—the possibility of mutual conversion in a context of dialogue (http://www.christianaggression.org/action_blacklist.php; http://www.christianaggression.org/features_nlft.php). The World Council of Churches (WCC) Commission on World Mission and Evangelism (1982) in its statement 'Mission and Evangelism—Ecumenical Convictions' (1997: 383) clearly states that 'Life with people of other faiths and ideologies is an encounter of commitments. Witness cannot be a one-way process, but of necessity is two-way: in it Christians become aware of some of the deepest convictions of their neighbours.' The ex-general secretary of the WCC, Emilio Castro, writing on evangelism in the *Dictionary of the Ecumenical Movement* (1991: 399) remarks that:

> The guidelines for our (Christian) relations with other faiths remind us that it is not just a question of co-existence or pro-existence of the different religious groups. It is also an attitude of dialogue...an attitude of respect for the neighbour...Consequently, our testimony to our faith should take place in a context not only of respect but of acceptance of the other.

These are examples of the multiplicity of positions in organised Christianity on issues such as evangelism and conversion—a diversity that is scarcely acknowledged by the media. The lived exploration of the Hindu–Christian meeting point by Swami Abhishiktananda (1969), Murray Rogers, Bede Griffiths (1983) and Jules Monchanin (see Rodhe, 1993) are further illustrations of convictions in mission that are undoubtedly an anathema to most evangelicals. However, the most powerful expressions of dialogue are communicated by the daily clatter of life experienced by various communities in India who live cheek by jowl in different locales and contexts. Presumably such unconscious, daily celebrations of difference and solidarity are grist to the fundamentalist mill.

While there certainly has been a mushrooming of a number of fundamentalist Christian and jihadi websites, the BJP era saw the growth of a number of Hindutva websites that are committed to protecting and defending Hindu identity and culture while simultaneously critiquing their enemies Islam and, to a lesser extent, Christianity. The presence of such websites has not gone unnoticed. In fact, the comprehensive and informative link site, Hindu Web Universe, refers to the work and worldviews of some of these organisations (http://hindulinks.org/Interfaith_relations/Seeking_conversion/).

www.Hindu.India

There has been a massive growth in pro-Hindutva websites over the last few years. HinduUnity.org is among the most radical of the Hindutva websites, with links to right-wing Jewish websites such as kahane.org and a number of pro-Hindu Kashmir websites. The global contestation between Islamic radicalism and the rest has led to a closing of ranks between religious fundamentalist groups whose common enemy is Islam. A case in point is the relationship between HinduUnity.org, a front for the Bajrang Dal in USA, and the extremist Zionist group Kahane.org named after the radical Zionist Meir Kahane who was killed in 1990. Raja Swamy (2004: 3), in an article on the relationship between extreme Hinduism and extreme Zionism, has observed that: 'The server with I.P. address 67.153.104.163, which hosts HinduUnity.org, Hindunity.com, and HinduUnity.net, also hosts BajrangDal.org, BajrangDal.com, and BajrangDal.net...along with Kahane.org, www.jdl-ny.org, New York chapter of the Kahane'ist "Jewish Defense League".' Goddess Durga as Mother India bestriding the Indian subcontinent and the 'Court Statement' of the RSS sympathiser Nathuram Godse who was charged with assassinating Mahatma Gandhi are featured on a number of these websites. These sites include Hindutva. com and those of the VHP, Hindutva Brotherhood, RSS (http://www. rss.org/rss/www/mission.htm), Shiv Sena, Hindu Swayamsevak Sangh (http://www. hssworld.org/ac/frbanner.htm), BJP (http://www. bjp.org/ home.html), Hindu Vivek Kendra (http://www.hvk.org/hvk/), Hindu Council, Bajrang Dal, Soldiers of Hindutva, Sita Ka Sanwar, Mera Bharat Mahan, the Saffron Tigers, the Global Hindu Electronic Network and the super link Hindu Web Universe (http://www. hindulinks, also see Swamy, 2002).What is perhaps the most striking aspect of these websites is their organisational streamlining—their attempts to represent a pan-Indian Hindu identity based on an aggressive vision of Indian futures in which the majority community clearly dominates the minorities. The task of women in India is to nurture and protect the family. The BJP website gives information on its history, rationale, organisation, leadership, its politics, its stance on issues and its overall philosophy, including statements by some of its key ideologues such as S. Gurumurthy and Arun Shourie. As the site of the current Opposition party in India, it does put forward its credentials as a Hindu *and* pro-minority party. That however stands out as a difficult and problematic juxtaposition. Jayaraman (1998), in an article that analyses the BJP's website in *Frontline* magazine, describes Hindutva's expectations of Muslims in India. 'And what about Muslims? If they have to choose between Mecca or Islam and India you must choose India... it is clear what awaits the sections of the population who do not go along with the BJP's vision.' The RSS site gives information on its founders and the Sangh Parivar's work in education, rural development, unionising, the fine arts, appropriate technology, heritage and communications.

The dominant narrative that links many of these websites is the legitimation of Hindu resurgence, and the need for updating the image and status of Hinduism in India from that of a 'wimp' to a strident and aggressive masculinity, communicated by the war-like images of Lord Rama and Goddess Durga. The project is one that effaces the received colonialist understanding of Hinduism and establishes in its place a post-colonialist understanding signified by Hindutva, the Hindu nation. It is about righting the wrongs inflicted by traitors, in the past and the present, a cleansing followed by the creation of a golden age of Hindu glory. The words of the BJP ideologue Mihir Meghani exemplify this rhetoric of manifest destiny:

Hindus are at last free. They control their destiny now and there is no power that can control them except their own tolerant ethos. India in turn is finally free. Having ignored its history, it has now come face to face with a repressed conscience. The destruction of the structure at Ayodhya was the release of the history that Indians had not fully come to terms with. Thousands of years of anger and shame, so diligently bottled up by these same interests, was released when the first piece of the so-called Babri Masjid was torn down.

While Muslims are, for the most part, the main targets of hate on these websites, christianaggression.org is specifically focussed on combating Christian mission in India and elsewhere. There is little information on its source although it is clear that it is US-based and carries a disclaimer: 'This website holds the Christian faith in high regard and is in no way anti-Christian. Rather, this website is opposed to the aggression practiced under in the name of Christianity.' Despite this disclaimer, it carries a variety of articles and features that are critical of Christian mission as well as missionaries in India and their activities, including conversion. While the website claims to be involved in unmasking the excesses of Christian mission in India, it is linked to a number of recognised websites that support the cause of Hindutva, inclusive of Hindu Jagran and the Sword of Truth. The site contains a lot of information on the activities of Indian and foreign Christian mission in India—for example, that of the openly fundamentalist and separatist National Liberation Front of Tripura (NLFT) that is allegedly supported by the US-based Southern Baptist Church—and a blacklist that names 70 Christian organisations in India that are involved in conversion-related activities. Interestingly enough, out of the 70 groups that have been mentioned, mainstream Christian groups inclusive of the Church World Service and Witness Unit of the National Council of Churches USA (NCCUSA), Evangelical Lutheran Church in America, Division of Global Mission, Lutheran World Relief, Presbyterian Church (USA) Worldwide Ministries Division and the United Methodist Church General Board of Global Ministries feature on this list, along with recognised Christian fundamentalist groups such as Gospel for Asia, Inc., Grace Ministries International, Inc. the CBN, New Tribes Mission, TransWorld Radio and MAP International, Inc.

There is no understating the objective of these websites. It is a fronting of imagined and real futures, towards a space and time in which the Hindus of India and the world will unite in and for the protection of the Hindu heritage. Needless to say, that space and time will, of course, not be to the advantage of people who belong to other religious traditions. Not surprisingly, this version of a predominantly Brahminical Hinduism is contested from within by websites fronted by Dalit organisations. Chopra (2006: 197–98), in an article on online Hindutva and Dalit discourses, has observed how these websites, 'embody the social logic of global primordiality, which manifests itself as a virtual rewriting of Indian history or cyber-historiography'. He cites a website which asserts that 'Dalits/Hindus are ur-communities of the subcontinent and the original inhabitants of the Indus Valley settlement, a civilization dating back to around 2300 BC.'

Manufacturing Communalism

The reading thus far has been rather cursory. More research needs to be conducted to unravel the links between the new media, exclusivist agendas and communalism in India. An obvious question that can be posed is—'So what, if there are religious web wars?' After all, in a country like India, those who have access to such technologies continue to be a minority. Such wars do not affect the majority who are moved by other considerations, food security and other basic issues of survival. Furthermore, there is little evidence that is indicative of a relationship between web content and changes in attitudes or behaviour. One can, therefore, argue that web wars merely amplify, reinforce and feed into a pre-existing situation and that, as such, one cannot even be sure of their impact. However, one can also argue that these websites do contribute to keeping tensions alive through their framing of other religions, creating an environment of expectations fuelled by myths, dreams and desires of a pure Christian or, for that matter, a pure Hindu Indian nation. A number of the Christian websites mentioned in this study are actively involved in soliciting funds by creating a particular image of India for global consumption—an image of starving children, heathen practices and broken cultures that can be healed through the 'blood of Christ'. It is possible that such websites function mainly for foreign consumption, although it is evident that Christian mission in India has begun to use websites for the marketing of products, information sharing and connecting to the faithful.

While there are non-media factors that are responsible for inter-religious conflict, it would nevertheless be absurd to claim that these factors are on their own responsible for heightening the levels of inter-faith tensions in India. The presence and role of the media in the creation of national public opinion in India has been demonstrated on many an occasion. In fact, the media has played a substantial role in interpreting inter-religious conflict in India. A prime example was the way in which the media in general reported the demolition of the Babri Masjid in Ayodhya in 1990. Instead of deflecting the political agenda of the Hindu right, the media gave rise to a great many dubious interpretive inflections on the reasons that led to the fall of the Babri Masjid. Among the inflections that were given prominent media space were the 'spontaneous' nature of the demolition, the release of long bottled-up Hindu righteous anger, making amends with past wrongs, the assertion of Hindu identity, and so on—some of these contained partial truths, but were nevertheless communicated without the benefit of any background information. Many reports failed to comment on the jigsaw of events that preceded the storming of the Masjid—events that point to a premeditated strategy. These events ranged from the unwitting influence of the tele-serials *Ramayan* and *Mahabharat* shown on state television in the mid-1980s; to the overt support given to religious nationalism on state television and in privately owned media, in particular through cable television, video and audio productions, and the press; and the symbolism mediated through national spectacles such as the religious nationalist pilgrimages or *Rath Yatras*. Aijaz Ahmad (1993: 33) has drawn attention to the rise of the Hindu right and the effective manipulation of symbols in their quest for political legitimacy:

The real ingenuity of the RSS was that it adopted at the moment of its own inception and consistently since then, the figure of Ram as the one upon whom all narrative structures converge, so that the later tele-vising of the *Ramayana* and the *Mahabharata* in quick succession cre-ated a sense of this mutual continuity, the story of Ram overlapping with heroic narratives of the sacred nation.... When Mr. Advani's *rathyatra* got going it was seen as an extension of the epics and no one was bothered by the simultaneity of symbols taken from both.

www.Interfaith.India

It is always difficult to project a strategic vision of inter-faith communica-tions in a context characterised by mutual distrust and simmering vio-lence. The Sangh Parivar has the avowed aim to Hinduise India, to de-secularise the Constitution and to reinvent institutions and systems, for instance, the educational system (Engineer, 1998; Omvedt 1998), in line with its own interpretative spin on the history of India and its fu-tures. Its external aims are no less belligerent, given the recent nuclear misadventures of its political ally, the BJP (Ram, 1999). While educational reform is necessary (there is a good case to revamp the potted, colonialist version of history presented in primary and secondary school text books) and there is much to be gained by a global ban on nuclear weapons as against the special set of rules for the recognised five nuclear weapon states, the long-term impact of policies adopted for the pursuit of narrow, exclusivist goals and short-term electoral politics is bound to keep inter-nal and external tensions alive. The convictions that accompany ethnic and religious identities run deep. And any call for forgiveness and recon-ciliation may well appear misplaced and premature in a situation where the 'healing' has hardly begun.

However, in spite of these larger constraints, there must be ways to ease this tension through the positive communication of the wealth of India's religious traditions. India carries the imprint of numerous reli-gions. And Indians are, in general, a religious people. Recognition of this fact is critical to any strategy aimed at restoring inter-faith amity. Igno-rance of this reality needs to be recognised as a key contributory factor to the tensions—ignorance that is manipulated by fundamentalists on all sides of the divide. The average evangelist in India is woefully ignorant of Hin-duism—his/her knowledge is often inadequate, couched in prejudice and determined by imported understandings that are insensitive to say the least. Unfortunately, the average Indian Christian too is often seen to share such views.

First, it would seem that, at the very least, all religious communities in India need to communicate their faith responsibly, without, in that process, attacking or undermining other faiths. Second, in the light of the deteriorating quality of faith reporting, religious councils in India could be jointly involved in drawing up an inter-faith media charter. These councils need to make an attempt to jointly work towards the creation of an ombudsman that would have the power to take action on those who violate this charter. Further, inter-faith efforts may be encouraged to set up a multi-faith cable television channel, along the lines of the Toronto-based inter-faith cable channel Vision TV. The objective of such a network will be to broadcast objective interpretations of faiths, religious traditions and spiritualities from and to the subcontinent. Such a service is needed to counter the present norm—the token space given to religion by state broadcasting and programmes that merely strengthens stereotypical perceptions of the religious other. At the least, such an initiative will create a shared space for imagining a different India. And last, it is necessary that religious institutions take seriously the challenge posed by inter-faith dialogue. In pluralist societies like India, where the issue of religion has become emotive and divisive, these institutions need to be called to create the basis for reconciliation and understanding. Bishop Tutu's (2004) affirmation, first expressed in Kigali, Rwanda, and reproduced in the Truth Commission's report from South Africa, that 'Confession, forgiveness and reconciliation in the lives of nations are not just airy-fairy religious and spiritual things, nebulous and unrealistic. They are the stuff of practical politics' communicates the fact that faith is both relational and grounded in the practical business of daily living. One cannot but love one's neighbour. Disregarding that simple human option can, as we only well know, result in bitter consequences.

Notes

1. *Rath Yatra*, literally 'chariot journey', is a highly politicised, symbolic modern day pilgrimage, in the tradition followed in the Hindu epics. The first *Rath Yatra* was organised by the BJP, which was then in the Opposition, and choreographed by the VHP and other members of the Sangh Parivar. The ex-Home Minister of the BJP, L.K. Advani, was at the helm of this motorised chariot pilgrimage. It started on 25 September 1990 from Somnath, Gujarat—the site of a famous razing of Hindu temples by Mahmud of Ghazni in the year 1026 AD—and ended on 30 October 1990 in Ayodhya, coinciding with the Hindu festival Debothan Ekadashi. For more details, see Davis, 1996. The Hindu right was also involved in organising other events, for instance, the

Ram Jyoti, another highly symbolic event in which a torch was lit in Ayodhya and sent to thousands of villages in India to light Deepavalli(Festival of Lights) lamps. Yet another was the Ram Shila Puja—the consecration of bricks from various villages in India to be used in the building of the Ram temple in Ayodhya (see Panikkar, 1993).

2. The 'nageswaram' is a south Indian wind instrument.

3. The Pancasila, meaning the 'five moral principles' governing the life of the state in Indonesia, was enunciated by Sukarno on 1 June 1945 and became state philosophy. The five principles are belief in one supreme God, humanism, nationalism, popular sovereignty and social justice.

4. The UN is seen by the right wing, in USA in particular, as the anti-Christ—a global institution whose sole aim is to bring about the downfall of the American way of life and in particular the power of 'white' communities.

5. The scale of church planting in India by indigenous churches is quite extraordinary. Daniel Samuel (1998), an independent researcher from Chennai, surveyed indigenous churches in and around Chennai. He came across 167 indigenous churches. Here are some interesting facts from his survey: 86.4 per cent of the churches surveyed were established after 1981; 75 per cent of these churches were Tamil-based; many were involved in saturation church planting activities; 98 of the churches were classified as free evangelical churches; 59 as Pentecostal/charismatic; 1 as historical; 8 as prophetic; and 46 of the churches were registered. Church planting is big business in India. While Chennai has generally been free from inter-religious strife, it would be the case that church planting in places like Varanasi are bound to lead to a rise in inter-faith tensions.

References

Ahmad, A. 1993. 'Culture, Community and Nation: On the Ruins of Ayodhya', *Social Scientist,* 21(7–8): 17–48.

Akkara, A. 1999a. 'India's Coalition Government Divided over Attacks on Christians', *Ecumenical News International* (ENI), No. 02, 17 February.

————. 1999b. 'After New Attacks on Christians India's Churches Call for Tougher Action', *ENI*, No. 06, 31 March, pp.18–19.

Ammerman, N.C. 1998. 'North American Protestant Fundamentalism', in L. Kintz and J. Lesage (eds), *Media, Culture and the Religious Right*, pp. 55–113. Minneapolis & London: University of Minnesota Press.

Basu, T., P. Datta, S. Sarkar, T. Sarkar and S. Sen. 1993. *Khaki Shirts, Saffron Flags*. Tracts for the Times/1. New Delhi: Orient Longman.

Brosius, C. 2004. 'Of Nasty Pictures and "Nice Guys": The Surreality of Online Hindutva', in *Sarai Reader*, pp. 139–51. Delhi: CSDS.

Castro, E. 1991. 'Evangelism', in N. Lossky, J.M. Bonino, J. Pobee, T. Stransky, G. Wainwright and P. Webb (eds), *Dictionary of the Ecumenical Movement*, pp. 396–400. Geneva: WCC Publications; London: Council of Churches for Britain and Ireland.

Gupta, Charu and Mukul Sharma. 1990. *Print Media and Communalism*. New Delhi.

Chatterjee, P. 1995. 'Religious Minorities and the Secular State: Reflections on an Indian Impasse', *Public Culture*, 8(Fall): 11–39.

Chopra, R. 2006. 'Global Primordialities: Virtual Identity Politics in Online Hindutva and Online Dalit Discourses', *New Media & Society*, 8(2): 187–206.

Dalrymple, W. 1999. 'Baptism by Fire', *The Guardian Weekly*, 20 March, pp. 20–25.

Dasgupta, M. 1999. 'Christians at the Receiving End', *The Hindu* (Bangalore Edition), 3 January.

Davis, R.H. 1996. 'The Iconography of Rama's Chariot', in D. Ludden (ed.), *Making India Hindu: Religion, Community and the Politics of Democracy in India*, pp. 27–54. New Delhi: Oxford University Press.

Doogue, E. 1999. 'Campaigner Warns Against Danger of Myths about India's Christians', *ENI*, No. 05, 17 March, p. 18.

Engineer, A.A. 1998. 'Education, the BJP and Hindutva', *The Hindu* (Bangalore Edition), 2 November.

Engineer, I. 1999a. 'Conversions in Dangs', *The Hindu* (Bangalore Edition), 22 January.

————. 1999b. 'Australian Missionary, Sons Burnt Alive', *The Hindu* (Bangalore Edition), 24 January.

Gautier, F. 1999. 'Western Indian Press', *Himal*, 12(3): 58.

Griffiths, B. 1983. *The Marriage of East and West*. London: Collins, Fount Paperbacks.

Jayaraman, T. 1998. 'The BJP on the Net', *Frontline*, 15(2). Available at http://www.hinduonnet.com/fline/fl1502/15021100.htm, accessed on 24 March 2003.

Kallen, E. 1998. 'Hate on the Net: A Question of Rights/A Question of Power', *Electronic Journal of Sociology*. Available online at http://www.sociology.org/content/vol003.002/kallen.html, accessed on 20 August 2003.

Manuel, P. 1996. 'Music, the Media and Communal Relations in North India, Past and Present', in D. Ludden (ed.), *Making India Hindu: Religion, Community and the Politics of Democracy in India*. New Delhi: Oxford University Press.

Meghnani, M. 'Hindutva: The Great Nationalist Ideology', pp. 1–4. Available at http://www.bjp.org/history/htrintro.mm.html, accessed on 15 February 2003.

Mitra, A. and E. Cohen 1999. 'Analyzing the Web: Directions and Challenges', in S. Jones(ed.), *Doing Internet Research: Critical Issues and Methods for Examining the Net*, pp. 179–202. Thousand Oaks/London/New Delhi: Sage Publications.

Nandy, A., S. Trivedy, S. Mayaram and A. Yagnik. 1997. *The Ramjanmabhumi Movement and Fear of the Self*. New Delhi: Oxford University Press.

Omvedt, G. 1998. 'Beyond Saffron and Secular Education', *The Hindu* (Bangalore Edition), 16 November.

Panikkar, M. 1993. 'Religious Symbols and Political Mobilisation', *Social Scientist*, 21(7–8): 63–77.

People's Reporter. 1999. 'Apex Indian Theological Body holds BJP Responsible for Violence against Vulnerable Minorities', *People's Reporter*, 1–15 March, p. 4.

Ram N. 1999. 'What Wrong Did this Man do', *Frontline*, 16(10): 1–15. Available at http://www.the.hindu.com/fline/f11610/16100220.htm, accessed on 21 March 2003.

Rodhe, S. 1993. *Jules Monchanin: Pioneer in Christian-Hindu Dialogue*. Delhi: ISPCK.

Samuel, D. 1998. 'A Report on the Study of Churches of Indigenous Origins in and around the City of Chennai', unpublished.

Shah, G. 1999. 'Politics of Policing', *The Hindu*, 12 March.

Swami Abhishiktananda. 1969. *Hindu-Christian Meeting Point: Within the Cave of the Heart*. Delhi: ISPCK.

Swamy, R. 2004. 'Zionism and Hindutva in the U.S. Update—May 2004', pp. 1–10. Available at http://ghadar.insaf.net/June2004/pdf/zionism.pdf, accessed on 22 May 2005.

Swamy, R. 2002. 'Zionism, Hindutva and Mickey Mouse Imperialism', *Ghadar*, 5(2). Available at http://www.proxsa.org/resources/ghadar/v5n2/zionism.html, accessed on 22 May 2005.

Tepper, M. 1997. 'Usenet Communities and the Cultural Politics of Information', in D. Porter (ed.), *Internet Culture,* pp. 39–54. New York & London: Routledge.

Tutu, D. 2004. *God has a Dream: A Vision of Hope for our Time.* NY: Doubleday.

Vanaik, A. 1994 'Situating Threat of Hindu Nationalism: Problems with Fascist Paradigm', *Economic and Political Weekly,* 9 July: 1729–48.

Venkatasubramaniam, K. 1998. 'Secularism or Anti-Hinduism', *The Hindu* (Bangalore Edition), 1 December.

Vyas, N. 1998a. 'The Ugly Face behind the Mask', *The Hindu* (Bangalore Edition), 3 January.

———. 1998b. 'Two Churches Torched in Surat District', *The Hindu* (Bangalore Edition), 29 December.

WCC Commission on World Mission and Evangelism. 1997. 'Mission and Evangelism— An Ecumenical Affirmation', in M. Kinnamon and B.E. Cope (eds), *The Ecumenical Movement: An Anthology of Key Texts and Voices,* pp. 372–83. Geneva: WCC Publications and Grand Rapids; Michigan: William B. Eerdmans Publishing Co.

Whine, M. 1997. 'The Far Right on the Internet', in B.D. Loader (ed.), *The Governance of Cyberspace: Politics, Technology and Global Restructuring,* pp. 209–227. London & New York: Routledge.

Websites

http://www.hindulinks.org/Interfaith_relations/Seeking_conversion/

http://www.rss.org/rss/www/mission.htm

http://www.hssworld.org/ac/frbanner.htm

http://www.bjp.org/home.html

http://www.hvk.org/hvk/

'Major Conversion Programs Operating in India'. Available at http://www.christianaggression.org/action_blacklist.php, accessed on 1 June 2003.

'National Liberation Front of Tripura (NLFT)'. Available at http://www.christianaggression.org/features_nlft.php, accessed on 1 June 2003.

www.Mission.India, accessed on 12 May 2003.

hinduunity.org, accessed on 12 May 2003.

http://www.ad2000.org/uterpeop.htm, accessed on 11 March 2003.

http://www.samindia.org/html/greetings.htm

http://www.wo.org/crusade.asp?sub=VY

http://www.aims.org/index.html

http://www.calebproject.org/cdecl/htm

http://www.aims.org/jaipur/html

http://www.ad2000.org/uters 4.htm

http://www.gfa.org/SEND/index.htm

http://www.joshuaproject.net/

8

BENNY HINN'S FESTIVAL OF BLESSINGS:

The Analysis of a Christian Crusade in India

Tofik Benny Hinn was born in 1953 in Jaffa, Israel, and is of Greek Orthodox descent. He is probably the best known tele-evangelist today and his syndicated show *This is your Day* is shown on hundreds if not thousands of cable and satellite channels throughout the world. His book *Good Morning Holy Spirit* sold a million copies. His travelling crusades are often held in mega sports centres, football fields, and the like, often attracting hundreds of thousands of people (http://www.bennyhinn.org/television/televisiondefault.cfm). He is a 'Word of Faith' minister with a reputation for healing and for his exposition of Prosperity Theology. In this latter sense, he is in the company of Creflo Dollar, Kenneth Copeland, and others. Benny Hinn is a controversial figure—not only for the unsubstantiated theological positions that he takes and his economising of the truth about his own upbringing, but also for his lavish lifestyle and frequent hyperbole.

> The Lord also tells me to tell you in the mid-90s, about '94, '95, no later than that, God will destroy the homosexual community of America. But He will not destroy it with what many minds have thought Him to be. He will destroy it with fire. And many will turn and be saved, and many will rebel and be destroyed (Benny Hinn, 2003).

Two very critical documentaries (*NBC Dateline*, December 2002 and a follow-up report, 6 March 2005) deal specifically with Pastor Benny's financial improprieties, while the documentary *Do You Believe in Miracles* on Canadian Broadcasting Corporation's (CBC) *Fifth Estate* and Trinity Foundation's *The Many Faces of Benny Hinn* asked serious questions about the effectiveness of his healing ministry. Critique has come from within the evangelical fraternity in USA, for example, MinistryWatch and the Evangelical Council for Financial Accountability as well as from without. T.J.S. George (2005), the Bengaluru resident editor of *The Indian Express*, has called him 'the world's most dubious trader in religion'.[1]

There is, in other words, no dearth of information available on the web and elsewhere on Pastor Benny's ministry. However, while the controversies rage, the show still goes on. This chapter attempts to contextualise the Benny Hinn crusade that was held in Bengaluru within the specific conditions of religious contestation in India—the reality of Hindu nationalism, the changing nature of popular religiosity, the growing influence of the market on religion and, last but not least, the search for meaning and spiritual healing that the mainstream churches seem inadequate to respond to. While crusades and revivals are certainly not a new phenomenon in India (the Maramon convention organised by the Mar Thoma Church in Kerala is more than a hundred years old), the Benny crusade, despite its continuities with extant traditions in India, is nevertheless different in the sense that Benny Hinn is a full-time global crusader, backed by a sophisticated global management and marketing machine, and is in the business of religion as spectacle. His religion is tailor-made for the era of wall-to-wall television and he himself is a representative of a resurgent, global and largely mediated form of Christianity.

While it is relatively simple to dismiss evangelists such as Benny Hinn as a dissembler, preying on the real emotional and spiritual concerns faced by people, the fact remains that he does attract huge audiences in hundreds of thousands and there is demand for his services. In order to make real sense of Benny Hinn, there is a need to unravel the manufacture of demand for such services—from the perspectives of audiences, the crusade economy, the symbolic economy, the religious products market, and, last but not least, local support systems that indicate the presence of networks, organisations and support systems for this form of resurgent Christianity throughout the world. What makes people go in their thousands to hear such faith healers? And how is that their very presence at such crusades is indicative of a shift in the meaning of the church in our times?

The success of Bengaluru as a centre for software development and India as the business processing centre in the world belies the fact that the country does have another side—millions of people below the poverty line, vast disparities between the rich and the poor, and the loss of faith in certainty.

Economic liberalisation has contributed to rising levels of prosperity in India for some. For the lower middle classes, changing India is a struggle. While salary levels have rocketed for those in the information technology (IT) sector, for many others insecurity is a constant reality. Medical bills are impossibly high for the lower middle classes—and it is not coincidental that a large number of those who take part in healing crusades hope to be healed for free. In interviews with those who had attended the Benny Hinn crusade in Bengaluru, I was told that many patients from hospitals around Bengaluru found their way to the Jakkur airfield to hear Pastor Benny, hoping for a miraculous recovery from their ailments.

The Culture of the Crusade: Festival of Blessings, Bengaluru, India, 2005

A crusade, according to *New Oxford Dictionary of English* (2001), is 'a medieval military expedition, one of a series made by Europeans to recover the Holy Land from the Muslims in the 11th, 12th and 13th centuries.' It is also used to refer to organised campaigns by political and religious bodies motivated by a desire for change. Modern day Jihadists are often termed crusaders, while, by the same token, the image of Franklin Graham riding into Baghdad atop a US tank communicates a symbolism that is replete with signs of a triumphalist Christianity liberating the evil empire of Baghdad and restoring it to civilised sanity—a project that, in hindsight, seems to have failed rather miserably. It would be fair to say that religious crusades such as those of the Hinn ministries are, at one level, forms of symbolic warfare aimed at making India a Christian nation—an avowed aim of global evangelical Christian mission—and, at another level, an attempt to create a unified theology and non-denominational Christian community. This Christian *umma* is the metaphorical, undivided Body of Christ, which is sustained by a theology that has an emphasis on certain aspects of Biblical doctrine as well as Pentecostal and neo-Pentecostal practice, inclusive of the slant towards miracles, the need to be born-again, the expectant, millennial longing for the second coming of Christ and an exclusive salvation for all those who belong to the body of Christ. By the same token, a crusade deals with the 'other' through symbolic conquest, through overt and covert forms of symbolic annihilation, and through the belittling of other faiths carried out by the manufactured aura of the crusade and the performative capital invested in the miraculous healing of a Hindu from the clutches of the Devil or illness.

A crusade is a visual feast and, in the case of spectaculars like the Festival of Blessing, a meticulous choreography; the spatial arrangement of the seating, the technology-based fit between the aural and the visual, the music and the careful build-up to the miracles contribute to the creation of expectation. Many were not converted by the experiences but were willing to suspend disbelief, even to believe that 'the cool, gentle breeze that blew across the airfield' was somehow related to the presence of God. The size of such extravaganzas and the presence of thousands of people all wanting a share of the miraculous make such gatherings unique. In fact, such forms of organised religion, at this level of sophistication, are hard to come by in India, although for sheer numbers, Hindu Godmen such as Satya Sai Baba and Sri Sri Ravishankar draw massive audiences.

The Crusade

One square mile, 215 acres, 300,000 chairs, 60 large 45-feet video screens, 45 sets of large speakers and 100,000 watts of sound, 50 miles of cable, 15,000 ushers, parking space for 60,000 cars and buses, a Gulfstream III jet, helicopters, 20 security dogs, a 100-strong private security network, two floors of the exclusive Leela Penta hotel, 10,000 state security personnel, billboards, television spots, advertisements in the key newspapers, many VIPs including an ex-Prime Minister of India (Deve Gowda) and the then Chief Minister of Karnataka state Dharam Singh (both have since been unseated from power), and at least a million people—you will be forgiven for thinking that all this was for a rock concert. But no—with a 2,000 voice backup choir and the support of 10,000 churches—the foregoing description is of an evangelical crusade organised by the flamboyant US-based tele-evangelist Benny Hinn at the Jakkur Airport Grounds, Bengaluru, 21–23 January 2005.

The stage is vast. Dignitaries are seated to the right. There are rows and rows of potted plants on the stage—carnations, chrysanthemums, roses—and a perfect row of anthuriums hugging the border of the vast stage. The stage is built like a mini grand stand and the back drop is occupied by a 2000-voice choir, the women in blue *salwars* and the men in black and white and ties. The band is on the left of the stage and to the near right of Benny Hinn is an organ and a rather demure looking organist dressed in blue. The first row in front of the state is for the VIPs. It is carpeted in red. In an off-white safari suit emblazoned with the logo of the Benny Hinn Ministries, the perfectly groomed Benny Hinn, with a full crop of white hair and a ring that sparkles as it catches the light, leads a rousing revival hymn. The crusade begins with the ex-Bollywood singer Vijay Benedict singing a song in Hindi 'Mera Bharat Mahan' that includes the words 'victory to India, victory to Jesus'. This the moment for patriotism and the Indian flag flies on the stage. The 'imported' vocalists including John Starnes and Sue Dodge follow with a repertoire that sounds straight out of vaudeville, followed by fast and slow revival hymns including the popular hymn 'Amazing Grace'.

The theme for the festival of blessing is that of 'miracles' and Benny Hinn begins with the words 'God Loves India, God Loves You, I love You.' The crowd itself is as Benny Hinn exclaims 'a miracle'. After the routine half an hour of songs, Benny Hinn begins a Biblical exposition on the theme of miracles—a standard feature during the three days—although the miracles chosen are different. The miracles are of a leper being healed— the story of Jairus, the cripple who is lowered from the loft. As he moves on from one miracle to another, the impression is that Jesus carried out all these miracles in the space of a single day—perhaps preparing the audience for what is to come. There is little theology. Every story is stretched and in some cases, the evangelist liberally peppers the story with his own imaginative flights—for instance, the story of the pool in Bethseda where Jesus healed a blind man. According to Benny Hinn, there were thousands of people with all sorts of infirmities around the pool. Those who were healed were the ones who asked to be healed. The miracles at this pool were greater than any miracle at any shrine. For Jesus is a gentleman who only heals those who ask. He then veers from this line of thought and exclaims that the first question that Jesus asked was: 'Are you looking for a miracle.' He then exclaims that he is not the healer and that it is God who is. And yet, when the healing is in full swing—it looks like it is Benny Hinn who is doing the healing. Like Jesus, Benny Hinn had work to do. As the evangelist builds up the atmosphere, he becomes all theatre—arms stretched, moving from one part of the stage to another, and his voice rising and falling, keeping time with the story of a particular miracle until the climatic end. By this time the choir is on its feet. And the stage is set for the main fare, the piece de resistance.

As the public healing session begins and testimonies tumble out from emotion-choked voices, the camera pans on to faces in the audience betraying all sorts of emotions—exuberance, incredulity, amazement and awe—at the sight of the blind seeing, the deaf hearing and the lame not only on their feet but doing back-flips. Benny's minders are on both sides of the stage. At his 'Henry, what's going on?' routine, the excited Henry has already begun the case history of the patient, sometimes with the theatrical flourishing of an x-ray or a written case history. Benny's minders personally usher in each of the healed, and publicly explain the before and after of the miracle, followed by the classic Benny 'slain by the Spirit' routine where the concerned individual collapses into the arms of the minders at the touch of Benny's palm. The testimonies are of those with leukaemia, all sorts of cancers, arthritis, even leprosy; those who are blind, deaf; and those who could not work. Some stories seem genuine, others stretch the bounds of incredulity—like the young man who proclaims that he is cured of blindness and who adds that his son has become a lawyer in the Supreme Court of London! Benny Hinn spends more time with them—for they are Hindus. He reassures a girl who is healed but worries whether Jesus cures Hindus. Again the moment lasts for longer than usual. There are times when Benny Hinn merely stretches his palms out, followed by an audible verbal command. The routine is theatrical and very business-like for there is little time to spare and many miracles to make. Some of those touched by Benny Hinn do not swoon and Hinn tries to fall to make it happen. This is an essential part of the routine and those who refuse to be floored are even hastily ushered out. There are audible gasps from the audience, very much like an audience watching a trapeze act, followed by clapping and shouts of 'praise the lord' and 'halleluiah' as the miracle is ratified as authentic by the person healed and blessed by Benny Hinn. There are those who claim that they were healed by merely touching the screen during one of Benny Hinn's *This is Your Day* programmes. This is a cue for Benny Hinn to look directly at the camera and implore the 'man with the heart disease' to touch the screen. The crusade becomes television. Since all media are seen as blessings— tools for the Great Commission—this is sanctified television. Never mind that at the flick of the remote, one can get violence and pornography and the dramatisation of all manner of venal sins. The capture of television is itself part of the struggle against Satan and his powers. The choreographed pauses, the soft renditions of classic revival songs such as 'How Great Thou Art' during the 'healing' and full-bodied versions at the climatic end of the healing session are part of the overall ambience, the spectacle. The DVD version of the Bengaluru crusade ends with a montage of the evangelist in white, arms outstretched, back to the camera, dissolving into a shot of clouds. Is this Benny Hinn the mortal, or is he an avatar of Jesus Christ? India is home to many avatars and therefore such forms of identification are not far-fetched. Most people have seen Benny Hinn on television. The crowd includes the curious, the sceptical, Hindus and

Muslims, along with the majority who belong to the evangelical and main-line churches.

This is of course not a one-off event. Benny Hinn was in Mumbai in 2004 and was scheduled to be in Hyderabad in December 2006, although this crusade is yet to be organised. And in between he travelled to Fiji, Seoul and other parts of the world. Modern day evangelical Christian crusades are made for television for they have all the necessary ingredients—information, entertainment and drama mediated by charismatic personalities. They bring together vast agglomerations of people. Crusades make for endless repeats on the many transnational Christian television channels such as GOD TV, Daystar, Christian Broadcasting Network (CBN) and the Trinity Broadcasting Network (TBN), and the many indigenous Christian cable channels found around the world. Since many of these channels rely on a maximum of 8 hours of programming per day, the rest 16 hours are filled with repeats. The crusades are an essential aspect of a programming strategy adopted by the Benny Hinn Ministries that includes the popular 15-year old syndicated television programme *This is Your Day* and the new programme *Manna from Heaven*, along with books, CDs, DVDs, posters and other religious paraphernalia. The DVD version of the Bengaluru event includes interviews with Benny Hinn, who is bathed in a soft light that is meant to enhance the ambience, and the warmth and aura of the person. The evangelist speaks of his friend Pastor Job, whose son was killed and who has started an orphanage for 250 children whose parents were pastors and who had all been killed for their faith—an incredible story for the consumption of his compatriots such as Pat Robertson. News stories of Benny Hinn's problems with the Hindu right on CBN are presented in an amplified manner and there is the suggestion that the triumph of the crusade against obstacles and adversity is the triumph of the Christian God.

The phenomenon of the global Benny Hinn road show can be seen from a number of perspectives. Its formulaic, predictable unity and its integration within a global and local events industry, economy and calendar is the triumph of a networked Christianity of the Spectacle. This is by no means a stand-alone project for it validates a Christianity that is practised by millions of people around the world. In this sense, the Benny Hinn crusade is the site at which the global validates the local at the level of the local. The accent on miracles and the miraculous is shared by millions of Christians around the world and Benny Hinn is first and foremost a miracle healer. The crusade is an expression of the globalisation of a particular form of Christianity, neo-Pentecostalism, and its related theologies, the Word-Faith Theology and Prosperity Theology. The crusade offers a stage in which faith, practice and belief can be corporately validated on a mass scale. This process of mass validation that is globally consumed via television and DVDs communicates the emergence of a globally consolidated Christian *umma* that is taking over from all the tired and bankrupt forms of traditional Christianity. It communicates a vision of non-denominational Christianity that is open to anyone and that is unhampered by tradition, ritual, status and authority. This is expressed in an idiom that is familiar to tele-visual audiences in India and elsewhere, longings that are validated on stage by Christian celebrities who have the perceived power to transform ordinary unfulfilled longings for market success and health into imagined if not real options.

One could also approach the crusade from a cultural perspective—as a site for a variety of audience negotiations including mediated healing, trauma relief, public vindications of the good, and the vanquishment of the Devil and evil spirits. The spirit world is routinely ignored by the rational theology of the mainstream churches. Crusades offer the space for people to witness on stage the battle between good and evil, the Devil and Christ, malevolence and the serenity that comes from giving one's life to Christ. The validation of this world of the unseen that the majority of Indians, irrespective of their religious persuasions, believe in reinforces the view that life at a very basic elemental level is all about a struggle between the forces of good and the forces of evil. Crusades offer a public space for the validation of the ministry of the new churches and the huge audience is a sign of popular dissatisfaction with the ministry of mainline churches. The presence of a million people at a crusade indicates people's need for emotional and physical healing of one sort or another. Religion remains an extraordinary source of personal, emotional comfort in a context in which the 'secular' is 'remote'. The economic promise of globalisation is always redeemed in a context—the habitus inhabited by individuals. Given the vastly different opportunities for individual fulfilment, religion will remain a potent source for individual empathy and a source of strength. The adjustment problems linked with employees at call centres in India is a case in point. The global ascent of Pentecostalism and neo-Pentecostalism has been accompanied by a perceptible decline in mainline church affiliations in many parts of the world. In Latin America, Africa, North America and Asia—the emerging tradition of Christianity is one form or another of classical Pentecostalism or neo-Pentecostalism. While church leaders belonging to the mainstream churches in India tend to ignore the competition, play down the threat and tend to assume that Christian growth has limitless potential in India, multi-church attendance has become widespread in India and elsewhere. The younger generation continues to play an important vanguard role in this movement away from traditional churches to the new churches.

One could, in the context of intrinsically religious societies such as India, a nation in which religion is an intensely contested reality, view the Benny Hinn crusade as an example of the contestation for the 'soul' of India. The prayer for India routine at the beginning of the crusade can be seen as an attempt to embrace India spiritually, to claim India for Christ. Such mechanisms of othering offer cues to other religionists and, for that matter, secularists who often view such fervent expressions of religiosity as a challenge to the status quo. These forms of othering basically reinforce the religious and political agenda promoted by conservative Christians in India and the global religious right inclusive of Pat Robertson, Franklin Graham, Ed Crouch, and assorted others. It is not at all surprising that Benny Hinn is a favourite target for Hindu fundamentalist groups and secularists. The Benny Hinn crusade can also be seen in terms of the new religious market that provides the necessary scaffolding for the consummation of a variety of salvific passions, the terms and tools for the negotiating of sacredness and salvation. The crusade in this sense is a gigantic, permanent marketing exercise that is reinforced by Benny Hinn shows on television and the sale of a variety of products over the Internet. The market is a perfect environment for 'Prosperity Theology' for it validates religious consumerism—the consumption of books, DVDs, CDs and other Christian paraphernalia that are necessary to 'making it' in life, to become someone, to become successful. The political economy of mediated religion is a story that is yet to be told. The Benny Hinn crusade is not a stand-alone project. It is an essential aspect of a larger, tele-visual political economy—the Christian satellite and cable industry, Christian broadcasting and Christian pedagogy peddled by a variety of Bible schools and seminaries.

Crusades and tele-evangelism in India are but aspects of a larger context of religions, religious cultures and practices, and expressions of religiosity in India. Since India boasts a variety of indigenous 'God men and women' for home and international consumption, Benny Hinn and others of his kind can be considered as just another addition to the colour and variety of religious communication in India. In this sense, Benny Hinn might be a threat to the Hindu nationalist and the avowed secularist, but is not a threat to the average Indian. The scale of the crusades and presentation of skills might be different, but Benny Hinn essentially belongs to a continuum of miracle makers who have from time immemorial practised their craft in India. Hindus such as Bhagwan Rajneesh, Satya Sai Baba, Mata Amritanandamayi and Sri Sri Ravishankar, and Christians such as K.P. Yohanan, Ezra Sargunam and Brother Dhinakaran have offered healing in a variety of specific ways. As Caplan (1987: 374–75) has observed in his study of Christian fundamentalism in south India:

A few charismatic prophets earn a reputation beyond their own congregations, and attract followings from outside their own immediate neighbourhoods. The more miraculous their achievements, the wider their notoriety. Some develop 'specialisations', that is, they become known for dealing effectively with particular kinds of problems: certain prophets in Madras are thought to have a singular gift for finding lost property, identifying thieves, exorcising spirits or even predicting whether a particular marriage proposal is likely to lead to a happy and successful union. Those who achieve supra-local fame do so because they are seen to stand above the innumerable local healers in terms of their charismatic powers. They are also acknowledged to be strong orators, able to ... present the word of God in a compelling and convincing way.

Crusades as an Aspect of the Marketplace of Religion in India

The globalisation of religion has led to a billion dollar New Spirituality market, a market where every human problem has a solution that often comes packaged and includes a hefty fee. During the period of Bharatiya Janata Party (BJP) rule in India, popular Hindu traditions, from numismatics to astrology, yoga, meditation and Hindu curative traditions, made a comeback aided by the advent of wall to wall television. Watching television early morning (6.00–6.30 AM) on 17 December in Bengaluru, I came across a number of cable and satellite channels, dedicated or otherwise, that offered a variety of religious fare (see Table 8.1).

The availability of diverse religious talk shows, sermons, spiritual help sessions and music on satellite and cable channels in India is among the most obvious, publicly visible aspects of the new market for religion in India. There are, however, innumerable examples of an evolving religious culture mediated by new technologies. One does not have to visit the Sri Venkateshawara temple in Andhra Pradesh or for that matter some of

Table 8.1 Religious Programmes on Television, 17 December 2005

Channel	Programme	Religion	Dedicated	Non-Dedicated	Language
Sanskar		Hindu	√		Hindi
Akshay		Hindu	√		Hindi
SAB		Hindu	√		
Amrta		New Age Hindu	√		Variety of languages
Doordarshan	Saptagiri	Hindu		√	Hindi
QTV		Muslim	√		Urdu, Hindi
ETC Ajabi		Sikh	√		Punjabi
Daystar		Christian	√		English
GOD TV		Christian	√		English
Teja TV		Christian		√	Telugu
Maa TV		Christian		√	Telugu
Zee	Satyavani Church of Christ	Christian		√	Marathi
Vijay TV	Joyce Meyer	Christian		√	Tamil
Surya	Joyce Meyer	Christian		√	Malayalam
Podhigai	Joyce Meyer	Christian		√	Tamil, Hindi

the other key temples in India. Today, you can buy your blessings over the Internet and download for free any number of Gods as wall paper for your PC screen. Television has become a site for popular veneration just as wall posters, calendars and statues of Mirabai. There is a huge industry around the Hindu God of prosperity Lord Ganesh, whose endearing image is ubiquitous on posters, t-shirts and figurines made out of every type of malleable material. Just as in the old days every new business venture began with a ceremonial blessing and the breaking of coconuts, today, given the economic boom in India, praying for economic success has become an art in itself with hundreds of self-professed gurus catering to the needs of stock-brokers, IT specialists, bankers, and the like. New Age Hindu books are part of a million dollar business and most book shops now have a well stocked section on Hindu spiritual self-help. And just as mediated Christianity has become integrally related to the global market, in India the very same corporatisation and marketing of religion has led to an agglomeration of sites where Hinduism is dispensed. Payal Bhuskute (2005), in an article in the *Deccan Chronicle*, describes one of the programmes of Sri Sri Ravi Shankar:

Art of Living is another great marketing model for would be spiritualists. It has differently priced packages for each city and more expensive advance courses in big cities. Besides, it has also applications in corporate training with the highly sought Apex (achieving personal excellence) course. The management programme has been personally designed by Sri Sri Ravi Shankar and encompasses everything from yoga and breathing exercise to improving peak efficiency. He speaks in 40 countries annually.

Benny Hinn: Text and Context

While it is relatively simple to write a subjective account of any given performance, be it a Sai Baba event or a Benny Hinn crusade, the challenge lies in assessing the discourse itself, relating text to context and understanding the specific conditions of consumption. Furthermore, it is critically important to understand the political economy of mediated religion, given the fact that this visibly cultural phenomenon is undergirded by a material edifice. Benny Hinn might be involved in preaching and his audiences in making meaning, but he and others of the same persuasion are, in a fundamental sense, involved in a global project related to competing for the monopolisation of the goods of salvation within the context of the industrialisation of religion in the 21st century. After all, this business of creating and mediating meaning is an intensely material project that involves a variety of capital resources—social, economic, symbolic—and, importantly, power. These organisations are involved in the business of cashing in on the need for healing, comfort and emotional support, on the one hand, and a political contestation for the 'harvesting of souls', on the other. This latter project of religious nationalism and globalised harvesting of souls is supported by the imperial politics of the hour. Not only does Franklin Graham ride into Iraq aboard a US tank, the religious right, as is only too well known, reflects Bush at prayer and accounts for the specific morality of the Bush administration and global policy.

Bourdieu's (1991: 23) specific observations on the antagonistic relationship between the established Catholic Church in France and the upstart prophet can be applied to understanding the contemporary competition for souls, profits, power and influence:

> In order to perpetuate itself, to the extent that it manages to impose the recognition of its monopoly...the church tends to prohibit more or less completely the entry into the market of new enterprises of salvation, such as sects or any form of independent religious community, or the individual search for salvation.... It thus gains or protects a more or less total monopoly over an instructional or sacramental capital of grace...by controlling access to the means of production, reproduction, and division of the goods of salvation.

One can therefore see Benny Hinn as a representative of neo-Pentecostalism's fratricidal moves to assert its authority over Christian religious capital. While the power of religious authority structures in the 21st century is certainly less obvious than it was a century ago, the human search for answers to life's small and big questions, and religion's role in catering to such needs has led to, in the context of 'civilisational clashes' and religious nationalism, the strengthening of religion as a framework for identity, claims and competing truths.

How live audiences respond to performances is one level of consumption. But the aftermath of an event is an equally important level, for it is during the aftermath that accounts of the event—negative, positive or neutral—circulate. The almost daily availability of Benny Hinn on Christian channels such as GOD TV further the reinforcements of meaning.

From a methodological perspective, one of the questions related to textual analysis is whether the many meanings generated via mediation and face-to-face encounters of events like Benny Hinn should or should not be open to value judgements in the light of, in this case, the larger objectives of this study—Christian fundamentalism and the media in India. While each one's personal effort at meaning making and interpretation should not be discounted, more so in a context in which low church 'spectacles' such as Benny Hinn are routinely critiqued by the mainstream church hierarchy, it would seem that the need to understand how and why people make sense of the world should not prevent one from coming to a reasonable understanding of how and why such events signify the contested reality of religions in India.

While the Benny Hinn event in USA is grounded in a largely 'Christian' country—extant traditions of popular religiosity and the political economy of the neo-Pentecostal movement—the context in India is very different. Christianity in India is a growing minority religion and post-Independence India has been through three decades or more of intermittent inter-religious blood-letting—for instance, Hindu–Muslim and, less frequently, Christian–Hindu riots have led to the deaths of thousands of people. The Bhiwandi riots, the Godhra riots, the killings of priests and nuns, the rise of the Sangh Parivar, the rise of Islamic fundamentalism, the routinisation of Christian triumphalism, the intentional conversions of India's 'tribals' and their re-conversions by Hindu religious nationalists, and external, mainly US-based, support for mission and evangelism in India are reminders of the very real struggles over access to and control over religious capital in India.

India continues to have this very contested public context of religion despite being a secular nation constitutionally. There are those like Madan (1991) and Nandy (1990) who believe that the inability of the architects of the Indian Constitution to recognise the intensely religious nature of Indians contributed to the creation of false dichotomies between the religious and the secular, to the privileging of the secular over the religious, and to contemporary divides between the majority and minority religions in India. While the architects of post-Independence India were, in hindsight, extraordinarily generous in their conceptualisation of and support for this vision, especially after the preceding agony of the Partition, present-day Hindu nationalists chafe at what they believe is a patently unjust constitutional mandate, given the numerical dominance of the majority community. This public context and the many sub-texts that accompany it are a powerful reminder of the materiality of these discourses, of the consequential nature of politics in India and of the struggles to maintain tolerance in the context of the many instances of intolerance.

In other words, the specific 'field' of religion in India is an arena that is currently marked by intense forms of contestation over resources and 'souls'. Muslim–Hindu clashes over the right to trade and over specific occupations, and Christian–Hindu clashes over property as well as over proselytisation are among the key sites of struggle. With Independence, church property was also handed over to Indian Christians, which in the case of the Church of South India (CSI) includes prime properties in all the major cities and in suburban and rural areas. While internal corruption has been responsible for the wastage of church properties throughout India, the prospect of prime real estate is nevertheless a key aspect of religious contestation in India. To come back to the specific field of Christianity, the perceived elitism of the mainstream church in India consisting of the Protestant, Orthodox and Catholic; the continuing dilemmas over caste within the church; corruption within the church hierarchy and, in particular, the open embrace of materialism by the church hierarchy; and the perceived lack of spiritual presence are some of the factors that have led to the mushrooming of a variety of indigenous and externally-supported churches in India.

Benny Hinn and others like him, in their conspicuous use of stadiums, fields and other public arenas, clearly communicate their preference for the church as a people signifying the wholeness of Christ, as against the rampant denominationalism and church structures that are intrinsically particular, congregated by those who have specific badges of identity—Orthodox, Lutheran, Mar Thomas, and the like. The poor, the sick and the lame, the Dalit and the upper caste-Christian, and the software engineer and the domestic help were able to sit in the Jakkur airfield and listen to Benny Hinn without having to look over their shoulders. The fact that a Benny Hinn event is driven by hierarchy is often not perceived as such by ordinary people who participate in order to be touched and healed by a powerful miracle-maker and publicly confirmed man of God. This open invitation to all—Hindu or Christian, poor or rich, via posters, radio and television messages, and newspaper advertisements—acts as a powerful incentive and a crowd-puller, especially in the context of an otherwise hierarchy-conscious society. These carefully choreographed, symbolic acts of solidarity are all that more effective because they come from a charismatic individual who not only draws the crowds but also the eminent—from politicians to industrialists. In this sense, Benny Hinn, on one level, exudes the same kind of personality as film stars such as the Bollywood actor Amitabh Bachan, although he is not as easily accessible as a Benny Hinn. The Benny Hinn who hugs a 'Hindu' girl who has been healed of a heart impediment is like the hugging 'Amma' (Ma Amrita) whose trademark dispersal of love is through hugging people. One can argue that such forms of personal identification contribute to the humanisation of God. And that television plays an important role in extending these terms of endearment. Mediation, in this sense, is grounded in context and reflects the specificities of the context. The fact that Benny Hinn sanctifies the screen can be dismissed as the ruse of a God man who is trying to cultivate a global audience, although the fact that people believe in the power of the sanctified screen and offer *darshan* through manipulating the cursor or keyboard indicates that mediation ought to be assessed for what it is and means to people. The context of religious mediation has changed. These technologies have become an essential part of their lives.

Media critics of new Christianity often belong to another generation of scholars. William F. Fore (1987) and Neil Postman (1985), who have critiqued tele-evangelism and tele-evangelists, have based their critique on 'essentialist' understandings of what the church is and ought to be, what Christ stands for, what the experience of the church is, and so on. While the critique is spot-on when it comes to an assessment of the structure of tele-evangelism, the difference between the suffering church as opposed to the prosperity church, the obvious disjunctures between Liberation Theology and Prosperity Theology, and their inability to understand and, more importantly, empathise with the cultural shifts that have taken place within Christianity makes them open to critique themselves. Postman (1985: 116–17), for example, believes that the essence of religion is 'enchantment' not entertainment: 'Everything that makes a historically profound and sacred human activity is stripped away; there is no ritual, no dogma, no tradition, no theology, and above all no sense of spiritual transcendence. On these shows the preacher is tops. God comes out as second banana.' It can be argued that new Christians move away from the established churches precisely because they are tired of religion as tradition. In other words, we need to move towards an understanding of the sacred, in all its variety and diversity, as it is practised today. The framework for understanding these new discourses ought to be the present as well as the past, the reinventions of traditions as well as new traditions, the habitus of the new Christian. The need for cultural understandings of mediation, however, does not diminish the need for grounded, empirical understandings of the structure and political economy of mediated religion.

In fact, at the heart of the globalisation of religion is the market. It is the market that legitimises the Prosperity Theology, which is involved in re-creating Christianity for this world rather than the other world. It is the market that reinvents the message of Christ in the light of the needs of the new economy and the economic success story, which however partial, has become the story of India. As Benny Hinn, Crefilo Dollar and, for that matter, Sri Sri Ravi Shankar advocate, to be prosperous is to be blessed by God. After all who wants to be poor? Since all goods and services are aspects of God's blessings and bountiful goodness, religion ought to nurture prosperity, communicate the feel-good character of the Gospel message and emphasise Christ's largesse rather than his empathy. The market urges the church to identify with success—with the testimony of stock brokers, financiers and IT specialists who have been blessed by God—rather than identity with failure and the poor.

India is yet to witness the full frontal marketing of Christianity as is the case in USA and elsewhere. The Hebron bookshop in Chennai seemed to be the closest expression of what Christian marketing could eventually become. The online marketing of Christian goods remains a fledgling enterprise. Most other Christian bookshops in Chennai, including the outlets of the Evangelical Literature Society, seem rather old-fashioned and bereft of Christian paraphernalia. However, it is during crusades and conventions that there are large business opportunities for the merchandising of Christian products. At the Every Tribe and Tongue convention that was held in Chennai in early January 2006, there were many stalls that sold all sorts of Christian products—from Bibles to DVDs, CDs, stickers, crucifixes, book marks, and the like. From a political-economy perspective, it was interesting to observe that the CDs and VCDs that were exhibited and that featured Gospel music, the sermons of popular tele-evangelists and local evangelists, and coverage of Christian crusades, sold for Rs 60–150 and were, for the most part, pirated. I did buy a pirated copy of Benny Hinn's Festival of Blessing held in Bengaluru.

Postscript

There is a web page set up by a few of those who took part in the choir at the Benny Hinn event in Bengaluru. This site contains a narrative, an account of what was an extraordinarily spiritual event for most of those who took part in the 2000-strong choir. However, at the end of the account, there is a request that Benny Hinn Ministries make available the VCD of the event at a reduced price to choir members. The published price of this VCD was US$ 40 (Rs 1,800 at today's rate of US$ 1 = Rs 45) and, therefore, unaffordable for most of those who took part in the choir. Well, their prayers have been answered. This VCD is now available for only Rs 150 (http://www.geocities.com/ronnie.johnson/bennyhinn_choir. html?200624).

Having an interest in the cultural politics of the 'copy' (Thomas, 2006), I am impressed at the delicious irony of the free availability of pirated copies of the Benny Hinn extravaganza. While Benny Hinn makes his millions, others, in this case, all fervent Christians, also cash in and probably do a service to his ministry by making him more popular. The copyright WARNING at the back of this VCD says it all: 'The national [sic] on this VCD is protected by the copyright laws of the United Status [sic] and may not be reproduced in any manner.' Was it not the availability of Bibles through copying responsible for the Protestant Reformation in the 17th century?

Note

1. Also see Riddlebarger (1992). The website http://www.rickross.com/groups/ bennyhinn/htm contains numerous reports on the flamboyant pastor's colourful life.

References

Bhuskute, P. 2005. 'Merchants of Nirvana', *Deccan Chronicle*, 31 July.

Bourdieu, P. 1991. 'Genesis and Structures of the Religious Field', *Comparative Social Research*, 13: 1–44.

Caplan, L. 1987. 'Christian Fundamentalism as Counter Culture, in William F. Fore (ed.), *Television and Religion: The Shaping of Faith, Values and Culture*, pp. 366–81. Minneapolis, USA: Augsburg Publishing House.

Fore, William F. 1987. *Television and Religion: The Shaping of Faith, Values and Culture*. Minneapolis, USA: Augsburg Publishing House.

George, T.J.S. 2005. 'How to Abuse God with Lies and Boasts'. Available at http://www. conversionagenda.blogspot.com/2005/01/t-j-s-george-how-to-abuse-god-with-.htm, accessed on 16 February 2006.

Hinn, Benny. 2003. Quoted in *Christian Sentinel*. Available at http://www.cultlink.com/ sentinel/hinnqs.htmilable, accessed on 12 May 2004.

Riddlebarger, K. 1992. The Theology of Benny Hinn, available at http://www. modernreformation.org/krhinn.htm, accessed on 12 April 2006.

Madan, T.N. (ed.). 1991. *Religion in India*. New Delhi: Oxford University Press.

Nandy, A. 1990. 'The Politics of Secularism and the Recovery of Religious Tolerance', in V. Das (ed.), *Mirrors of Violence: Communities, Riots and Survivors in South Asia*, pp. 69–93. New Delhi: Oxford University Press.

New Oxford Dictionary of English. 2001. Second Edition. Oxford & NY: Oxford University Press.

Postman, N. 1985. *Amusing Ourselves to Death: Public Discourse in the Age of Show Business*. NY: Penguin Books.

Thomas, P.N. 2006. 'Uncommon Futures: Interpreting IP Contestations in India', in P.N. Thomas and J. Servaes (eds), *Intellectual Property Rights and Communication in Asia*. New Delhi, Thousand Oaks, London: Sage Publications.

Websites

http://www.bennyhinn.org/television/televisiondefault.cfm, accessed on 12 May 2005.

http://www.rickross.com/groups/bennyhinn/htm, accessed on 12 April 2006.

'Singing with the Strength of the Lord! The Benny Hinn Crusade Choir, Bangalore'. Available at http://www.geocities.com/ronnie.johnson/bennyhinn_choir.html?200624, accessed on 12 April 2006.

TOWARDS ANOTHER RELIGIOUS COMMUNICATION

9

COMMUNICATION AND THE SEARCH
FOR INTER-SUBJECTIVE FUTURES

Preceding chapters in this volume have dealt with low- and high-intensity versions of Christian fundamentalism in India reflected in Christian mission, the rise of Pentecostalism and neo-Pentecostalism, Christian broadcasting and online provocations. The failure of the mainstream churches to deal with the rise of aggressive forms of Christian mission is, as I have pointed out, a consequence of the perceived need for Christian unity in the light of the revival of Hindu nationalism, an attitude that has resulted in the accommodation of charismatic forms of expression within mainstream Christian traditions of worship. How to preach the 'Good News' in the context of the new India and its many confident religious communities remains a challenge to new and old churches, which remain impervious to the need to go beyond their representation of the other as a 'non-Christian'. This residual colonial arrogance needs to be contested by concerned Christians committed to another vision of religious pluralism in India. I have also tried to argue that contemporary expressions of mediated Christianity, with its narrow understanding of Christian identity, along with aggressive conversion drives, and India as a recipient of gross exports of Christian fundamentalism—missionaries, missions, dollars—have contributed to a rise in inter-faith tensions. While there is no denying the project of Hindutva and the aggressive attempts by members belonging to the Sangh Parivar to disrupt the freedom to worship and prevent celebrations of the Christian community, I have taken strong exception with the view that inter-faith tensions in India between Hindus

---

177

and Christians are caused exclusively by one community alone. GOD TV's Christian Zionism and brand of exclusive Christianity, the political machinations of local Pentecostal leaders in Chennai, evangelical spectacles such as the rallies organised by Benny Hinn Inc., and the organisation of militantly pro-conversion events such as the Every Tribe, Every Tongue convention in Chennai contribute to raising the ante—communicating a version of exclusive Christianity that a liberal Christian like myself along with many others in India certainly have serious misgivings about.

While India's tolerant traditions of existence and co-existence certainly have accommodated the most extreme types of religious radicalism over the centuries, contemporary forms of Christian fundamentalism are not by any stretch of the imagination wholly indigenous expressions of Christianity, but rather integrally related to agendas that have been created and globalised through predominantly US-based Christian missions and visions. The '10/40' window of the Joshua Project can be dismissed as a grandiose project of little consequence, although in relation to the Every Tribe, Every Tongue convention that I had attended in Chennai in January 2006, it took on a whole new meaning. While the broadcasting of religious television can present a larger than life picture of any given religious community as against their actual involvement in mission and conversion, the image conveyed by broadcasting can, in a context in which religious tensions are at significantly high levels, result in misunderstandings of the 'other' and their activities.

I have argued that low-intensity and high-intensity forms of Christian mission have contributed to the decline and, in some cases, the demise of common values in India. It has been suggested that the impact of this divisiveness is clearly visible in the breakdown of the moral community. This, in turn, has clouded the efforts by India to renew itself and to reinforce its identity as a nation of nations. Indians are yet to provide firm answers to that central question. Should that history be defined in the consolidations of a single community or the celebration and fulfilment of its many communities? The country seems to be engulfed by competing definitions of 'truth' and 'legitimacy'. These definitions often openly discount the need for common ground. In the presence of such divisive processes, it would seem absurd to suggest, let alone hazard, an exploration of common values. But the very presence of such negative trends provides the strongest rationale for engaging with the politics of the possible. There are no blueprints or shortcuts but plenty of barbed wire and fences, no answers but a myriad of questions, no light at the end of the tunnel, only a host of uncompensated memories and little prospects for any meaningful reconciliation. The questions then are: How does one make stable a mere flickering light? How does one practically engage in a context marked by non-engagement? How does one make a leap of faith precisely in the situation of a paradox, in the face of the absurd, in a context characterised by seemingly irreconcilable contradictions? There are other quandaries. To whom does it fall to make this leap of faith? Who is ultimately responsible for common values—the state, which some would claim say is withering away or, as the case may be, reconstituting itself in the light of the pressures of globalisation? What about the role of community, in particular the religious community, in the making of common values? What about civil society, that rather nebulous entity that is frequently given the mantle of humanisation? And what role should the media play in the making and communication of these values?

The making of common values is, in my way of thinking, the joint responsibility of the state, its 'nations', particularly its religious nations, civil society and the media. It is a joint project. It cannot be otherwise. Let us take up each in turn, these three major societal institutions that ought to be responsible for the initiation of projects and programmes linked to the extension of common values. While these three institutions are to be dealt with separately, they really ought to be seen in terms of their inter-relationships and their connectivities, mutually enriching the pursuit of common values.

The State

The Indian nation-state, or 'nations'-state has had a long, at times illustrious, at times woeful, record in the making of common values. In a sense, post-Independence India had no choice but to grapple with issues related to the project of common values. The Partition had torn the heart out of India, and the Indian State was faced with the unenviable task of building up a united India from the fragments, the simmering discontent and the bitterness. The plural visions of Mahatma Gandhi and Jawaharlal Nehru of a new India were not only destroyed by communalists within the Congress Party, but also by the exit politics of the British Raj as it manoeuvred its way out of a mess that it was partly responsible for creating in the first place. However, despite the birth of independent India in the context of violence and bloodshed, the Congress Party had, at its core, leaders who were visionaries committed to new plural beginnings for India. It is often said that it was the British who were responsible for carving India out as a nation from the many warring feudal nations that made up the land called Hindustan. Seen from an administrative perspective, that assumption is right. India was the 'jewel in the crown' and it was necessary that its nations were made part of a colony called India, at the least to expedite trade, commerce and the efficient exploitation of its resources. However, this making of colonial India was primarily a political project linked to the aspirations of empire-building. It was only secondarily and very loosely linked to a social project—the conscious creation of a plural nation. In fact, this latter intent was only sporadically affirmed, particularly during the times when the British were not at war with dissident groups in India, such as the challenge mounted by the southern king Tipu Sultan. In fact, the British left the many fiefdoms and principalities that made up their empire in India for the most part to their own devices. As long as taxes were paid and the rajahs and nawabs (Indian rulers) genuflected periodically to the King or Queen in Britain, there was little interference from the colonial power. There was quite a bit of 'divide and rule' but then that was a hallmark of the empire.

And so at Independence, the Congress Party inherited a number of 'Western' institutions—education, transportation, particularly the railways, administration, the judiciary, and so on. It also inherited a social fabric that was relatively untouched by the presence of the empire. For instance, it was only in the early 1970s with the abolishment of the Privy Purse, that the rajahs and nawabs were shorn of their many privileges. There were, of course, other factors too—the caste system, particularly its economic basis for exploitation and its links to bonded labour, widespread illiteracy, and so on. In other words, there was a huge gap between the institutions inherited by the Congress Party at the time of Independence and the masses of Indians who had little knowledge of what these institutions stood for or what Western forms of democracy were all about. The very idea of Delhi as the capital of India must have sounded strange for the ordinary Indian whose idea of the nation must have been limited by the boundaries set by caste, community and other immediate factors. In fact, even today, many Indians have little idea of where Delhi is located, let alone what it stands for. It is, in other words, too remote from the daily grind of ordinary people. Equally, other institutions such as education and the judiciary continue to remain at a distance from the expectations and experiences of the ordinary Indian.

So what did the Congress Party do to impart common values? Its primary response to the making of common values was by way of the Constitution. This was framed by a multi-religious and multi-cultural group of people who believed in common values engendered through respect for unity in diversity. In hindsight, these constitutional decrees did contribute to the making of a democratic and plural India. These constitutional guarantees were reflected in the policies on education, law and order, and the management of society adopted by central and state governments. Its agenda included options for the poor—affirmative actions related to employment, development, health, education and nutrition. Planned development furthered a programme of production linked to redistribution. Land reforms were enacted by both the central and state governments, although, with significant exceptions, these were not successful given the power of vested interests.

Like most constitutions, the Indian Constitution is not a perfect document and is vague on notions such as Indian identity. The notion of Indian culture and Indianness in the Constitution is, for example, not based on an understanding that reflects the reality of multi-cultural and multi-religious India, but instead based on an essentialised understanding, that is, Indian culture as coterminous with Hindu, Sanskritic culture.

In fact, it became clear from very early on that constitutional guarantees could not, by themselves, close the gaps between principle and practice, for instance, on the issue of land reforms or, for that matter, on caste-based discrimination. There has, of course, been some progress on these fronts, but not consistent, deliberate progress linked to a change in worldviews, behaviours and attitudes, for instance, on matters related to caste-based discriminations. These guarantees did not prevent government institutions from identifying with and communicating a specific expression of identity. An example of such divergence comes from the annals of broadcasting. All India Radio (AIR), the state-run network that today is the largest of its kind in the world, was formed under imperial auspices. The Reithian imprint on AIR was significant in its early days, although the concept of public broadcasting adopted was resolutely different from that of its mother institution, the BBC. One of AIR's stated objective was public service. The intent was as much to ingrain as to inform. The purpose of radio was to educate the ignorant, and to make people appreciative of Indian culture and its aesthetic traditions, in order to validate the all-Indian significance and legitimacy of this tradition. This discourse was in line with the Mathew Arnold/F.R. Leavis tradition in the UK that valued high culture above 'popular' culture (see Hoggart, 1957; Williams, 1958). AIR had a core of traditionalists on its staff, and for many years the music featured on AIR was predominantly Indian classical or religious. Before AIR realised the limits of such exclusive fare, its audiences deserted it en masse for Radio Ceylon that had a more enlightened 'music' policy, with an emphasis on the broadcast of Indian film-based music. This example is by no means an isolated one. It is no accident that the early serials on Indian television, the *Mahabharat* and the *Ramayan*, indirectly and directly contributed to the electoral prospects of the then nascent Hindu right wing.

In a sense, these examples illustrate the fact that there are significant limitations to making constitutional guarantees by decree and hoping for the best instead of following up on such guarantees through negotiating a culture of rights and responsibilities. The failure of the Pancasila, the constitutional guarantee for inter-faith amity in Indonesia, to protect the unity of the country is a striking example of the limitations of rule by decree. Similarly, the failure of Tito's Yugoslavia is another example of the limits of forced political and cultural unity.

There is a strong case for the state to distance itself from any involvement in the religious affairs of both majority and minority communities in India. If it is proving to be impossible to legitimise a uniform civil code as is the case in India today, then it is necessary for the state to try and evolve other ways by which its many communities can come to a greater self-realisation. The greater the self-realisation of the many communities that make up India, the better the prospects for a united nation.

In other words, what is needed is greater decentralisation on matters related to religion and the state in India. A uniform approach to management, based on a poor reading of pluralism, often results in the creation of bland, half-hearted strategies and in across-the-board type of solutions that do not offer justice to the multiple demands made by a heterogeneous polity. Take, for instance, the judicial system in India, which is an inherited institution. Its institutionalisation has led to the de-legitimisation of older forms of arbitration rooted in the traditions and cultures of village communities and indigenous groups. India is home to one of the world's largest population of indigenous communities —concentrated in some parts such as the Chota Nagpur Plateau in central India, but also living in dispersed settlements throughout the length and breadth of India, in the context of a great variety of habitats and environments. While the judiciary at the national and state levels has been responsible on occasion for landmark judgements leading to greater freedom and justice, its manifestations at regional and local levels have resulted in many travesties of justice. It would be an understatement to say that this labyrinthine system of justice has scarcely benefited the ordinary Indian who is yet to understand the workings of a city court let alone its judgements. And yet, all indigenous communities have their own systems of justice. These may not be perfect, but the possibility of gradual reform from within makes infinitely better sense than any tinkering with official systems of justice that are often encumbered by the sheer weight of their infrastructure, institutions, traditions and power brokers. I have, on a couple of occasions, witnessed the ways in which ordinary people, who are totally ignorant of the workings of the justice system, are treated in the local courts. In fact, the estimate that there are 30 million pending cases in the Indian courts, with an average of 20 years for dispute resolution, merely points to the fact that it could well be in the interests of the state to explore alternative bases for justice in addition to what is already in existence. The distance between such public institutions and the public signifies the larger failures of India. If the greatest need for communities in India is a sense of 'certainty', of being able to believe and belong, then our existing public institutions must go through a process of reform, and space ought to be given to the exploration of local solutions for local problems. Core identities need to be made secure. Only then will the many nations that inhabit India feel that they belong to the Indian nation.

These suggestions, in favour of state reform, do not imply that the state must forego its role in the shaping of India. Most definitely not. In fact, the state needs to play an important role in creating an environment for change and for supporting the institutions for change. In the present context of Indian politics, these responsibilities will have to include the reining in of the religious right wing in India, the espousal of inclusive national policies and support for the project of nation building, based on justice for all.

While the present Congress-led coalitional government will baulk at the prospect of engaging with minority religions in India, given the record of the previous government, it nevertheless needs to be involved in maintaining the framework for democracy in India. In this regard, and in the context of the subjects discussed in this book, there is certainly merit in the proposed Broadcasting Services Regulation Bill, 2006, that is intended to provide a framework for satellite and cable televisions—enterprises that have, for all practical purposes, been left to develop without the benefit of broad regulatory oversight. The proposed Broadcast Regulatory Authority of India is needed in a context in which multiple broadcasting means have gone ahead of the reach of the state's regulatory power. One can, of course, agree with the view that after decades of centralised control, media diversities ought to be guaranteed. Cable and satellite channels have certainly contributed to the creation of regional identities, and enabled the celebration of creativity and innovation in the areas of tele-visual information, entertainment and education. However, as it has been noted in Chapter 6, monopoly broadcasting remains a reality in the era of cable and satellite broadcasting. Together with the state monopoly on terrestrial television and most types of radio, private monopolies have begun to define cable and satellite television and FM radio. While the media industry and the Opposition have predictably critiqued this Bill for its perceived excesses, the fact that it has addressed issues of public concern inclusive of the issue of media ownership, the need for a level playing field, genuine media diversity and public service obligations makes it important for the public and civil society. The fact that the public was not involved in the making of this Bill remains a serious concern that has been raised by the Indian media academic Ammu Joseph (2006), although her critique does commend the Bill's inclusion of issues related to media ownership. The subject of media ownership is absolutely critical. And it would seem that both corporate broadcasters who are spearheading the broadcast revolution in India today and the Indian State that has used licensing as a means of raising large amounts of revenue routinely ignore the 1995 Supreme Court ruling which affirmed that the airwaves are public property. If this indeed is the case, then the state has a responsibility to ensure that those who are licensed to use a scarce public resource, use it in the best interests of the public. This includes the need to regulate religious broadcasting in the interests of maintaining religious harmony.

The following section from the draft Bill (2006) highlights the government's powers to restrict broadcasting that is deemed to be against the public interest:

> Central Government to exercise certain powers in public interest: The Central Government may at any time, if it appears necessary or expedient to do so in public interest, in respect of any broadcasting service, which is considered prejudicial to friendly relations with a foreign country, public order, communal harmony or security of the State, direct the Licensing Authority to suspend or revoke its license or direct the service provider to stop broadcasting its service or transmit in its broadcasting service such announcements in such manner as may be considered necessary, and the service provider shall immediately comply with all or any such directions.

While there needs to be transparency and due process in the government's implementation of such action, this clause needs to be seen primarily in its role in deterring broadcasters, inclusive of religious broadcasters, from broadcasting prejudice. The freedom to broadcast cannot be an absolute freedom. And broadcasters within the country, from the Christian Broadcasting Network (CBN) and GOD TV to local religious channels, need to abide by the responsibilities of broadcasting in a multi-religious and multi-cultural society. While private news media players have critiqued this Bill's content restrictions, I think that it is important that we clarify the nature of news, and the difference between news and religion-based news, in particular the version found on *The 700 Club* and Alec and Wendy's news reports on GOD TV. The project of common values is jeopardised by agendas such as the following highlighted on GOD TV with the title 'God has not forgotten the Sikh':

> Unlike Southern India where Christianity has made more of an impact, the North of India has been spiritually dry up until now. But thanks to the work of many missionaries and their organisations, the labour of past years is starting to bear fruit and a rich harvest is at hand. God TV is privileged to contribute to this by playing an effective role as media missionaries, with a divine mandate to reach the lost and equip the church through television (http://us.god.tv/Publisher/ Article.aspx?id=1000007742).

There may be those who are prepared to dismiss this rhetorical style as merely a case of excess verbosity. However, if the text is not just seen as language but also as a vehicle that is the basis for communicative action for discordant ends, then there is a need for the state to be involved in creating the framework for broadcasting rights and responsibilities in an era of convergence and new media. Free speech should not be used as a pretext for denigrating people of a faith that is not one's own. In the present context of the war against terror, the need for us to be especially careful is obvious enough.

Media Ownership, Scarcity and Religious Broadcasting

De-regulation, privatisation, and the easing of restrictions on monopolies and cross-sectoral media ownership have not only led to the emergence of a breed of local entrepreneurs, but also to business convergences between old business families and new economic opportunities. The Tatas, the Ambanis, the Thapars, the Modis and the Birlas are among venerable business families in India that, today, have substantive interests in the telecom and media sectors. In fact, these groups have cornered large sectors of the media market. Consolidation is the name of the game today.

This very same pattern of consolidation has affected the Internet Service Provider (ISP) market. In 2006, there were 183 ISPs in India out of which 49 had all-India licences. It is interesting that these 49 companies over-represent the ranks of the already advantaged, with the Tatas involved in at least four companies—Tata Communications, Tata Teleservices, Tata Internet Services Ltd and Tata Power Company. (This is a moving feast and things change fast in this sector, given all the mergers and alliances. Tata Power Company obtained an ISP license in 2000.) The Tatas are also involved in Direct to Home (DTH) television services through Tata Sky— a collaboration with the Rupert Murdoch's UK-based Sky Broadcasting Group. Consolidation has also characterised the FM radio market in India. The Chennai-based Sun Network—owned by the Maran family and currently the second largest media house in the country—owns 20 television channels along with seven FM radio stations and has significant interest in the Tamil vernacular press. Suryan FM is currently the market leader in Tamil Nadu and Andhra Pradesh. Bennett, Coleman & Co. Ltd, owned by Samir Jain, is the largest media house in India with significant interests in print (*The Times of India*, *The Economic Times*, and so on) and FM radio (Radio Mirchi) as well as online interests inclusive of the top Internet company Indiatimes.com. The satellite and cable television market has also been affected by consolidation. The Zee TV empire, which is the largest of the home-grown media empires, has become even larger following its acquisition of the south India-based Asianet channel.

There is a case to be made that the media is a scarce commodity. It is a commodity with a difference because unlike ordinary commodities—soap, toothpaste and biscuits—media products affect consciousness, what we think, and how we assign value to ideas, ways of behaviour, and ways of conceptualising the world and 'others'. So it does matter what we read, see and hear on a daily basis. While there is a school of thought that believes people have the innate capacity to figure out texts for themselves and make sense of the version of reality on offer (and I would agree that some people do this habitually), for the vast majority of us, media products are a given and we are not, as audiences, inclined towards deconstructing texts. One can argue that the average Indian Christian who listens to Joyce Meyer or Benny Hinn, listens to the message in order to learn something about the connections between religious values and everyday life, and to reinforce and validate personal experience and attitudes. While Benny Hinn as a person and institution can certainly be deconstructed, his audiences do not do this as a matter of course, nor, for that matter, does the average devotee of Sai Baba spend time dissecting his message or his lifestyle. Thomas and Mitchell (2005), in their study of television viewing among Mar Thoma families in Kerala, make the point that unlike audiences in the West for whom non-religious media commodities have become a source of spiritual values, these families ascribe religious values only to specifically religious products. One can, in other words, argue that the specific and pervasive reality of established religion as practised in India, routine modes of religious identification and pre-existent traditions of religion as popular culture, pre-empt and prevent audience identifications and negotiations of religion with secular media products—for example, the popular programme *Buffy the Vampire* in USA.

So what does the preceding section on media ownership have to do with the religious television market in India? Media concentrations can result in the commodification of culture. More importantly, however, media concentrations can lead to one-dimensional productions of meaning as an exercise of power. Both Fox TV, which has backed the US government's military interventions in Iraq, and the Australian national newspaper *The Australian*, which supported the previous government's anti-terror campaign, are owned by Murdoch's News Corporation. Mergers and acquisitions have not yet affected the religious television industry in India. Given the fact that the Christian television market in India is quite small, and there is limited possibility for using it as a platform to sell religious goods and services, it would seem that for the foreseeable future, this industry will remain as it currently is, with perhaps a few enterprising Christian businesses using the Internet for a variety of online services including radio and video on demand, for example, Num TV, which is owned by the Chennai-based Jesus Calls. There are no local channels to 'consolidate' as it were and the scenario is, therefore, different from that in Brazil, where the Rede Record TV Network owned by the neo-Pentecostal Universal Church of the Reign of God has been used in the wars of position being waged against the Catholic Church and its de facto supporter TV Globo (Birman and Lehmann, 1999).

In India, sooner than later, there will be attempts to start family oriented, Christian values-based channels, given the potential for a larger multifaith audience and the possibility, therefore, of spreading the message of the Gospel to 'non'-Christians. For the moment, the ability of conservative churches to control flows of mediated discourses on Christianity will restrict the circulation of multiple understandings of Christianity and meanings that are not a part of the Pentecostal and neo-Pentecostal imaginary.

The correspondences between the worship experience on a Sunday, rallies such as those organised by Benny Hinn and local evangelists, Christian networking and mission, Christian radio and literature, and tele-visual worship experiences has led to a circulation of singular meanings, to the making of narratives that can be accessed in a living room, alluded to during Sunday worship in church and in the context of a crusade. This vertical and horizontal integration of meaning making, offline and online, has contributed to the making of a relatively new public discourse of Christianity in India. It is in this sense that one can argue that contemporary Christian television in India has played a key role in privileging Christian discourse characterised by limited discursive openness. And in this context, Bourdieu's analysis of the contestation between priest and prophet, and the politics of 'misrecognition' certainly applies to Christian broadcasting in India.

One question that remains to be answered is the extent to which Christian broadcasting in India has strengthened and reinforced the notion of belongingness to a Christian *umma*, and the extent to which that has weakened ties with the idea and reality of India as a nation. Is it the case that globalised pentecostalism, a 'religion made to travel', has led to a fracturing of national identity and towards the creation of larger and wider allegiances beyond the territorial confines of any given nation-state? Has global Pentecostalism in India led to the formation and assertion of a specific Indian Christian identity and to the displacement of the mainstream version of Christian identity? While politicians in India routinely occupy prominent space during religious rallies in India, the fact that the Finance Minister of India P. Chidambaram and a variety of local Dravida Munnetra Kazhagam (DMK) leaders were present at the Every Tribe, Every Tongue convention and that Pentecostal leaders are respected by politicians for the vote-banks that they represent, seem to indicate the shifts that have occurred from the dominance and influence of 'Great' mainstream Christianity towards the dominance and power of the 'Little' traditions of Pentecostal Christianity. While there are a number of differences between the context of Pentecostalism in Brazil and the rise of the Universal Church of the Reign of God, on one hand, and the situation in India, on the other, the following quote from Birman (2006: 54), illustrates the ways in which mediation has helped a little church in Brazil become a dominant player, a process that is also now germane to the situation in India:

By generating new meanings for religion and politics, while simultaneously mixing the religious with business and finance, the Universal

Church creates spectacular events and media personalities out of the ways in which various distinct levels and spheres are associated, hierarchized, altered and extended. Despite its quasi-official standing and its enduring links with the Brazilian state, the Catholic Church has so far failed to match the success of the Universal Church in projecting a close association between state, pulpit, and the virtual domain on such a grandiose scale, a success that now threatens the catholic hegemony.

I strongly believe that the moves to create a 'federal' future in India will certainly allow not only imagining a new India but also living in a new India. There are those who believe that the state is congenitally incapable of delivering on its promise of common values and that this task ought to be left to civil society. While the track record of the Indian State certainly leaves a lot to be desired, there have been occasions, such as during the post-Emergency period, when the country was united in its defence of common values. In spite of the fact that this interregnum was brief, contradictory and non-sustainable, it nevertheless did provide the intellectual resources to think through the making of another India.

Civil Society

Civil society has routinely been assigned the task of creating a new vision of India. But this rather nebulous term has always been taken as a given and rarely been interrogated. In the context of India, it is a term that is closely identified with the rhetoric of the global left to describe the progressive, democratic sector, and the activities sponsored by this sector towards the creation of a new, just India. This interpretation of the meaning of civil society stands in contrast to one of its original meanings—as the sector that the state uses to legitimise and facilitate its hegemony over society and rule by consent. This Gramscian understanding of civil society needs to be revived for it enables more complex readings of civil society. While there are 'a million mutinies' against the established order at any given time in India, these would not all fall under the purview of 'civil society' as the term is globally understood to be—the space between organised politics and the market, inhabited by those who give substance and shape to people's rights and to a functioning democracy. The rubric of civil society offers the space for a variety of actors involved in a variety of causes that have progressive and regressive objectives.

The reality is that there are multiple groups and interests at work in India today. Some are working towards making the state accountable—making sure that it fulfils its constitutional guarantees with respect to freedom, justice and equality. Others are involved in creating local spaces for human freedom—the emancipation of bonded labourers, Dalits and women. There are numerous groups involved in fighting to keep the privileges of caste, class and the established order. Still others are involved in preserving and maintaining traditions—traditions that may be deemed conservative by Western liberal standards, but that are essential to keeping community ways of life and a sense of certainty alive. In the context of a mono-cultural globalisation, with all its attendant anxieties, the struggle to hold on to 'tradition' is now being waged as a struggle for freedom. The blanket invocation of civil society is made complicated by the fact that institutions on the right, most prominently the fascist Rashtriya Swayamsevak Sangh (RSS), have, in the past, pursued anti-globalisation and pro-people policies with more vigour than the traditional left. Granted that such organisations are motivated by a communalist agenda, such examples nevertheless point to the complex nature of popular struggles in India that can never be fully understood within received understandings of civil society.

These freedom struggles that are being waged at different levels and intensities, sometimes in the pursuit of contradictory, sometimes progressive, sometimes even reactionary, goals constitute in their entirety and complexity, the public expressions of India. These are, despite the contradictions and divergences, the most valuable spaces for the creation of common values.

The church does play an important role in some of these struggles, although its visions of liberation are sometimes just too particular to make sense to ordinary Indians. It is also the space where experiments in living, in the extensions of the 'daily dialogue of life' and in the making of inter-subjective futures, are being explored. These projects range from intentional initiatives in the areas of inter-faith dialogue, inter-faith projects aimed at combating communalism, projects aimed at heightening the awareness of traditions of tolerance within faith communities, their literature, culture and ethos, on the one hand, to countless instances of people living their lives as they always have, on the other. Even Ayodhya, the location for what was perhaps the most trying moment for the 'secular' state in independent India—the demolishment of the Babri Masjid, has had traditions of religious tolerance and inter-faith relationships that Indians outside that city hardly know of. Muslims and Hindus had co-existed for years in Ayodhya.

Such traditions of daily discourse stand in marked contrast to the attitude of 'Born again' Christians for whom traditions of consangnuity are an anathema. I am reminded of a story narrated by the ecumenical theologian and inter-faith dialogist Wesley Ariarajah (1999: 126–28) in his book *Not Without My Neighbour*. He was travelling by train from Jaffna to Colombo. The person sitting next to him was a scholarly Hindu with whom he had a conversation going. When the train stopped at a station, a group of young 'train evangelists' boarded the train. These are people who go from compartment to compartment distributing evangelistic literature and giving personal witnesses. One of them came over to where Wesley and his fellow traveller were seated and proceeded to narrate his testimony. The testimony dealt with how he had led a dissolute life and how he had come to find a new life in Christ. When the young man had completed his discourse and moved on, Arairajah, who was embarrassed at this uninvited preacher's lack of sensitivity, asked his Hindu neighbour what he had made of the sermonising.

> Did the testimony of the young man force my Hindu friend into a reflection on the fleeting nature of human life? No, it turned out that he was in fact thinking about the young man and his testimony. 'How old do you think this young man would be?', he asked me. 'Well, perhaps sixteen or seventeen,' I replied. There was silence. And then, the question: 'Now that he has found salvation at the age of seventeen, what is he going to do with the rest of his life?' (ibid.).

Reflecting on his comment, Ariarajah points out that this question was by no means meant as a slight. It was wholly genuine. For in the particular Hindu tradition his co-traveller belonged to, Saiva Siddhanta, salvation was a life-time's pursuit that was by no means assured even for those who were 'born again'.

Community

The search for common values is critically also the responsibility of communities in India. By community I mean collectives of people, contiguous or dispersed, who are united by tradition, culture, ethnicity, religion, gender, enthusiasm and belief, who inhabit local or transnational spaces and who connect offline, online or both. Rather than deal with community as an abstraction, I would like to briefly focus on the Protestant Christian community in India.

The singular Christian community in India, in reality, consists of a great variety of traditions and denominations. There is, for instance, variety even within the Orthodox tradition—the two larger churches in this tradition co-exist with smaller churches (for example, the Knanaya Syrian Ortho-dox Church), which are presided over by a single bishop and made up of a few parishes. The Protestant tradition is inclusive of the mainline churches—those who are a part of the conciliar movement, along with those from the evangelical, Pentecostal and neo-Pentecostal churches who inhabit both the centre and the periphery. The Mar Thoma Church is distinctive, unique and different from other churches in the Protestant tradition and yet it is, at the same time, related to these other traditions. Commonality and difference or commonality in spite of difference is a fact of life as it is encountered through the institutions that structure our lives. However, the larger objective of conciliation is, I would argue, despite some success, constrained by the reality of denominationalism and by a lack of identity. The latter problematic—the identity of the Indian Christian church—continues to be, in spite of numerous attempts to de-fine it, the central blind spot of the church in India. There have perhaps been too many efforts to define identity and not enough efforts devoted to practising it. As it has been all too often the case, definitions of Indian Christian identity have been constructed by theologians, church-based knowledge-brokers, those who sit on committees and those who exercise power. The ordinary member of the church in India has seldom been given an opportunity to express his or her views on such issues as Christian identity. Inevitably, therefore, the understandings that prevail are the ones that are couched in the tradition of grand ecumenical narratives that are often strong on the rhetoric of 'justice' and 'peace', but weak on everyday practicalities, in particular on the need to root this identity in everyday life. And in the era of televised neo-Pentecostalism and the market, ro-bust, separatist versions of Indian Christian identity are available for pub-lic consumption. A number of questions that have been posed by Christian groups in the past await answers. What does it really mean to be an Indian and a Christian living in present day India? How does one be a witness for Christ in India? How can this witness be best made in a context characterised by a multitude of faith traditions? How best can that faith be communi-cated through our practice of faith—in the ritual and everyday spheres of life? While there have been isolated instances of indigenisation such as experimentation with indigenous liturgies, these have, more often than not, been communicated in the rarefied environments of theological semi-naries and/or in the context of international ecumenical meetings.

The fact that such expressions have become little more than a tourist attraction to be gazed and gaped at, often by bewildered visitors, is a comment on the state of indigenous expressions of Christian faith in India. The church as the corporate witness of Christ does have a long way to go in making Christ meaningful to India and Indians.

Communion

So what minimum rules are required for a sharing of common values among the faiths in India? For a start, shared respect for the diversity of faith expressions in India. India is not only the birthplace of Hindu tradition but also of Buddha, Mahavira, and the multifarious 'little' traditions of popular Hinduism and indigenous 'tribal' faith expressions. Add to it the presence of an albeit tiny Jewish tradition, an ancient Orthodox church and the continuing presence of Sufi traditions, along with newer faith expressions, and what you have is the most religiously diverse country in the world. Such affirmations of faith need to be seen as the heritage of the country—the basis for its renewal. This is a blessing and a gift, the wonder of India. However, matters are not made easy by pronouncements like, for example, the recent one made by the Pope in which he rather casually marginalised the Islamic tradition as a tradition of violence. In the context of a highly charged inter-religious context, such arrogance only creates opportunities for counter-arrogance and unfortunately also for inter-religious conflict. It merely reinforces the vision of a crusadic church, irrelevant to the needs of a modern world, like the vision captured in Ingmar Bergman's classic film *The Seventh Seal*.

The conciliatory church, on the other hand, is one that embraces the vision of Christ for all, expressed through all his people. This, however, is no mean task. For, the church needs to be prepared and ready to understand the 'other'. Unfortunately, that preparation today is at the level of the mind, not at that of the heart. The church is readily critical of other faiths but only rarely recognises the spiritual gifts inherent to other faith traditions. Swami Abhishiktananda (1983: 5–6), in his book *Hindu-Christian Meeting Point*, describes the attitude needed by a Christian and the impressions that may result from such an encounter. Honesty and acceptance can sometimes result in rewards far exceeding expectations.

When he meets this experience, which has been handed down through countless ages and is still living in the hearts of the holy men of India,

193

the Christian can only adore in reverent silence the mystery of God and the unsearchable ways of his providence. As long as he is conditioned by his Western upbringing, he may well be disconcerted by the outward expression of this experience at the level of religion—prayer, formularies, rites, etc. But, if the Spirit has already communicated to him some awareness of the innermost depths of his own soul and has made him sensitive to the unfathomable silence of God, when he first comes into contact with the true spiritual tradition of India, the words which he reads or hears will awaken a profound response within him, as though they had been born from the depths of his own spiritual experience. Then, still unable to understand, much less explain, what is happening, he will find himself exclaiming 'This is the finger of God!'— the finger of God who is the Holy Spirit, as the Fathers perceived in their meditation on the Gospel (cp. Matthew 12:28, Luke 11:20).

How can one translate 'communion' into an authentic broadcasting? Should there be moves to establish multi-faith broadcasting services in India that are run by representatives from faith communities? What stands in the way of the establishing of such initiatives? I believe the current domination of Christian broadcasting in India by neo-Pentecostal or charismatic groups is not a healthy situation because this broadcasting does not reflect the diversity that is Christian India. Prosperity Theology in the Word-Faith tradition that is promoted by the Sam Chelladurai Ministries, D.G. Dhinakaran, Christian Zionism, support for US imperial conquests and geo-politics, a narrow understanding of the Gospel message, the negation of other faiths and the vision of pluralist India that is a stock feature on *The 700 Club*, Gospel for Asia, GOD TV and other channels—such expressions need to be challenged through another approach to broadcasting.

A 'Vision TV' for India?

I have, in this book, referred to the Canada-based Vision TV as an example of what religious broadcasting could also become. Launched in 1988 in Toronto by an ecumenical council including the Uniting Church of Canada, it is now owned by S-VOX, a multimedia enterprise that is specifically involved in faith-based initiatives that include One: the Body, Mind & Spirit channel, Vision TV International and a pod-casting service called myGodPod. Featuring documentaries, lifestyle programmes, drama and reflective, Vision TV's two programming streams, *Mosaic* and *Corner-stone* showcase the diverse religious and spiritual heritage. Seventy-five faith groups from seven religious communities including Hinduism, Sikhism, Islam, Judaism and Christianity regularly feature on Vision TV. Evangelical Christians also feature, though this group prefers to remain on uncontaminated platforms. Vision TV has not only supported innovative programming, won industry awards and supported independent production, but also demonstrated that faith communities can share a common broadcasting space and platform. The need for such a service in multi-religious societies like India need not be underemphasised. There is a lot that can be gained from an inclusive approach to religious broadcasting—from a larger appreciation of different religious traditions to a greater understanding of one's own religion in the context of other faiths.

VISION TV, Canada's Faith Network, was created to illuminate and reflect the broad range of religion and faith subscribed to by our country's diverse population. Our purpose is to affirm the journey of faith and to promote understanding, tolerance and where possible, cooperation between faiths and cultures. We are licensed to broadcast religious programs produced by the full spectrum of eligible religious and faith communities, and to present general interest programs that explore, or are inspired by spiritual, moral, ethical and humanitarian concerns (Vision TV).

The success of the project of common values is dependent on our coming to grips with and finding equanimity in the midst of the paradox expressed in the following lines: 'Liberalism, tolerance and pluralism incline us to find pleasure in the idea of a multiplicity of visions; the desire for objectivity, and universality, on the other hand, leads us to desire that truth be but one, not many' (Gellner, 1985: 83). To those of us who have lived in the midst of plural environments, this is a challenge we cannot but face. Perhaps this tension is destined to haunt us, exposing not only the frailty of the human condition but also the human urge to transcend that condition.

The Church and Communication: Then and Now

There was a time and period when the encounter between religion and media was a two-way process in the sense that there was once some reciprocity in influences—for example, there were close correspondences between the emergence of text-based communications in the West, even broadcasting in its early days, and the ethical framework of public communication which, to some extent, reflected sensibilities and priorities purchased from Christian ethics. I am aware that one must not overstate the case, for the advent of text-based communication also led to the gradual de-centring of religious 'authority', to the reinterpretation of hitherto closely guarded texts, to the reading of multiple meanings, to the eventual privatisation of relationships with God and to the increasing emphasis on the democratisation of communication. In the context of the church in post-colonial India—characterised by a loss of privilege, the reality of pluralism, rampant secularisation, the ascendance of image-based technologies, the decentring of the written text and the rapid spread of consumerist values—it would seem that no religion in India has sufficient influence to bear on the ethics of public communication. As the gulf between technological change and the shrinking capacity of religion to influence such changes continues to grow, religion has fast been reduced to a mere consumer of technology. This is of course a global phenomenon.

The Malaise of Instrumentality

Convinced of its objectivity, neutrality, and power and capacity to regenerate the fortunes of the church, there is a tangible move by some churches in Asia to contemplate mega-media projects. The dissemination of this way of thinking about technology has led to a pervasive instrumentalism that is extremely difficult to counter. To some extent, this tendency towards instrumentalism has been germane to the mainstream church in Asia, but it was constrained by national media legislations and the need for capital-intensive investments. All this is beginning to change. Economic liberalisation, deregulation and new technologies, along with shrinking costs, have given the church new options. The evangelical churches have traditionally been pacemakers in this respect. These traditions are normally founded on the primacy of 'proclamation' rather than that of 'witness'. They implicitly accept that every successive communication technology is a gift from God to be used to further the Kingdom. They have plugged into this revolution with great gusto all over Asia. Their approach is instrumentalist, intensely pragmatic and in tune with the commercial logic of the times—they sell God as a product for a living and their task is limited to persuading people to consume that value-added product with its promise of salvation. To them, new technologies are merely new weapons for an old crusade. Their clearly enunciated, singular plan of action is visible in the objectives of the Trans World Radio, the Far Eastern Broadcast Association (FEBA), GOD TV and Shalom TV, and the websites of organisations such as AD2000 and the Accelerating International Mission Strategies.

Many church leaders belonging to the mainstream churches in Asia have been tempted to do likewise—for instance, to get into broadcasting in a big way. This has led to the creation of multi-million dollar institutions such as the Christian Broadcasting Service in Seoul and, predictably, to spectacular failures as the demise of the Bangkok-based Asian Christian Television (a Thai Sky Company owned Catholic satellite television service). Behind such forays is an implicit belief in the power of the media—that ownership of the media will somehow revitalise the presence and power of the church, in a context in which that power is rather severely proscribed by cultural, economic and political factors.

The late Indian Jesuit scholar Anthony de Mello, in his book *The Song of the Birds* (1998: 97), has a story that can be used to illustrate the predicament and the consequences of accepting the power of the status quo, be it related to technology, politics or economics:

> The philosopher Diogenes was dining on bread and lentils. He was seen by the philosopher Aristippus who lived in considerable comfort by fawning on the king. Said Aristippus 'Learn subservience to the king and you will not live on lentils'. Said Diogenes 'Learn to live on lentils and you will not have to cultivate the king'.

If the church in India is truly concerned with communion and solidarity, I think that it is time that it does not take a back seat on such issues. In a context characterised by a surfeit of media opportunities, will the church jump on to the media bandwagon or will it opt for an approach that will lead to larger solidarities and to the extension of the right to communication. Given the choice, will the church in India, for example, opt for an exclusively Christian broadcasting channel or will it opt for an inter-faith approach such as the successful Vision TV in Toronto, Canada? Is the church in India willing and in a position to make this leap forward or is it doomed to replicate an instrumentalist and narrow logic in its uses of communication? Not as long as it continues being parochial when it should be denominational, being denominational when it should be ecumenical, and being narrowly Christian when it should be human?

Almond et al. (2003), in a book entitled *Strong Religion*, have observed that the rise of Christian fundamentalism in south India has been a response to Hindu revivalism. I have argued in this book that this reason certainly needs to be accounted for in any attempt to understand the growth of Christian fundamentalism in India. However, it is not the only reason. There is a need to reckon with the political economy of global Christian fundamentalism, the export of aggressive forms of Christianity, the political power wielded by the Christian right in USA (Mike Allen [2006: 32], in an article in *Time Magazine*, has claimed that the 'republican evangelical base...makes up nearly a third of the party's electorate'), as well as the war of position being fought within Indian Christianity today between the mainstream churches and the Pentecostal and neo-Pentecostal churches, and there is a need to interrogate Christian broadcasting's role as a foot-soldier for the cause of conservative expressions of Christianity. David Harvey (2003: 191) reminds us of some aspects of this new imperialism:

> The influence of the Christian right cannot be underestimated. The failure to place any constraints on Sharon's violent repression of the Palestinians (interpreted by fundamentalists as a positive step towards Armageddon) is a case in point. And in the conflict with the Arab world it is hard not to let these attitudes slip into the rhetoric of a Christian crusade versus an Islamic jihad.

Last but not least, there is a need to contest the tendency by these groups to:

> interpret local disputes as part of a larger pan-regional and pan-Indian conflict...embrace the literal and political interpretation of Scripture and/or the supernatural charismatic authority of individual leaders and spiritual adepts...and emphasise corporate identity, promote symbols of 'true' Christianity, and repudiate emblems and forms of worship that express common ground with Hindus and Muslims in the same densely populated sacred landscape (Almond et al., 2003: 183).

Likewise, systematic questionings of the cultural environment that we are all a part of needs to become an important part of Christian practice for the church in India. The question related to who should participate in and control the cultural environments that we all live our lives in cannot be directed to or answered by the political, economic and cultural Caesars of our world. That is a task for all concerned communicators including those belonging to the church in India.

Combating Mediated Religious Fundamentalism

In October 2006, Prof. Scott Appleby, University of Notre Dame and one of the co-editors of the five-volume series on fundamentalism (University of Chicago Press), presented a keynote at a conference on fundamentalism and the media held at the University of Colorado, Boulder. In an address entitled 'Waging Peace through the Media: What We Can Learn from the Fundamentalists', Appleby presented five 'media-savvy practices of fundamentalists' (pp. 13–14) that could form the basis for a counter-response from 'peace builders'. In the context of this book, these five practices relate to the need for concerned Christians in India, who may or may not be part of the mainstream church, to:

1. Reclaim the symbolic narrative of Christianity—the Jesus truth—and frame the myth in such a way that it communicates Christianity as a dynamic, inclusive religion that has commonalities with other faiths and people. Illustrate this dynamism through stories of Indians, past and present, from Gandhi to a Medha Patkar, people of faith and for that matter no faith who have through their life and works communicated the essential message of Jesus Christ—peace, love and justice. This narrative of the 'Great Commission' will stand in stark contrast to understandings currently propagated by fundamentalist churches.

2. Propagate this ideology of peace, love and justice as the message of the Gospel, through images but also through text. The need for the mainstream church in India to engage with images and intervene through images is of critical importance. While mainstream Protestant churches in India traditionally have had a problem with 'images' and the symbolic, it cannot stand by in an era in which hyper-textuality has come to define life itself.

3. Get involved in 'spinning' alternative truths. Scott Appleby refers to the truth of peace-making in Belfast. There are any number of stories of reconciliation, peace-building and communities involved in justice in India. Such stories of social change, not charity; people 'doing' the Word, rather than preaching it; the message in action, rather than the message itself, which is the stock in trade of tele-evangelists; communicating the miraculous and miracles; and healing as the result of communities working together and bringing about reconciliation and social change, rather than the result of intermediaries like Benny Hinn or Sarah Hughues need to be highlighted in our communication and media strategies.

4. The need for concerned Christians to get involved in the media—old media and new media—and for church leaders to understand that 'in the 21st century, the mass media, especially the electronic media, is *a*, perhaps *the*, paramount interpreter, framer, creator of meaning and mobilizer'(Appleby, 2006: 15).
5. The need for concerned Christians to continually present, demonstrate, validate and re-validate the core of these alternative messages—since on any given day Christian television channels have a maximum of 4–6 hours of original programmes, while the rest are repeats, and repeats reinforce the message.

In addition, there are a number of other strategies that concerned Christians ought to consider:

1. Seriously consider the need for an inter-faith broadcasting channel or/and faith-based broadcasting based on values that are different from those espoused by tele-evangelists.
2. Reclaim public space through organising rallies that celebrate community, peace-making and reconciliation.
3. Consider adopting outreach strategies perfected by the neo-Pentecostalists—from effective pastoral ministries to youth-based initiatives that recognise the needs, problems and solutions for people living in either the slipstream of globalisation or at its very core, losers and winners.

References

Allen, M. 2006. 'Can a Mormon be President', *Time*, 4 December, pp. 30–32.

Almond, G.A., R.S. Appleby and E. Sivan. 2003. *Strong Religion: The Rise of Fundamentalisms around the World*. Chicago & London: The University of Chicago Press.

Appleby, S. 2006. 'Waging Peace through the Media: What We Can Learn from the Fundamentalists', paper presented at the Fundamentalisms and Media conference, University of Colorado, Boulder, 10–12 October.

Ariarajah, W. 1999. *Not Without My Neighbour*, Risk Series. Geneva: WCC.

Birman, P. 2006. 'Future in the Mirror: Media, Evangelicals, and Politics in Rio de Janeiro', in B. Meyer and A. Moors (eds), *Religion, Media, and the Public Sphere*. Bloomington & Indianapolis: Indiana University Press.

Draft of the Proposed Broadcasting Services Regulation Bill. 2006. Available at http://mib.nic.in/informationb/POLICY/BROADCASTSERVICESREGULATIONBILL.htm, accessed on 9 November 2006.

Birman, P. and D. Lehmann. 1999. 'Religion and the Media in a Battle for Ideological Hegemony: The Universal Church of the Kingdom of God and TV Globo in Brazil', *Bulletin of Latin American Research*, 18(2): 145–64.

de Mello, A. 1998. *The Song of the Bird*, 16th Edition. Anand: Gujarat Sahitya Prakash.

Gellner, E. 1985. *Relativism and the Social Sciences*. Cambridge: Cambridge University Press.

Harvey, D. 2003. *The New Imperialism*. Oxford: Oxford University Press.

Hoggart, R. 1957. *The Uses of Literacy*. Harmondsworth: Penguin Books and Chatto & Windus.

Joseph, A. 2006. 'Sound and Fury over the Broadcast Bill', *India Together*. Available at http://www.indiatogether.org/2006/jul/med-bcastbill.htm, accessed on 10 December 2006.

Nandy, A., S. Trivedy, S. Mayaram and A. Yagnik. 1997. *The Ramajanmabhoomi Movement and Fear of Self*. Delhi: Oxford University Press.

Swami Abhishiktananda, 1983. *Hindu-Christian Meeting Point*. Delhi: ISPCK.

Thomas, S. and J.P. Mitchell. 2005. 'Understanding Television and Christianity in Marthoma Homes, South India', *Studies in World Christianity*, 11(1): 29–48.

Vision TV. Available at http://www.whitepinepictures.com/seeds/partners/vision.html, accessed on 21 May 2006.

Williams, R. 1958. *Culture and Society 1780–1950*. Harmondsworth: Penguin Books and Chatto & Windus.

Websites

'God has not Forgotten the Sikh'. Available at http://us.god.tv/Publisher/Article.aspx?id=1000007742, accessed on 21 May 2006.

ABOUT THE AUTHOR

Pradip Ninan Thomas is Associate Professor at the School of Journalism and Communication, University of Queensland. He is also the Vice Head of the Participatory Communication Research Section at the International Association for Media and Communication Research (IAMCR).

He has written extensively on a number of issues related to the media—communication rights, communication and social change, refugees and the media, the political economy of communications in India, and religion and the media. His recent publications include the co-edited volumes *Indigenous Knowledge Systems and Intellectual Property in the Twenty First Century: Perspectives from Southern Africa* (2007) and *Intellectual Property and Communications in Asia: Conflicting Traditions* (2006). He contributes regularly to journals such as *International Communications Gazette, Global Media and Communication, Media Asia, Info, Journal of Communication for Development and Social Change* and *Economic and Political Weekly*, and was co-editor of the journal *Media Development* during 1995–2004.

He is currently co-editing a Communication and Social Change reader and researching indigenous knowledge systems in Vietnam. His other interests include natural history and trekking.